ECSTATIC RELATIONS
A Memoir of Love

For Brook and Jesper —
with gratitude for being
such lovely neighbors!!
Blessings at Solstice —
Carolyn
Berkeley
December, 2006

ECSTATIC RELATIONS

A Memoir of Love

CAROLYN NORTH

SENTIENT PUBLICATIONS, LLC

First Sentient Publications edition 2006
Copyright © 2006 by Carolyn North

A paperback original

Cover design by Kim Johansen, Black Dog Design
Book design by Sara Glaser
Cover art: *Sacred Marriage* and *One* by Jerry Wennstrom,
    photo by Ed Severinghaus
Masks by Sharon Strong
Cosmic Dandelion by Meredith Stout

Library of Congress Cataloging-in-Publication Data

North, Carolyn, 1937–
    Ecstatic relations : a memoir of love / Carolyn North.
    p.   cm.
    ISBN-13: 978-1-59181-052-0
    1. Friendship. 2. Love. 3. Friendship—Miscellanea.
4. Love—Miscellanea. 5. North, Carolyn, 1937–   I. Title.
BF575.F66N67 2006
152.4'1092—dc22   2006029514

Printed in the United States of America

10 9 8 7 6 5 4 3 2 1

SENTIENT PUBLICATIONS
A Limited Liability Company
1113 Spruce Street
Boulder, CO 80302
www.sentientpublications.com

All the particles in the world
Are in love
And looking for lovers.

Jelaluddin Rumi

The Zero Point Field is an ocean of
microscopic vibrations in the space
between things. If the Zero Point
Field is included in our conception
of the most fundamental nature of
matter…then the very underpinning
of our universe is a heaving sea of
energy—one vast [Unified] field. If this
is true, then everything is connected to
everything else like some invisible web.

Lynne McTaggart
The Field: The Quest for the
Secret Force of the Universe

CONTENTS

Introduction

In these times of chaos and confusion, we've got no choice but to feed the world with beauty in every way we can. So I offer here six of my love stories to help you remember your own and to suggest that, in essence, the universe itself is a vast love story based not upon competing forces, but upon the forces of attraction, magnetism, and connection.

Ancient wisdom traditions from all over the world have known of this underlying field of attraction, and they have called it by many names: *Brahman, Tao, the Primordial Ocean,* to name a few. Mythology tells numerous allegories about the love affairs between the gods, and between the gods and their Creation.

In our time, the field that unifies all phenomena has been referred to as the Zero Point Field, the Free Energy Field, the Unified Field—all terms connoting an all-embracing source of magnetic energy within which matter, form, life, and intelligence have their being. In these pages, I will refer to it as the Unified Field.

Beyond our human concerns of right and wrong
there is a Field. I'll meet you there.
Our souls, sinking onto that fragrant grass,
*Will be too filled with ecstasy to even speak...**

said the eleventh-century Persian mystic and poet Jelaluddin Rumi. To Rumi, the Field was the miraculous, sacred love that transcended

---

* Taken from several different translations of Rumi, this is my own version.

all forms and yet permeated all forms. He knelt and kissed the ground of this Mystery in a hundred ways, with the certainty that love was the ultimate reality—the wild dance of the cosmos in continuous passionate creation: it was his beloved.

Until quite recently, contemporary astronomers defined space as empty—a vacuum. Nothing was out there; our solar system floated in a void and we were alone in the universe. But this notion is changing, and new data are showing that outer space is filled with some mysterious energy and matter. *Nothing* has become *something*—*dark* matter, *dark* energy. Could it be that what has been called a "vacuum" is actually more like an invisible, infinite field of conscious, magnetic force?

One of the earliest known hymns of Creation comes from the Hindu *Rig-Veda* and includes this verse:

> *Before there was night or day, birth or death*
> *Could there have been some knowing, invisible Spirit,*
> *some essence of goodness like a conscious, infinite Presence*
> *breathing with windless breath?*
> *In this darkness shrouded by darkness,*
> *In this fathomless ocean of featureless, still water,*
> *Could this unmoving force have caught its breath with longing*
> *And roiled the dark waters into hot motion,*
> *Planting the primal seed—born of desire—*
> *Into the heated void?** *

This interests me, this longing that roils dark waters into hot motion, planting primal seeds filled with desire into heated voids. I long to know what it might feel like to be a universe, to be a dark

---

* Taken from several different translations of the *Rig-Veda*, this is my own version.

sea of passionate power in a constant state of desire. I want to know for myself the ecstatic force that holds the universe together, the cosmic glue that connects all the parts, uniting everything with everything. And I would suggest here that the deep bonds we feel with people we love are that same primal glue—a human, earthly expression of the cosmic Unified Field.

I wonder, often, about the intelligence that caused the big bang in the first place. Was there some longing in the darkness, as it says in the *Vedas*, that roiled the world into being—some yearning to know embodiment and its challenges, to experience the glories of human love itself? And might this longing, I wonder, have expressed itself more as a gasp of desire than as a big bang?

Capturing the ineffable seems to be impossible, but being captured *by* it happens to me whenever I fall in love. I become breathless with an irresistible force of attraction—a pulsing magnetism, a desire at least as strong as the pull of the moon upon the earth's tides. I feel shot through with potency, flooded with the longing of the whole cosmos towards union with my friend. In that state, I know how compelling these forces are. It is as if nothing else mattered but to achieve intimate union, letting the universe express itself through me. Colors are dazzlingly vivid, the world is wondrous, and every joke is wildly funny. I cannot help but live at 100 percent of myself when the sacred force field of the whole cosmos makes me an emissary of its love.

In the thrall of love, I recognize the place just at the edge of memory that I had almost, but not quite, forgotten. I remember it as "home"—where I come from and to where I will return—and know without a doubt that I belong to it. Loving, I remember who I am, what is real, and what I'm here for.

So naturally I make a point of falling in love often.

From time to time, even during the forty-five years I have been happily married to my husband, I meet a person who has some quality that catches my attention, and I am drawn like a moth to a flame. Sometimes the feeling is mutual, and we begin a delicious courtship, discovering who is there behind the other's eyes. It is a soul quest, I believe—an ongoing search for kinfolk, and when the match is right we fall in love.

When I was young and exploring the world, I fell in love with dogs and gym teachers and piano players with red hair. Rarely did I fall in love with boys my own age. Over the years, the pattern has persisted and I find these friends of my heart in the bodies of babies and elders, men and women, people gay and straight. Once it was even an intriguing little calico cat named Trinity.

What makes these relationships different from other loving friendships is the quality of physical attraction I tend to feel. Longing to be in the presence of the beloved is part of it: we want to touch, to be in deep communion—in the ecstasy. Sexuality has often not been appropriate to our relationship, but sensuality and the desires that accompany it have been, and I have been shaped by these relationships like stones in a riverbed.

So here are my stories of five wonderful people I have loved deeply and well, and of Dukie, my childhood dog, who initiated me into the mysteries. I have chosen these particular stories to tell not because they are the only ones, but because they represent the spectrum—male, female, gay, straight, young, old—and because recounting these adventures will give me, during these perilous times in the world, more pleasure than I can say.

Many names, including my own, have been changed to suggest that these stories could belong to anyone, and I have fictionalized and telescoped events at will to keep the book a manageable size. If

I remember these beloveds as too good to be true, it is because I was, after all, madly in love with them, but the delight of our adventures is as close to what actually happened as I could convey. I hope you enjoy reading these stories as much as I delighted in writing them.

After each story, in the tradition of Talmudic commentary, is a short discussion of the aspect of universal law addressed in that story. These commentary chapters might be considered a survey of "sacred science" as I understand it, but the stories stand on their own. So if sacred science is not your cup of tea, by all means skip over them.

My real goal in this book, through story and discussion, is to suggest that science and religion are not separate quests, but find their place along the same universal continuum of, in my granddaughter's words, "the invisible love glue" from which we all come.

To my husband, Herb, goes the closing love story in the book, and to him and our children Ethan, Rebecca and Michael, their partners Anne, Susan and Sofia—and our grandchildren—Alexandro, Robert, Camilla, and Elizabeth—I dedicate this labor of love, with gratitude for our journey together all these years, and for all the attraction in the universe.

Carolyn North
Berkeley, California

ONE

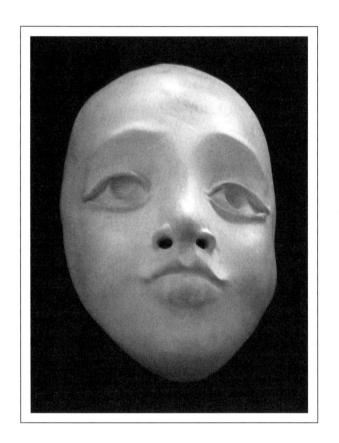

Duke

Dukie simply arrived at our house one summer evening—just like that.

I was turning the page of my book, holding my other hand clamped over my ear to shut out the sounds of my little sister fighting with my mother in the kitchen, when my father came home from work and climbed up the porch steps. I was at the part in *The Secret Garden* where the robin had just shown the orphan girl, Mistress Mary, the key to the ivy-covered door.

Just as Mary was about to see the secret garden for the first time, my mother yelled, "Take that dress off this minute!" which made Simone stamp her feet and wail harder. I turned over on the living-room floor and pressed both hands tighter over my ears. My father would have to deal with those two. Sometimes I tried to stop their tiresome battles, but I had learned it was mostly useless because then they both would gang up on me and I'd feel even worse. So I pretended I didn't hear their yelling, and I kept on reading.

That was when my father opened the front door and came in with a strange look on his face and his hands behind his back. He stayed right there in the hallway waiting for us to notice, and then he stepped aside to reveal a hairy black and gray dog with a white throat and a long pink tongue hanging out of its mouth.

"He's called Duke," was all he said by way of explanation, "and he's had all his shots."

Until that moment, the word 'dog' had never even been spoken in our household. We were a family of second-generation Russian Jews living in an Irish section of Brooklyn, my parents still too crazed with fear to find themselves comfortable with anybody, much less working-class Irish Catholics. People like *them* killed people like *us*, I was told harshly, even though I couldn't figure out who in the neighborhood might want to kill me—unless it was the ones with blonde hair and blue eyes, different from us, with our black hair and brown eyes. Or maybe they meant all the ones living in the brick apartment buildings that surrounded our one-family house with its own porch, and so it made some sense that they might want to kill us. Anyway, we had just moved into this awful house and I hated it.

For our family, pets were not even a category. At the age of eleven, I knew nothing of other creatures; like my parents and little sister, I was a stranger to all things even slightly wild. My one experience with another species had been with a miniature turtle in a bowl, an episode that had resulted in disaster when a teasing uncle had threatened, fork in hand, to eat it for dinner and I threw up in my panic to save it.

To my parents, the whole world—not to mention the neighborhood—was dangerous. The Sacred Heart Church around the corner was the most dangerous place of all, and the Irish and Italian kids who roller-skated on East Seventy Street, the suspect foods 'those others' ate. I was warned 'within an inch of my life' about going anywhere near any of these, and I was punished when I transgressed.

So the appearance of a dog—and a pretty scruffy one at that—was like a visitation from another reality, though there he was, right in our front hall, real and smelly. His back legs quivered with fright, and his tail hung between his legs as we all gathered around him.

"C'mon, boy," my father said ineffectually, tugging at Duke's leash. But the dog just lay down, too scared to move. I figured that in this house, where mistrust was considered a virtue, he would fit right in.

Duke, it seemed, was a castoff dog. An accounting client of my father's had gotten him as a puppy for his own little girl but she had lost interest, so Duke was passed on to us. Daddy, whose specialty as an accountant was finding ways to keep tax evaders out of jail, received a lot of gifts for his services. Most of the time they were doodads I figured other people didn't want: a dozen green wine-glasses, gallon bottles of perfume, imitation leather purses. Even our new house had come to us as 'a favor' from some client who had to unload it quickly. But Daddy always said yes to his clients, no matter what. Anyway, Duke was the first authentic, living thing he ever brought home with him.

None of us had any idea what to do next. My mother was afraid of dogs and wouldn't let Simone touch him. My father looked embarrassed and tried to untangle the leash from between the dog's legs. I just stood there, my heart pounding in my chest and one hand timidly reaching towards its nose. It sniffed my hand and then backed away.

Dogs went for walks—I knew that. They had to eat and needed water. What the hired boy Dickon said to his mother in *The Secret Garden* was that you had to be "friends to the animals, for sure—that's how you made 'em thrive." But what if this dog peed on the rug? What if he barked?

But Duke didn't bark; he just looked from one of us to the other with sad brown eyes and panted, dribbling tiny drops of water onto the floor of the dark hallway.

My father pretended he knew what to do with dogs and handed me the leash. I took it, scared as can be, and with trembling hands I pulled gently to see if Duke would follow me into the living room. At first, he resisted and wouldn't budge, but when I squatted down to his height he decided to take a step and go with me. We all breathed out when he did. It felt as if the king of Persia had suddenly shown up at our house, or maybe a wild tiger from the zoo. We were in the presence of the unknown.

If my mother was the unhappy outsider on East Seventh Street in Brooklyn, then my father was its resident bully. Surrounded as we were by 'the others'—a polite way to indicate non-Jews—he bullied any kids who dared come anywhere near me or Simone. He targeted the boys more than the girls, especially the boys who were from poor families. I never knew how he told them apart from the rest because they all looked alike to me, but every night when he came home from work, any kids who were slow to scatter from near our house would find themselves hauled by the collar and pushed hard against the lamppost while he lambasted them. Why nobody ever called the police, or why their fathers didn't form a gang and beat him up, has always been a mystery to me. Maybe, since we lived in the fancy house on the corner, they thought we were rich. Whatever the reason, it hardly made me a popular playmate for the other kids on our block, especially around early evening when my father was likely to show up.

So, when Dukie came to live with us, he and I became each other's best friends, both of us thankful, I think, to not be so alone anymore. At first he wasn't allowed to sleep in my room, but he would curl up right outside my door and jump up in the mornings when he heard me get out of bed. Simone liked him too, but she would poke at him and step on his tail, with the result that he clearly identified himself as my dog. It was my job to feed him, to walk him, and to brush his blackish coat with a wire brush. We both enjoyed all these chores, he and I, and he would prance excitedly around me all the way to the kitchen, whatever was happening, as if the most wonderful treat was about to be bestowed.

"Just on this block!" my mother would yell through the sound of the vacuum cleaner as I left the house to walk him every morning. "Just on this block!" she would admonish again later when I took him out in the afternoon.

For the first few weeks after he arrived I followed Dukie everywhere, entranced. I would crawl along on the carpet with him, trying to feel out the sequence of being on all fours; hunker down by his water bowl as his soft, pink tongue curled at the edges to lap up water. I learned to read the moods of his thumping and wagging tail, and I wondered what it meant when he circled one place on the floor, around and around, before he curled up to go to sleep. I was, it seemed, an avid student of Dog, testing his patience by lifting up his jowls to examine the curve of his canine teeth and spreading his claws to feel for the soft fur between his rough footpads.

My mother didn't like the way he smelled, so she made me brush him out on the porch. Simone would come too and sing her heart out by the wooden railing while I bent over Dukie on the stoop, running the brush through his coat until it shone. The kids hanging out by the lamppost would watch, but of course they never came up to the porch. But then I would clip on Duke's leash and bring him down to be admired by the kids at the corner and when I took him down the block for his walk, some would tag along.

"Can I hold him?" asked Carole one day as Dukie peed against a garbage can in the middle of the block. She glanced around to my house, her eyes asking the unspoken question about whether my father was home or not. It always made me feel ashamed when kids did that, and I shook my head.

"It's safe," I muttered, looking at a crack in the sidewalk. I gave her the leash and she slipped her hand into the loop and held on tight as Dukie sniffed at the sidewalk and followed some scent to the hedges; then he zigzagged back to the curb and then to the fire hydrant, where he peed again. We ran after him breathlessly, but when we got to the mailbox on the far corner of the block she had to hand the leash back to me because I was not allowed to go farther.

"He's really nice," Carole said, looking both ways before stepping off the curb. "You're lucky to have a dog."

I watched her go while Dukie squatted by the mailbox to poop. Nobody was passing at that moment, so I leaned over to watch his hole spread open for the poop to come out like brown toothpaste, hot and stinky. It made a steaming pile on the sidewalk, and as soon as he was finished and had scratched the pavement behind him in a futile gesture to cover his traces, we turned and walked quickly back up the street toward the house. Every day—twice a day, at least—he tugged me up and down the block, exploring the neighborhood at his level. I began to notice brand-new things that had always been there but I had never seen before—like birds hiding in the hedges and weeds growing out of cracks in the sidewalk and people stopping who had never talked to me before.

I was *very* lucky to have a dog.

On one of those muggy, misty days of midsummer, Dukie and I lay curled up on my bed, me reading my book and he leaning his whole warm weight against my thigh. While I read I stroked idly at his muzzle, sometimes reaching for the edge of a silky ear to rub between my fingers, and when I got too absorbed in my book and forgot to pet him, he poked his nose insistently in my hand to remind me.

The orphan girl Mary stood in the doorway of the secret garden, astonished by all the beauty that had been hidden behind the walls. She picked her way through the tangle of rose vines and bluebells and weeds, wondering why the garden had been locked away for so long. *"It was magic that sent the robin to show me the key! she thought. I know it was magic! There must be magic in the world, but people don't know how to make it."*

I looked up from my book and leaned over to rub my cheek against Dukie's head. He gave a big sneeze, banging his nose into my arm and then licked me wetly. I felt a soft, creeping sweetness come into my body, like the beginning of being happy.

Mary went on, *"Perhaps the beginning is just to say nice things are going to happen, until you make them happen."* Right at that moment, Dukie opened his mouth in a big, singing yawn, stretched to a stand, and jumped off the bed as if he knew exactly what I had just read in the book.

Later, when we got to the mailbox at the end of the block, Dukie kept on going, pulling me around the corner and I kept on walking—it was as easy as that. He smelled another dog and followed the scent, his tail wagging furiously. Right around the corner was a little reddish spaniel and its girl, who looked about my age, and when the two dogs met nose to nose, both tails circled around like lassos.

Both of us were shy, the girl and I, and we held tightly onto our dogs' leashes while they sniffed at each other and leapt up to play, dancing around until their leashes were all tangled up around their legs and ours. We laughed as we twisted and turned to untangle ourselves, finally exchanging leashes to extricate our bodies from the dogs'.

"What's your dog's name?" the girl asked.

"Duke…umm, Dukie," I replied, twirling around once more and grabbing the leash from between Dukie's legs.

"Really?" she said, her blue eyes gaping wide in surprise. "Mine's Duchess!" We both sucked in our breaths and stared at each other at the coincidence. Then she said firmly, "Maybe it means we're supposed to be friends." She had curly blond hair and blue eyes and freckles—just the kind of girl I was supposed to keep away from—and when she smiled her cheeks had dimples and her teeth were perfect and white. I thought she was beautiful, but wondered if I was betraying the history of my people for thinking that.

"My name's Mickey," she said, "short for Michelle, but everyone calls me Mickey. What's yours?"

"I'm Clara," I mumbled, suddenly self-conscious of my name and my dark hair and my brown eyes, wishing I could be a Pat or a Suzie with yellow hair like everyone else. She must not have noticed, because the dogs started chasing each other down the street, and we both had to run to keep up. Both dogs were pulling us as hard as they could, choking from their collars. Like a blind person not knowing where she was being led I stumbled along, following them where they went.

"I always take her for a run in the schoolyard at Sacred Heart," Mickey called over her shoulder. I nodded dumbly, my heart going cold in my chest. "You can take their leashes off and let them play, because it's all fenced in," she explained, keeping up her chatter and asking me questions all the way to the schoolyard. For me, it was like pacing the last mile to a hanging, but my feet took one step after another as she told me that Duchess was her Christmas present from her parents last year, and that she had two older sisters,

Delores and Patty, and that she went to Sacred Heart Parochial School and the nuns were nice, but she couldn't stand the green uniform she had to wear every day.

We discovered that we were in the same grade, but I went to Public School 215, and that her Mom always baked Toll House cookies and I could come and have some whenever I wanted. I told her Dukie was a present from my father, too, but I said it in a very low voice so I'm not sure she heard. By that time we had reached the forbidden fence of the schoolyard, and I had a stomachache.

The sky was clouding over, and the air felt heavy and hot. I did, too, but the dogs pulled us right through the chain-link gate, and when Mickey unhitched Duchess' leash, I snapped Dukie's off too. We stood close together watching the dogs race off after the rubber ball she threw. Both dogs went like the wind, skidding and colliding as they caught up to the ball. Duchess got it first, tossing it around in her mouth before she got a good grip on it, and then she came racing back to Mickey for another throw. I was still tight with apprehension, darting looks over my shoulder for fear one of my parents would find me here, but Mickey was lighthearted and easy, romping freely with the dogs as she retrieved the slimy ball and threw it again.

A statue of Jesus stood in front of the school, His arms spread out to the sides, and on His chest was a big heart with sun lines coming out from it. He had long hair and a kind face, and he didn't look anything like a man who would chase kids away or hate someone for being Jewish. I took a deep breath, totally confused.

Dukie galloped back and jumped up on me, dropping the grungy ball at my feet and leaping around expectantly. His eyes stayed fixed on me and his tongue hung out of grinning jaws. I picked up the ball just as Mickey had done and threw it as far as I could. The dogs took after it at a million miles an hour, like it was the most important thing in the world.

Gradually, the ache in my stomach faded, my arm got stronger at throwing, and I forgot to be scared. We laughed a lot at the dogs' antics, and we ran after them, talking and making jokes. Mickey told me about her school, answering the questions I kept asking her, and I hardly noticed that the sky had gotten much darker and the wind was picking up.

"Storm's coming," Mickey said with excitement. I began to panic and snapped Dukie's leash back onto his collar. At that moment, the whole schoolyard lit up for a second, and the flash was followed by a rumble of thunder somewhere far away. Mickey squatted down on the ground, quite relaxed, her arms around Duchess. She said, "Let's stay and watch. My dad and I just love storms, even though it scares my mom. We'll get wet, but it'll cool us off and we can change when we get home."

Truth be told, I was as scared as her mom—as my mom, in fact—but I pretended I wasn't and squatted down next to Mickey and hugged Dukie to my chest. Inside me, everything was turning upside down. I had never before heard anyone be glad about a storm coming, but I knew that was the way I wanted to feel if only I were allowed to. But I wasn't allowed to. But I wanted to be. But I couldn't. It was like when Mary discovered the crippled boy, Colin, in his room down the forbidden corridor; she had to go where she was not allowed to go. If she hadn't, she would never have found him. She was much braver than me. But she was just in a book...

My mind was a buzzing nest of bees. The wind picked up, and I held Dukie even more tightly to me. We were both trembling like mad, and I felt my teeth clunk together.

When the schoolyard lit up with lightning again I nervously laughed out loud. The flash disappeared as suddenly as it had come.

"One Mississippi, two Mississippi, three Mississippi..." Mickey counted as the rumble of thunder, a bit louder this time, broke out from the sky. Dukie whimpered high in his throat, but so did Duchess, and Mickey just held her tighter, so I laid my head against Duke's neck to reassure myself as well as him. Mickey's very blue eyes shone like *Puree Kabolder* marbles, and when the next streak of lightning came we could see it for a second above the houses as a jagged streak of light in the sky. Moments later, the thunder cracked as if the world was coming apart.

"One more," Mickey shouted above the noise, "and then let's run for it!"

I was breathless—as the wind started blowing in earnest and the air took on a new smell—as much out of exhilaration as out of fear.

Right then I made a vow to myself that from that moment on, I would be brave and look for real things, even if they were scary. My eyes started tearing—from the wind, of course—and I shifted my weight so that my legs could take off and run fast at the right moment. The wind blew even harder, tossing my hair into my face as the lightning and thunder broke at exactly the same time, filling the whole world with light and sound and sending huge drops of rain down on our heads.

"Run for it!" shouted Mickey, and we both jumped up with our dogs and dashed out of the schoolyard, she racing to the left toward her house and me racing to the right, leaving the statue of Jesus to get wet in the rain with His arms still outstretched, His face still smiling, and His heart still open and shining on his chest.

My mother was out on the porch when Dukie and I came running home. She was nearly hysterical.

"Where were you?" she cried in a squeaky voice, grabbing Dukie's leash from my hand and tying it to the porch railing. He kept shaking to get the water out of his fur. "Where were you? Didn't you realize it was raining? I thought you'd been killed!"

My mother always made things sound so much worse than they were, that it was hard to answer her questions. Except she was serious. I unlaced my sopping shoes and left them by the door and shrugged.

"You went off this block, didn't you? Answer me—didn't you?"

I tried to think of a good lie but I couldn't, so I told her the truth, or at least most of it. I said I had met a girl with a brown cocker spaniel, and we went dog-walking together, and her dog's name was Duchess—wasn't that funny?—and then it started raining and then we went home. She narrowed her eyes in suspicion.

"Do I know her mother?" she demanded. I shrugged again.

"She's called Michelle," I mumbled, but my mother shook her head impatiently, not caring about that. I told her I didn't know her last name, or her mother's name, and I repeated that Duchess was the feminine for Duke, but she didn't care about that either and she pushed me inside and upstairs, leaving Dukie tied up on the porch. His head was cocked and his ears stood straight up. He didn't know what was going on, either.

But I knew that she got crazy when she was scared, so I would probably get one of her tight-lipped warnings, which would leave me confused and humiliated for having tried to have fun. This was my mother, like it or not.

Each time I felt so mortified I wanted to die, but if I didn't pretend she was a good mommy, then someone might find out. That would be worse. She stomped after me to my room, muttering, not trusting me to change my clothes by myself. Angrily, she handed me a towel.

"Who is this girl?" she demanded again in an accusing voice. She closed the door and faced me, making me feel as if I had done something really bad. Had I?

"Who were you with?" she repeated with tight lips.

"Just a girl." I heard myself start to whine. "Michelle, she said her name was. And she has this little dog…"

In my mind, but not out loud I added that she had blonde hair and blue eyes and perfect teeth, and her mom made Toll House cookies every day and her dad liked to watch storms. My mother's face sized me up for lies, and she looked at me with her sharp-edged glint. I kept my face very straight and tried not to cry. Then she softened—this was the scariest part of all because it came when she disappeared into her craziness—and she sat down at the edge of my bed and looked at me imploringly.

"It's for your own good I'm telling you this," she in that false gentle voice, where I could see blood behind her eyes. I tried to look down, but she grabbed my chin and made me look at her.

"Keep away from them!" My throat went hard and I couldn't have said anything if I had tried. I wished I could be anywhere but there—like back out in the rain, which was still pelting on the roof. I felt nauseated, sullied. If only I could feel clean again the way I did when Mickey and I watched the storm come in. If only Dukie was right here with me, and not tied up alone on the porch. If only I was in a different family, or far away where Simone and I and Dukie could be safe.

"She's good…" was all I could whisper.

"Not for you!" she spit out. "You may think she's nice, but they'll stab you in the back when you're not looking. We're different from them! We don't belong with those people!" She said this through clenched teeth, and she banged her fist again and again on my bed. I was too scared to move.

"These people don't even give their children piano lessons or braces for their teeth!" She gave another angry thump on the bed, and I went numb with terror. All words left my brain, my eyes stopped seeing, and my ears stopped hearing. Blankness filled me down to my bone marrow, and I sank into muffled sand.

I don't know how long she stayed in my room or if she had more to say, because I disappeared into a stupor. I vaguely remembered that Dukie was still tied up on the porch, but my body was too heavy to move, and with eleven-year-old despair I disappeared into a dreamless sleep where nobody knew my name.

For the next few days I hid in my room. At dawn I crept outside to walk Duke, and then again once it was dark, but I stayed close to the house and avoided any other kids who might be around. I certainly didn't want Mickey to see me, and I was glad I hadn't told her where I lived. I hoped she thought I lived in one of the apartment houses. I could hardly swallow, and I couldn't talk to anyone, even Dukie. On my dresser *The Secret Garden* lay unread.

The only things I knew for certain were that I would never, ever take piano lessons for as long as I lived, and that if my parents ever took me to an orthodontist for braces, I would throw up all over him.

On the fifth day after the storm I was still sunk in despair, but with just enough will to pick up *The Secret Garden* again. The hired boy Dickon was saying *"you can do anything as soon as you stop being afraid."* I lay the book down and stared up at the ceiling, wondering how it was possible to stop being afraid when fear was filling your breath and your air and your whole mind. The tears crowded into my throat but I swallowed them down, still hurting too much to cry. Then I remembered being in the storm and how I had promised myself to always be brave enough to face real things, even when they were scary; then I wondered what was *really* real here.

Was it real to hate Catholics even when they were nice? Was it real that our family was better than Mickey's family? Were people who played the piano the only good ones, and people who didn't, all bad? That didn't sound right. But can parents not be right, and if they're not, then who is?

Dukie nosed his way into my room, his nails click-clacking on the linoleum floor, and he put his front paws up on my bed and made a small whimper under his breath. Dickon had just said to Mary, *"animals will always understand if you're friends for sure, but you have to be friends for sure."*

I turned my head and saw Dukie's brown eyes pleading with me for something, his tail thumping slowly against the floor and his nose burrowing in the covers near my hand. For the first time since the day of the storm, my throat loosened and my eyes brimmed with tears. I rolled over to grab Dukie up onto the bed and then sobbed helplessly into his fur, crying until there were no tears left. He licked my face and my wet hands—he was my friend, for sure— and then we both climbed down off my bed.

At the bottom of the stairs, still hiccoughing, I grabbed his leash and snapped it onto his collar, and then we left out the back door, heading directly for the schoolyard of Sacred Heart, where I hoped we'd find Mickey and Duchess.

They were not there, but I stayed a while anyway to watch the rollerskaters whiz around with their hockey sticks before I continued walking slowly around the block. Dukie stopped at every hedge and lamppost, checking out smells carefully and leaving a spurt of his own for any dogs who came after him, but on Mickey's block his tail started circling and he dragged me up the street, barking. Duchess was there, right in the middle of the block, with Mickey and an older, dark-haired boy who was fixing his bike. He had the bicycle upside down and was pushing a pedal with his hand to spin the wheels. I tried to approach them slowly, but Dukie wouldn't let me. My heart was pounding in my throat and I felt my face go hot.

"Hi!" Mickey called, holding onto Duchess' leash with both hands. The dogs met with a frenzy of happy barking, nipping at each other and romping so that Mickey and I were quickly tangled up in their leashes again. I felt embarrassed, as if her ears had heard what my mother had said about her, but she laughed in a carefree way. I noticed that her teeth, just as I had remembered, were perfectly straight. She would never need braces.

"I wondered where you went to," she laughed breathlessly, twirling out of the leash's grip and stumbling after the prancing dogs. The boy tightened a bolt on his bike with a spanner, and turned around to watch the crazy scene with the dogs. He was a brownie, like me—dark hair and eyes and eyebrows—and his nose didn't turn up at all. In fact, he even wore braces! He looked like what my parents would call "one of ours."

"This is my new friend Clara, Sammy," Mickey introduced us, pointing first to me and then to him. "Sammy's my big sister Delores' boyfriend." She giggled as she ducked away from his friendly slap, but he seemed very pleased to be called Delores' boyfriend. I found myself trying not to stare too hard, but my mouth went dry and I felt a prickling flush start at my heels and rise right up through my whole body. Boyfriend? But he looked Jewish. His eyes, even though they sparkled with fun, had that hint of sadness that all of us had. How could he be...?

"There, it's all fixed," Sammy announced, giving the oilcan a final tweak and straightening up again. When he lifted the bike to turn it over, his arm muscles bulged a little, and when he flung his leg over the seat his motion was smooth, like a dancer's. He took off down the street fast, turning around at the corner and whizzing by us again before he stopped short right where the dogs were playing.

"Is he really your sister's boyfriend?" I whispered to Mickey.

She nodded. "He gave her his pin last week—they're going steady."

"But..." I began, quite short of breath.

"But what?" she prompted.

"But, but...he looks Jewish!" It took a while for my voice to come out and when it did, it cracked.

"Yeah, he is," she said, as if it was the most normal thing in the world.

Like a sleepwalker, I followed them into the apartment-house lobby, and then into the dark elevator—Sammy with his bike, Mickey with Duchess, and me with Dukie. I automatically looked over my shoulder to check for my father, but then I stared straight ahead with defiance. They'd never find me here. And if they did, I'd run away!

The dogs piled out of the elevator first, pulling and yipping, and a door at the end of the hallway opened up to let us in, dogs and bike and all. Mickey's mother, with her hands clasped against her apron, welcomed everyone with smiles, and we followed her into a cozy, old-fashioned apartment smelling of baking cookies.

A tall, slender version of Mickey with a deep dimple in one cheek—her sister Delores—came out and greeted Sammy with a quick hug; he turned all rosy, gazing with his brown eyes into her blue eyes as if nobody else were there.

Their kitchen, now crowded with five people and two dogs, was as bright and cheerful as our kitchen, with its drawn shades, was dim. Mickey's mom crouched down to meet me and Dukie, and regarded me with a kindly face, no doubt noticing the puffy redness around my eyes from my recent bout of tears. Then she took me into her arms. Her red-checked apron smelled deliciously of flour and onions and cabbage, and I burrowed there for a moment. She felt like Dickon's *"comfortable, wonderful mother creature,"* just like I had always longed to have.

She patted Dukie's head and said, "Loverly to meet Mickey's new friends! I'm just about to take these cookies out of the oven—would anybody like some?" A shout went up in the kitchen, and laughter and the scraping of chairs, and the dogs set up a racket and skidded into the hallway, chasing each other back and forth. Then there was a yell from the back room where Mickey's other sister Patty was trying to study; the toilet flushed in the bathroom, and Mickey's dad, Mr. Mahoney, came out in his undershirt, scratching at his chest and yawning.

"Settle those dogs down, would you?" Mrs. Mahoney told Mickey and me while she poured milk into glasses and turned the chocolate chip cookies out onto a baking rack to cool.

"This is Clara," she said when the rest of the family squeezed into the kitchen, "and her dog is Dukie. Fancy that!"

Delores rolled her eyes at the bedlam, and Sammy grinned from ear to ear, the braces on his teeth like silver train tracks without the trains. Mickey and I scampered after our dogs and sat them down in the hallway, petting them slowly until they reluctantly simmered down.

"Calm down, boy, it's alright; calm down, girl...," we kept murmuring with each stroke, holding them firmly against us each time they started up again. "Not in the house..."

My chest quivered as I let out a big shaky sigh, feeling safe. Mrs. Mahoney called me "darling," and I felt my face go hot with blushing. It was too noisy and chaotic for anybody to notice, but it wouldn't have mattered if they did, because nobody would have made fun of me for it.

I felt as if I were in a movie or a dream where everybody loves you, and the chocolate chip cookies were so delicious with cold milk, and Mr. Mahoney was in his undershirt and Sammy called him "Sir," and he was Jewish so it was alright for me to be here too. I felt so relieved, it didn't even occur to me to be jealous.

School would be starting in a few weeks and then it would be the High Holy Days, when my parents always made me go to synagogue—even though we never went there at any other time. Mickey and I met at the schoolyard almost every day that was left of the summer. We ran the dogs and talked about everything in the world, from dogs and sisters, to the shapes of our belly buttons. Sometimes the skating crowd was there—Carol and Larry and Regina and Boss and Huey and Richie—and we would watch, or Mickey would be out there skating with them. The metal wheels scraped against the pavement as they chased each other round and round with their hockey sticks, and the tin-can puck flew into the air and landed with a satisfying 'ka-ching' while they all skated after it with their sticks. My legs trembled with the longing to be racing around with them, taking long, rolling strides and laughing my head off when I caught up with the puck.

One day, Mickey spun out of the pack and skated up to where I was standing by the fence, slowing herself down with the heel of her skate.

"Hi!" she said breathlessly. "Why won't you skate with us?"

"Don't have skates," I admitted miserably, not adding that I didn't know how to skate either.

She regarded me thoughtfully for a moment, leaned down to pat Dukie on the head, and then declared, "We've got extras. Delores'll lend you hers—I know she will. She never uses them anymore." I had never felt more like the poor little rich girl, who lived in the fanciest house on the block but whose parents didn't love her enough to buy her skates.

What Mickey, or anybody else, except maybe Simone, didn't know was that I had been practicing on the slick linoleum of my bedroom floor in my socks. The stride was in my body—slide out and skim; slide out and skim—but there wasn't much space in my bedroom and it would of course be different once I got on wheels. What I could *not* do was ask my parents for roller skates, because then they'd track me down to the Sacred Heart schoolyard and all those kids they couldn't stand; what might happen after that I couldn't bear to think about. But if I used borrowed skates—Delores' skates—then nobody in my house needed to know, and I could hide them under the bushes in my backyard where my parents would never think to look.

Mickey probably understood that something weird was going on at my house, and even though she soon found out I lived in the big house around the corner she knew that, for reasons I couldn't talk about, she couldn't come over.

So I went to her house, and I was mostly spared from answering questions about my own. What her parents thought, I never knew, but I imagine they wondered if my father was a drunk or my mother a snob, in any case feeling sorry for the little girl who often looked so sad. If they guessed at the real truth, they never let on, and Mrs. Mahoney took me in like another daughter. She listened to me when I talked, fed me in her kitchen, and hugged me when I most needed a hug. Just like the way Colin felt about Dickon's mother, I wished with all my heart that she could be mine as well.

By the end of that summer I was not only a good skater, but a fast one. I loved the feel of moving through space with the wind at my ears, my weight shifting easily from one side to the other as I balanced on rolling wheels. Leaning into a wide arc, my eye on the puck and the stick in my hands, I felt the freedom of speed as my legs crossed one over the other as I made a turn, striding to catch up with Larry, who now guarded the puck, and Carol, who tried to beat me to it. Mickey shot in for a try at the skittering puck and stole it right out from under my stick. We both shrieked loudly, laughing as she got away with it, but then I zoomed in to steal it back. Dukie and Duchess ran back and forth, following the game in excitement and barking their heads off for all they were worth.

Every day that it wasn't raining we were out there playing hockey, and when the weather kept us indoors, I was either sneaking around the corner to hang out at Mickey's house, or I was in my bedroom practicing new tricks in my socks: one-legged glides, jumps and landings, and backward strides.

To my mother I always said I was going to see Myra, a girl from my class who picked her nose, but I only went to her house once. All I wanted to do was skate, think about skating, and talk about skating. My legs longed to balance on one foot, to twirl, and to crouch close to the ground. My arms loved stretching to the sides while I threw my head back. And when my whole body was lifting itself up, breathing in and arching itself backwards, I knew what it felt like to be *real*! It was sort of the way Jesus must feel, with his arms held out, his face aglow, and his chest so wide open that his heart showed right through.

If my parents had guessed any of this, they would have killed me.

The first day of school was the worst day of my life. Simone was starting first grade, and my mother took both of us to school, dropping me off at Mrs. Bildersee's classroom first. Mrs. Bildersee was the strictest teacher in P.S. 215, and we all had to sit exactly in the center of our seats and were promised demerits if we were caught looking either to the right or to the left.

For the first hour I tried hard, but after that it was pure torture. I itched all over and had to scratch, I bit my pencil, my fingers went numb, and my legs began to twitch. She gave me two demerits by lunchtime. The windows were kept closed, and my head began to hurt from the stuffy air. By the end of the school day I could hardly breathe and I wanted to cry, and my throat hurt from holding it back. When we finally were dismissed, my mother and Simone were waiting for me at the fence.

"He got out," my mother said without preamble. At first, I didn't know what she was talking about. "The back door was open while I was hanging out the laundry, and he was too fast and I couldn't catch him." My stomach squeezed into a fist and my mind forgot how to think.

"When?" I managed to whisper. It was in the morning after I left for school, she told me. He hadn't come back. She had walked all the way back to school to see if he had followed me, but he was nowhere to be found.

"Did you call him?" I demanded. "Where did you look? Are you sure he didn't come back and is lying down in the backyard?"

Actually, I wondered if he hadn't gone to Sacred Heart looking for me, or to Mickey's apartment house, but I couldn't even mention that to my mother or try to go there now. So I went home with her and Simone before I raced out again, after they were inside and away from the windows.

The last bell of the day was ringing when I dashed up, all out of breath, to Sacred Heart while the kids poured out the doors in their green uniforms and Buster Brown shoes. When Mickey saw me she ran over, and through the chain-link fence I told her Dukie was lost.

"He might have come here," I gasped, "or maybe even to your house. Help me look?"

"Yes, yes," she breathed, and together we clattered down all the stairwells to the school basement, poked through all the bushes, and called his name at every alleyway between Sacred Heart and her house, listening for his answering bark. But Dukie never came; the air was completely silent of him.

Mickey took me by the hand and brought me home with her, whispering to her mother what had happened, and Mrs. Mahoney held me tight while I wept shuddering sobs into her bosom. The sobs turned into hiccoughs, and she wiped my face and smoothed back my hair, holding me against her and saying, "We'll find him. He'll come back. Dogs always do. He missed you, that's all. He'll be back—you'll see, he'll come back."

But Dukie didn't come back. Not that night or the next day, although my father took me out in the car, driving in widening circles from the neighborhood, calling out the window for Dukie and searching up and down every alleyway we passed.

"We'll get another dog," my father tried brightly. "We can get a better one this time—a puppy."

But my father never understood anything, and all I did was shake my head. I didn't want another dog, I wanted Dukie—right now! He was my friend for sure, and when I imagined him dead by the side of the road, or stolen by somebody and shut up in their dark basement, I wanted to die myself.

For the next two days I sat in class in the middle of my seat like a zombie, and after school I wandered the neighborhood, disconsolate. Even in my sleep I listened for his bark or whine. On my way to school, I passed by peoples' windows, and searched for him inside, and I stared up and down every street, my throat as dry as flannel and my eyes fuzzy with grief.

On the third day, when I had all but given up hope, my mother and Simone met me after school with excited faces.

"He came home!" Simone yelled. "Dukie's back!" She was skipping up and down, and my mother was smiling the biggest smile I'd ever seen on her. My heart jumped into my ears, and I couldn't say a word. I could hardly breathe. All I could do was run all the way home, leaving them way behind, and then wait on trembling legs while they caught up and unlocked the front door to the house.

There he was, lying on his side on the living-room floor, his fur matted with blood and his eyes glazed over. But he thumped his tail weakly when he saw me and tried to get up.

"Dukie," I choked, dropping onto the floor beside him, almost too afraid to touch his body. "What happened to you? Where were you?"

A huge red gash at the top of one leg went right down to white bone, and cuts on his head and neck bled freely. He licked my fingers with the tip of his tongue, his body shivering uncontrollably and his wounds showing purple against his black fur. When I felt his nose it was dry and hot, and when I put a finger near the big red gash he jerked in pain.

"We gotta take him to the doctor," Simone announced. I nodded, dizzy with fear.

"He hasn't eaten," I said, taking charge to cover up my panic, "and he needs water. Bring me his bowl."

Simone rushed into the kitchen to bring it, and we scooped water into our hands, letting him lap it from our palms. But after a few drops he was too tired, and a low moan escaped from his muzzle and he lowered his head again to the floor. My mother hovered nearby, helpless, and I kept one hand protectively on Dukie's back, vowing not to leave him even for one minute until he was all well again.

"We gotta take him to the doctor," Simone repeated as if she, at least, knew what to do when somebody was sick.

"When Daddy gets home," my mother promised. And indeed, when my father walked in, even before he had his dinner, he and I took Dukie to the doctor.

"He's been hit by a car," the veterinarian told us, examining Dukie's wounds and staring with a light into his eyes. "Another day without food or water, and I don't think he would've made it, but let's try and patch this pooch up."

Dukie just lay there, barely breathing. The doctor gave him a shot and then cleaned out his gashes, scraping away the infected flesh and covering all the bloody places with sprinklings of pink powder. One of his legs was broken, but the doctor set it and put on a plaster cast, saying it would heal fine.

"The real danger here is dehydration, and of course he needs to eat in order to get well. But, young lady," he said, addressing himself to me, "once I let him go home, it will be your job to make sure he takes water every half hour. Can you do that?" I nodded vehemently. "Your doggie has been pretty badly hurt, and we hope we can save him, but we'll need to keep him here for observation tonight, and if he makes it through the night you can take him home tomorrow. But he's going to need round-the-clock attention. Are you sure you can do that?"

"Yes!" I shouted, but then in a smaller voice, "How will he go pee?" My father admonished me with a poke of his elbow, but the doctor didn't mind and answered me right away.

"Twice a day, or whenever he asks for it, you carry him outside and stand with him until he does his business. Then bring him right back inside—you understand?"

"Yes."

"He's still in deep shock from the accident and the exposure, and he shouldn't be left alone for at least the next week. Call me in the morning, and we'll take it from there."

Dukie did make it through the night, and the vet let us take him home. The Jewish High Holy Days started just then, so I was allowed to stay home from school and spend every minute with my dog. We carried him upstairs to my room, and for the next two days he barely lifted his head. I had to force him to take his pills and water, and he was so weak I was afraid he was going to die. When I thought he might give up, my heart hurt right down into my stomach. In the book when Colin wouldn't try and stand up, Mary had *"gabbled under her breath as fast as ever she could, 'He can do it! He can do it! He can do it! He can!"*

I did the same thing. Holding a bit of cooked meat just under Dukie's nose, I didn't try to force him to eat, but I held it there, sometimes for half an hour, all the while whispering under my breath, "You can do it, you can! You can do it, you can!" Meanwhile, I stroked the soft whorl between his eyes, following the lay of his hair gently with my thumb.

In the book, Mary says that the robin knew that *"nothing in the world would make her startle him in the least tiniest way. He knew it because he was a real person—only nicer than any other person in the world."*

I made up a song for Dukie about how he was a real person, only he was nicer than any other person in the world. I think he listened, because he began to open up his mouth and delicately take in his teeth the bits of meat I offered him, occasionally swallowing them down.

For two days and two nights I sat with him, listening to him breathe. I held his leg cast in my hands as if the very heat in my body could heal the break. Sometimes my eyes closed and we slept together head to head, and once when he was shivering I had a shivering fit too. We were blood relatives and I could smell his blood seeping through the bandages and hear it pumping near his heart. I bled too.

I was fighting for his life with him, and I heard his meaning with each of his sighs and groans. I knew, without words, what his brown eyes were saying and what his every twitch meant. Sometimes I talked to him in whispers, telling him about Duchess and the dog biscuit Mrs. Mahoney was saving for him, that Sammy had come to visit him twice and waved at the window, and that my father hadn't chased him away. I told him that made me so happy it was, all by itself, a reason for him to get well. Maybe someday we could all have a party at our house—wouldn't that be fun? Wanly, he started to lick my hand, but it was too much of an effort to keep his head up, and he fell asleep again.

Each day he got a little bit stronger, and for a week I hardly left his side. Sometimes my parents came and stood at the door of my bedroom and watched, and sometimes Simone, but mostly it was just me there, feeding him his pills and offering him water and tempting tidbits to eat.

One night, after the rest of the family had gone off to the Kol Nidre service at the temple, he thirstily lapped up most of his water and wagged his tail when I brought him food. I watched him lick the bowl clean, and when he fell back asleep I kissed him on his muzzle, almost spinning with relief. I crept downstairs to breathe the outside air, and for the first time since he was hurt I began to cry. The tears seemed to come up from my knees, which went so wobbly I had to sit down on the back steps, and my whole chest flung open like a window that had been stuck shut but was suddenly pried loose. I sobbed great, gulping sobs that shook my whole body, and my nose ran all over my hands, which I wiped on the grass. The stars were my witnesses, along with a night bird that flew across the yard in the dark, fluttering. The crying turned to laughter, and the laughter turned to a longing for Dukie so strong that it pulled me back to him as if I were the one on a leash.

I heard a moan come from me as I stumbled through the back door and raced up the stairs two at a time until I was with him again, my face touching his face and my arms circling his battered body. I dropped to my knees by the bed, still crying, and keened his name over and over—Dukie, Dukie, Dukie...

He opened his eyes and nuzzled his nose into my hands, the warm weight of him pressing against my fingers, alive and quivering. I kissed him on his whiskers and tasted his stiff hairs on my mouth. He sneezed, and his nose was wet and cool for the first time since he came back. A laugh burbled up into my throat, along with drool, and I kissed his whiskers again, and his ears. Then he sneezed again and shook his head hard. The laughing shout that came out of me was the song that wanted to be sung, and I buried my face into the velvety pelt of his neck, crooning and crying softly into his warm, healing body.

By Saturday, Dukie was well enough to walk around the block with me to Sacred Heart, at a dignified, limping pace, and we were both glad to be out of the house and in the fresh air again. A few cars whooshed by too fast and he cringed and leaned against me, but I tightened the leash around my wrist to let him know that I was holding him safe. Delores' skates were flung over my shoulder, and each person we passed wanted to know the whole story of his recovery. Everyone stroked his head and admired his true grit and courage. I was so proud of my dog, the hero of East Seventh Street!

The kids were all out skating in the schoolyard when we got there, and the puck sailed into the air above their heads and landed with a ringing clunk on the pavement. They took after it, the metal of their wheels scraping and sparking crisply on the pavement. Larry hit it hard, *ka-ching!* and Huey took off after him fast, shouting, and his stick got caught and toppled him over. I laughed so hard it hurt, even though it wasn't funny.

Helen gave him a hand up and then made a graceful circle around the group before she came in closer. Dukie and I watched by the chain-link fence, and I told him what I thought would happen next.

"See, Helen's gonna wait until Mickey goes for the puck, and then she'll zoom in…" and while I was telling him this, my focus blurred and I saw the kids as if I were a bird flying high above them. It looked like the kids were in the middle of a rainbow wheel going round and round—a wheel with spokes stretching out beyond the schoolyard to the far ends of the world. My friends were right at the hub, and the wheel was the whole wide world.

I saw it with my eyes, but my heart really was doing most of the seeing. The kids from East Seventh Street were right in the center of everyone who had ever lived or who would ever be born anywhere on the earth. Like magic, all those people were in the Sacred Heart schoolyard with Dukie and me.

The whole world was there too, not just East Seventh Street in Brooklyn. I could see every country and all the oceans, and space in all directions with stars and planets and galaxies going forever. Of course! Everything, for all time and everywhere, was right here, right now. Always.

It was such a great joke to be in the Sacred Heart schoolyard on Yom Kippur, with Jesus smiling down on me, a Jewish kid. He smiled down on the other kids too, and on the policeman stopping to watch their game, and on the baby in the baby carriage, and the guy who owned the barbershop, and the old lady passing by on her way to the store.

And He was smiling down on Dukie, too. I knelt and held my dog as tightly as I dared, rocking him in my arms and singing him a little song. He licked my face and gave two sharp barks, and then he barked again as Duchess charged over to greet us, with Mickey following close behind.

"Hey, they're back!" she called to the others. "Get on your skates," she told me, slapping her knees impatiently.

I hauled in a breath and plunked down on the ground, attaching first one skate and then the other onto my shoes. I tied both straps, tightening the clamps with my skate key, and I pulled myself up on the chain-link fence. Then I knotted Dukie's leash to the fence, told him he'd better just watch quietly today, and skated across the schoolyard to join the game.

THE UNIFIED FIELD

The universe originates from one completely subtle sound that gives rise to all the other more gross vibrations. One might say there is a descent of sound from the subtlest and most impalpable to the densest and most palpable. Yet, unlike a hierarchy, there is no separation between levels. The subtlest incorporates the most gross. The untrained person is often aware only of the grossest levels.

From a creation hymn of the Kashmiri Hindu Shaivites

On the night Dukie began to rally, when I went outside to gaze into the night sky, and then a few days later as I watched my friends skate in the schoolyard, I had my first conscious experiences of ecstasy. My heart, having been flooded by love for my wounded little dog, emerged from despair and opened to a bright, boundless world in which everything was vivid and alive.

I 'felt' this grand luminosity rather than 'saw' it. The world was in Technicolor, and the kids in the Sacred Heart schoolyard seemed to be skating in midair above me. Of course they could fly if they wanted to—anything was possible!

Between one breath and another my world disassembled and then reassembled right before my eyes, becoming vast and wondrous enough to contain everything that was or ever would be. With every blink of my eyes I saw things link up: the policeman standing by the fence, the birds flying over his head, the woman with the baby carriage, and the statue of Jesus—with Dukie in the center of it all, the most gorgeous creature in the whole wide world!

I could not know it then, but much later I would understand that I had received a classic mystical vision that day—my first initiation into the Mystery.

There are two essential elements to this Mystery, as recorded in most ancient wisdom traditions of the world.

First, there exists a single Source, an all-encompassing field of consciousness beyond time and space from which all phenomena come. The Source holds the potential for all form and all life in all realms, and nothing—absolutely nothing—exists outside of it. Everything belongs. Ancient cultures speak of this Source as a primal field of force whose center is everywhere and whose circumference is nowhere—it simply *is*. I am calling this Source "the Unified Field."

Second, every form in existence—animate and inanimate, seen and unseen, this moment and forever—is permeated with the intelligence of the Unified Field. That means that everything is related to everything else because everything is interconnected, mutually dependent, and interacting continuously, everywhere and always.

This has been called "the Relative Universe." It is the manifest world we live in, and it nestles within the Unified Field, level by level, the way Russian dolls nestle one within the other.

The Unified Field and the Relative Universe *together* comprise what we refer to as "God."

I believe that what I experienced that day in the schoolyard was this understanding of God, and the rest of my life has been spent searching for it like a cat stalking a skittering bird through shadows in the grass.

Imagine a rainbow, a spectrum of light banded into colors by the changing frequencies of the light. The colors appear to be separate, but actually they merge gradually one into the other. Ultimately, they are all phenomena of the spectrum of light.

I think of the Unified Field as similarly banded, level after level of decreasing frequency, or increasing density, down to the solid forms of the earth. From where we stand, we are mostly aware of a world that is limited to what we can see, feel, and touch, but the magnificence and multiplicity of the natural world, phenomenal as it is, is only the frosting on a vast, many-layered cake way beyond our imaginings.

The one has given rise to the many—"the ten thousand things," as the Buddhists say—which come continuously into creation and, when their appointed life spans are over, eventually sink back into the Source from which they came.

Thus we exist in a divine universe of consciousness and love, sound and motion, thought and dreams, rocks and rivers, jungles and savannahs, parrots and alligators, horses and worms and hummingbirds, and all the human children and their parents of every gender, every color, every culture, every size and every temperament in the glorious diversity of this sacred world we call ours.

THREE

Danilo

Before I ever met him, I heard him. He told a joke in a deep voice, and his French—as much as I could hear of it through the partition that separated the women's dormitory from the men's at the Chartres Youth Hostel—was strongly accented. He had the sound of someone who enjoyed himself immensely, and through the wall I could feel his laughter vibrate in my chest. I pictured a tall fellow, blond and muscular, in a black turtleneck sweater, from Denmark maybe—a struggling artist here to paint the famous cathedral.

I was, if the truth be known, a highly suggestible girl of nineteen who was barely squeaking through college as an art history major, and who had come to France to find herself. Taking a break from school in New York, I came to study medieval iconography at an institute of medieval studies as a way of trying to understand what religion was all about. Really though, I was just trying to figure out what I was all about.

In Brooklyn everyone thought I was out of my mind—a Jewish girl going all the way to Europe to study Catholics? My father was sure I'd be raped before I even got off the boat; my mother didn't know why anyone would want to go back to 'the old country.' What they did not understand, though, was that I was looking for God, and specifically the God portrayed in Christian churches—like the Jesus at Sacred Heart. I felt there was a clue there, especially in the medieval period when all of life revolved around religion and I wanted to understand why the church art spoke so strongly to me, especially scenes depicting heaven and hell. My parents thought I was crazy.

In the fall I would be entering the Centre d'Études Médiévales in the small town of Poitiers, but for the summer I was wandering through rural France, practicing my French and going from one ancient church town to another, spending my nights in cheap *pensions* and youth hostels along the way.

Admittedly, it was a bit scary to be traveling alone—*une jeune fille toute seule?* people remarked in dismay—but it was also exhilarating after the suffocating hothouse of my extended childhood. With the encouragement of my favorite art professor, I had managed to procure a French government fellowship for study abroad in Poitiers. Then I found a live-in position as an *au pair* girl with a local family, so my parents, although full of admonitions, had to let me go. It was past time.

Even in the drizzly gray morning, the sculpted figures on the porch of Chartres Cathedral were full of life. "The Mob at Chartres" was the way my professor had referred to them, and indeed they were tucked into every nook and cranny of the entryway—standing and sitting and flying and lying in bed—all carved in stone. It was Dr. Frances Godwin, in fact, an émigré artist from Vienna, who had introduced me to Romanesque sculpture, recognizing that I was languishing in the stuffy confines of academia and needed a way out. She showed our class a sculpture from the Abbey church in Moissac, a sensuous and soulful figure of the prophet Jeremiah, and when I all but swooned at the sight of him she had encouraged me to go to France to find him.

"Go fall in love with him," she had said with a knowing smile. "Go fall in love with life altogther!" she had added with a wink.

So I did, and I now stood in the light rain greeting the crowded portal of Chartres Cathedral, wishing that she were here to see it with me. My sleeves were damp by the time I was ready to enter the sanctuary and I walked the steps reverently, filled with anticipation of what I would find.

The light inside was dim, and while my eyes adjusted I stood in the narthex just breathing it in. Centuries of candle wax and incense hung in the air, and my footsteps on the stone floor echoed through the nave as I slowly walked in.

On either side of the nave granite columns rose like massive trees, branching way overhead into ribbed vaults that disappeared in shadow as if the ceiling itself dissolved in the night sky. I felt the presence of generations of others who had walked down this nave, lit their flickering votive candles, and kneeled at this same altar. They were still here, hovering in the shadows of the side aisles and intoning soundlessly from the spiraling pulpit.

It was my turn now—this untested girl from New York in the mid-twentieth century, drawn forward toward that altar by stone columns and tiers of stained-glass windows rising between them, windows that could only hint, at this hour, of the spectrum of color that would stream from them in full daylight. I stopped midway, feeling the silence pulse beneath me in layers: in the crypt beneath the stone floor; in the packed earth of the ancient pagan grove beneath the crypt.

The cathedral felt as if the grove itself was transmuted into stone trunks and arched branches. Were the old ones still here somewhere, the people who worshiped rocks and trees? Would I recognize them if they showed themselves? I dipped my fingers into the font of holy water and flicked some droplets into the air. Later I would add my candle to the banks of votive flames near the altar.

I was finally here! Turning slowly in place, I took in the cathedral from each perspective: north, south, east and west, up and down. The rows of chairs pictured in every photograph I had ever seen of Chartres had been removed, so the space seemed much grander than I had imagined, and on the stone floor was incised a huge labyrinth I had never noticed in the pictures. The lines circled in a complicated pattern that seemed to twist back on itself again and again; I tried to follow it with my eyes but was quickly lost. In the center of the design was a petaled flower large enough for several people to stand in, and I thought to walk directly toward it, but I couldn't. Something compelled me to find the place of entry and follow the path round and round as I was supposed to.

Back and forth the lines took me, turning first right and then left and then right. I lost all sense of time and seemed to be getting no closer to the center. I'd think I was almost there, and then the path swung me out again to the periphery as if it were starting all over again. Then, when I least expected it the path went quickly in, straight as an arrow to the open hub in the middle. The sudden stillness disoriented me.

Some people had entered the nave by this time, and their footfalls rang in the echoing space, their whispers sibilant like breaths in the hallowed stillness. I just stood there, entranced, until it felt like time to do the walk in reverse. I considered cutting across the lines and walking straight out of the labyrinth, but again I couldn't do it. So I followed the path, no longer wondering how long it would take, no longer trying to figure out the pattern.

When I at last emerged I stood still with my eyes closed, feeling strangely calm as if all that twisting and turning had sorted out something in my head. It reminded me of how, as children, we would spin and spin until we were dizzy and then flop down on our backs to watch the sky spin above us, feeling the sweet calm when the dizziness passed.

"*Bonjour.*"

I came out of my dreamy state to the sound of the same deep voice I had heard through the partition in the dormitory the night before.

"I watched you walk the labyrinth," he said, greeting me with a genial grin. I faced a fellow about my own age and height with tousled black hair and a long moustache, who could have been a movie version of a Slavic farmer. His face was broad and ruddy with high cheekbones, and his beaked nose curved right over his moustache. His eyes, though, were the most intensely green eyes I had ever seen on a person and I found myself staring. So much for a tall Danish artist in a black turtleneck! His smile was contagious, and I smiled back.

"*Bonjour,*" I responded. "You're at the hostel, aren't you?" My rudimentary French gave me away as a foreigner.

He nodded, raising his eyebrows. "How did you know?"

"I heard you last night," I admitted, suddenly shy.

"My voice is very loud," he commented with a theatrical shrug of his shoulders. "My parents used to kick me out of the house when I sang." His eyes crinkled when he smiled.

"No, I thought it was distinctive," I declared, making up a French-sounding version of the word 'distinctive.'

"My accent, you mean?"

"Your voice and your accent. Where is your accent from?"

"Czechoslovakia," he said shortly. I had never met a Czech person before. I probably couldn't place Czechoslovakia on a map if I had to. I now felt not only shy, but ignorant as well.

"You have an accent too," he observed with interest. I giggled.

"*Oui*! I hardly can speak French yet," I admitted. "I'm American."

"Ah, *bon*!" He rubbed his hands together delightedly. "I can practice my English with you!"

As parishioners began entering the cathedral for the morning Mass we ducked into a side chapel, talking in whispers. The language we spoke was a whimsical patois of French and English and what must have been smatterings of Czech, along with much gesturing on his part, and a repertoire of facial expressions that kept me staring at him in fascination. He found out more about me in ten minutes than I think I had ever told anyone before, which was doubly amazing given that we spoke in whispers and barely had a language in common.

"And you live now in Czechoslovakia?" I asked him.

"I was born there, but now my family lives in Switzerland—in Zurich. We lived near Prague until the Russians came, and then we left—pffft!" He gestured their flight with a sweep of the hand. His face sobered and we both looked down. After a breath, he continued. "So, now I am studying chemistry in Basel, but my real passion is *les vacances*."

He found his own joke very funny, and we both bent over double to keep our laughter from echoing into the cathedral. We slumped to the floor and sat cross-legged against the *prie-dieu* with our heads close together. In a whisper, I prompted him to continue.

"Your passion is vacations…?" He nodded.

"*Je fais l'auto-stop.* I hitchhike and go wherever my rides take me, so I have adventures and meet interesting people and think new thoughts. It's good."

"I love that," I murmured, wondering if I would ever be brave enough to hitchhike alone. "Where are you going next?"

He shrugged and, eyeing me speculatively, said, "Who knows? We'll see."

The first organ chords cascaded around us, filling the cathedral with sound and resonating off the old, pitted stones. My heart started to pound.

"Tell me why an American should be so interested in this old Europa?" he asked. I felt the sound vibrate through my bones, and tears sprang suddenly to my eyes. I slumped further down, too filled to speak. Maybe this was what I had come to old Europa for. He offered me his handkerchief, which made the tears spill even more. He waited, and then he took back his handkerchief from me with care. We said no more until the last notes of the organ died away, fading into the high air.

"I'm Danilo," he whispered. "Call me Dani."

"I'm Clara," I whispered back, rolling my r the French way. Holding back a giggle, I kept my face straight and added, "Call me Clara." Even with my poor French, he got the joke.

"*Bonjour,* Clara," he said, offering me his hand.

"*Bonjour,* Dani," I repeated as our hands met in a handshake. My fingers felt the warmth of his and I took it in like a breath, smiling.

We left with the others at the end of the Mass, quite chilled by this time; it was still raining outside, and he suggested we find a café and get something hot to drink. As people reached the narthex doors, they turned around to face the altar and genuflected, dipping their fingers into the font and touching themselves in the sign of the cross. Dani and I walked straight through the doors amongst them, but we didn't stop.

"You didn't kneel," Dani observed.

"Neither did you."

"Because I'm a Jew!" he said fiercely, challenging me. I was surprised at myself for not realizing it right away.

"*Moi aussi*," I said, challenging him in return. "Me too."

We sat across from each other at the little round *café* table, warming our hands around steaming bowls of *café au lait* and smiling a lot. He had the kind of lips that turned up even in repose, like a happy gremlin.

"A nice Jewish girl from America, eh?" He said this in broken English, and his accent reminded me of my grandparents. "You're lucky."

I leaned in closer, prepared to argue the point. If he only knew. "Why lucky?"

For a while he didn't answer, and we concentrated on taking small bites of our croissants. Then a crumb got caught in the edge of his moustache and I couldn't take my eyes off it. Finally, he hauled in a breath, placed his bowl down on the table, looked me straight in the eye and said, "Because we didn't get out when we could."

"Oh!" I remembered family stories of fleeing from Russia as refugees, but having been born in Brooklyn myself, I had no personal experience of that time. I really knew very little about the war, and virtually nothing about Czechoslovakia except that soon after the Germans were gone, the Russians had invaded the country. "Tell me," I said, bracing my hands against the underside of the table.

"The short version is what you'll get," he announced tersely. Everything about him seemed electrified, his amazing green eyes sizzling with intensity.

"OK. My parents met each other in our lovely German concentration camp, Terezin, and they managed to keep each other alive until the Americans came."

His lips were taut, and his face searched mine for understanding. I held his gaze, but it was hard. He closed a fist around his spoon and I wanted to put my hand over his, but I didn't. Around us, men talked and shuffled their feet and scraped their chairs against the floor. Spoons clinked against glasses, and people called greetings across the room. Dani and I could have been alone there, caught in a wrinkle in time that included only us.

"Were you born there?" I choked on the words and had to clear my throat twice before the sounds came out.

"No, after. After they went back to the same small village where my father had first been betrayed!" His nostrils flared with anger, and he slapped the palms of both hands on the cafe table, hard. Next to us, a man glanced around and turned back to his drink.

"My grandparents were the only Jews there when my father was growing up—and hard to believe, but he went back there after the war and took my mother with him!"

"And then the Russians came," I said in a hushed voice.

"C'est ça, mon amie. The Russians came. By that time, all three of us kids were here and we had to escape in the dead of winter, in the dead of night."

He stared up at the ceiling and stretched out his legs, recalling the terror of their flight.

"So after the refugee camp we found our way to Zurich, where my father got a job, and so now I am Swiss!" He glared at me provokingly across the table. I could hardly breathe. He was right—I was lucky. "And that's my whole story," he concluded with a sigh. "And now let's hear yours."

For the next few hours, after our café au lait we went on to onion soup and then to bread and cheese, our elbows propped on the table and our heads close together, talking. The rain continued unabated outside, and across the square the cathedral, in all its gray grandeur, stood like a giant ship with two tall masts. How it had managed to survive the war intact with two spires like beacons for airplanes to home in on, I could not imagine.

We talked about how churches had been preserved in Europe even when the cities around them had not been, and I told him about my fascination with medieval art.

"I've always had a thing about religion," I explained. "I just wonder why people can compose this glorious music and build churches like this one, and then are willing to kill each other over it. I'm missing something."

"Maybe people are crazy," he suggested. "Or so scared they'll do anything they're told to do. Or maybe we're all stupid."

"But probably thousands of people worked on this cathedral for centuries," I insisted. "And it's so beautiful, at least some of them had to be smart and spiritual."

"Perhaps, but look at what evil has been done in the name of the church!" he countered. I had nothing to say.

We spoke of our parents—he with caring and me with caution—and our siblings and our favorite friends and the things we most loved to do. He was a daredevil, I learned, with a passion for seeing the world from high places—mountains, airplanes, hang gliders.

"I may be the first doctor of science in the hang-gliding club," he told me with a laugh.

"What do your parents think about you jumping off cliffs with fake wings?" I asked.

"They have no idea, of course," he replied, tilting his head with a crafty grin. "Say, there's another thing I love to do! I love to go walking in the rain."

"You do, really? That's my favorite thing!" I exclaimed. "People at home think I'm nuts!"

"Then let's go," he declared, tossing some bills on the table, putting on his jacket, and pulling a battered beret from his pocket. I grabbed my windbreaker from the back of the chair and wriggled into it, tying a kerchief around my head.

"*Andiamo ma baboushka!*" he cried in the patois that was to be our private language, and led us out into the rain.

The rain wasn't driving hard, but it had come down steadily since morning. The moisture seeped into every pore of our bodies, but it didn't seem to matter.

"Which way?" he asked, indicating the various streets that radiated out from the square. "You choose."

His eyes sparkled with fun, and a droplet hung from the tip of his nose, which he wiped away with the back of his hand.

I pointed to a narrow alleyway behind us. Gallantly he offered me his soaked sleeve, and we set off down the slippery cobblestone passageway.

Everything was funny, and we outdid each other with wit. Already, it felt to me as if we'd been friends forever. We pretended to be tour guides of the cathedral; we discussed the prices of houses we decided to buy; we fantasized about the lives of people who lived in all the places we passed. A window-box garden became an outlandish treatise in botany, and a storefront became an exercise in creative advertising.

We passed one dwelling with a postage-stamp garden and a watering can sitting on the step, disconsolate in the rain—and full. Danilo could not let that go by. With an actor's timing, he picked up the little brass can and brought it to a border of primroses, carefully watering the sodden soil around their base and never cracking a smile. Giggles rose up in me like bubbles, melting everything in their path. I could not stop laughing.

We wandered along the river that wended its way through the town, soaked to the skin. Danilo, in fine form, turned everything into a game: sticks became baseball bats and shot puts; stones got skipped in the river; all manner of flotsam was tried on as hats. I became as silly as he. We entered a shop to get out of a brief downpour, and in the jumble of household goods in the back we found a child's orange kite and the spindle and string to go with it.

"Of course," he breathed, his mouth a delicious smirk of mischief beneath his dripping moustache, "it's a day to fly kites!" Carrying the package to the counter, he sang softly in anticipation, "tada da-da-da-da" while the woman wrapped it up and handed it to him. *"Andiamo, mon amie!"*

He took off skipping, and I had to run to keep up with him.

"You're so great!" I called breathlessly after him. "You have the most fun of anybody I know, even though you've been through the most horrible things!"

He stopped as if putting on the brakes and stood stock still in the rain until I caught up with him. Slowly he turned to face me, droplets caught in his eyebrows, his eyes piercing green, and said in a quiet voice, "Not 'even though'—*because*. What would be better—to cry?"

It was quite a hike down the road to get to open country where we could fly the kite. The land was flat and trees were few. We found an ideal spot, and with ceremony we tore open the package and tried to attach the string to the kite's struts in the rain. Several times we collapsed in hysterics, getting even wetter on the ground, but at last the kite was ready to fly.

Dani put up a finger to test the wind, ran across the field for all he was worth, and let the kite go. It bounced a few times and then got snagged on a bush. Next, I held the kite above my head and we both ran as hard as we could. I let go of it as soon as I felt a gust of wind, flinging it over my head and jumping out from under it. It flew!

"Yaaayyh!" Dani shouted, tugging on the spindle and letting the line spin out as the kite picked up the wind and took off into the sky.

"There she goes!" we shouted jubilantly in a variety of languages. The little orange kite whipped to and fro in the air, twisting and turning as it tugged on its string to get higher. It was like a live thing. Dani reeled it in and out, playing with its pull while I cavorted alongside him, splashing heedlessly in puddles, the two of us shrieking into the wind. Whipping us around as the wind changed direction, the little orange kite rose in the air above the road, where, in the misty distance of the world behind us, the two unmatched spires of the cathedral bore witness to our flight.

By the time we finally made it back to the hostel, we were freezing and soaked to the bone. Neither of us had a real change of clothes in our backpacks, so we carried kindling to the fireplace in the common room and started a fire. Our clothes would have to dry on our backs.

"Where have you guys been?" the other residents asked as we staggered through the communal kitchen with loads of firewood in our arms. My teeth chattered uncontrollably, and my hair was plastered all over my face. I could hardly see where I was going.

"Flying a kite, of course," Dani informed them, his face a study in innocence and his eyes shining like beacons in a lighthouse.

The kindling went up in dry crackling sparks, and once the bigger pieces had caught we had a bright fire roaring up the chimney. We huddled as close to it as we could, bowls of steaming vegetable soup in hand, and slurped hungrily. I undid my barrette and shook out my wet hair, tossing it over my shoulder for the heat of the fire to dry. Danilo ate his soup thoughtfully, staring into the flames and nudging burning logs back into the firebox with his boot when they shifted.

One by one the others joined us with bowls of hot soup, and for the next three hours we shared the fire, the common stew, and good conversation with this random community of people who, only yesterday, had never heard of each other. By the time our clothes were dry we were all good friends, and when we all started yawning it was after midnight, with much still to be said. But we were all too tired, and with handshakes all around we left the circle one by one and went off to bed—Dani to the men's dorm and me to the women's.

I had never had such a fun day in my life! This was what it was like to feel alive. And we hadn't done anything much, really—talked, walked, played—but with Dani every little thing was magic. I liked myself with him, and that made even walking down the street something special. I could hardly wait to see him in the morning, but…what if he did this with a different girl every day? What if he was gone when I got up, or if he preferred somebody else's company? What if…but I was so tired I flopped into bed like a stone and fell asleep right away.

In my dream Dani is showing me how to sing a person. First, you draw the person's outline with a pencil and write numbers so you can follow the dots of his body. At number 1 you start singing the notes of his body, tracing his torso and arms and neck with your song. That's how he comes to life from the picture on the page, with your voice. Knees and thighs and crotch and hips…I am singing his armpits and chest, my voice rising.

Dani tells me that everyone has a different song, and that he likes when I sing him. Then he sings my body, his voice deep and purring, and I feel his notes tickle my skin. I can hardly breathe for the exquisite pleasure of it, but he doesn't stop singing, he doesn't stop singing…

An alarm clock woke me, and the sun was already filtering through the casement onto my upper bunk.

Stretching, I sighed and heard my ribs crack as I twisted, completely awake now and absolutely, completely and deliciously in love.

Once I was dressed in my stiff-dried jeans and had come out into the empty common room, I got scared. I was so certain he would go off with someone else for the day that I left the hostel at a run even before he got up.

The early light in the cathedral was soft and subtly colored by the stained glass it came through. I took out my notebook and camera, telling myself that I was here to work. Dr. Godwin had mentioned how extraordinary the rose window was by morning light—well, here I was. I was a student of medieval art history this year. I told myself that I had to be serious, no matter what. I told myself everything except the truth—that probably Dani would choose somebody else to spend the day with, and I couldn't bear it.

He found me, not fifteen minutes later, lighting a penitent candle up at the altar.

"Up early," he observed lightly, though I noticed that his eyes were a little guarded. I nodded, having difficulty looking up. I could still feel his dream song on my skin, and the sound of his voice was doing provocative things in my belly. "Have you walked the labyrinth yet?"

"No." My heart was beating entirely out of my control. I felt like a six-year-old.

"Want to walk it with me?" His hand came toward my shoulder, stopping just short of touching me. I nodded but couldn't speak, and I followed him up the nave to the ancient labyrinth on the stone floor. Pools of reds and blues and golds played on the gray stones, shifting as the sun rose higher and lit the stained glass. From the clerestory above, rays of dust-moted gold illumined the upper reaches of the keystone arches in the heights, and the windows circling the altar shone more brightly as the sun rose in the sky.

He led the way and I followed a few paces behind him, matching a slow stride to his and trying not to gaze too obviously at his back and buttocks. His jeans were as wrinkled as mine, and his shirt even more so. We circled and turned in phases, sometimes walking in the same direction for a while, sometimes passing each other on adjacent paths. When we passed we smiled self-consciously, but otherwise we stayed focused on the path. The way seemed endless, again, although I could have walked it with him forever. We were on the same road, following each other round and round, together in the circle. We took one step after another, circling at last way out to the periphery, and then we shot straight into the center. Home.

The light was higher now, and the church was perceptibly warmer when we stood facing each other in the center, lit by a ray of sunlight that had reached that very spot the same time we did. Eyes closed, he lifted his face to the warmth. His moustache glistened and his lips beneath them were pink and soft. I was stealing peeks, trying to still the agitation in my belly. When his eyelids fluttered, I quickly shut my eyes so he wouldn't think I was watching him. Cat and mouse, we took turns peeking until we caught each other at it and then both looked away quickly

The first notes of a Bach organ prelude poured out into the sanctuary as parishioners began entering for the morning Mass. In the center of the labyrinth we stood right in everybody's way, and I wanted to move to the side, but Dani showed no signs of being disturbed.

"*Reste.*" he whispered. "Stay." So I stayed, and through the rippling fugue we stood side by side in the center of the cathedral listening to each other breathe.

"Tomorrow—you'll stay here?" he asked in a slow whisper as the last crashing chords were fading into the shadowed vaults. My eyes opened to see his gaze steady on my face.

"I don't know…I think so," I fumbled, wanting to be wherever he was and not brave enough to say so. He rubbed his nose and sighed. Then he scratched his moustache, then his chin. Yes! Yes! I wanted to shout to his unasked question. He cleared his throat. I didn't know where to look. He cleared his throat again, began in French, then in English, "Would it you please—ummm—you would like to be *sur la route* with this guy?"

Two days later, backpacks on our backs, we left at dawn after walking the labyrinth together one last time. We decided to head west toward Bretagne where, Dani said, there were mysterious stone circles and *dolmens*, megalithic stone chambers all over the countryside that he had always wondered about.

"Nous sommes sur la route!" he exclaimed gleefully as we left the town behind us and walked along the same road we had taken to fly our kite; when was that—three lifetimes ago? "We're on the road!" Our plan was to catch a ride that would take us westward, and to travel as far as we could in one day.

After we had trudged for most of an hour, seeing cars pass only on the other side of the road, Dani said philosophically, "Not yet have we reached the magic spot."

"Not yet," I agreed. My backpack was beginning to chafe. For now, I was happy to simply follow him down some road towards an unknown destination, feeling what it was like to 'not be there yet,' as he had felt since fleeing Czechoslovakia.

"How about right here?" I asked when we reached the shade of a large roadside oak, already shrugging out of my heavy pack.

"It is a very magic spot, no?" he agreed, squinting down the road from where our ride was sure to come and dropping his backpack onto the ground. I lowered myself into a squat, my arms hanging over my knees.

"Hey, Dani," I asked, "when you go on your *vacances*, are you really looking for the place you want to live?"

"For home, you mean?" he asked, holding out his thumb as a car materialized in the distance. For the first time in my life I dared hold out my thumb too. "I suppose so," he mused, peering hopefully at what was looking more like a truck as it got closer. "*Bon!*" he exclaimed, "*un camion!* Truck drivers always stop for hitchhikers. Eh!" he sighed, continuing his thought. "Where does somebody like me belong? I'm a wandering Jew—I live everywhere and nowhere."

"Like me," I echoed softly just as the lorry, with a hiss of brakes and a grinding of gears, pulled to a stop before us.

The young red-haired driver pushed open the cab door and called from his high seat, "Where you going?"

"West," shouted Dani above the engine's noise. "We're going to Bretagne."

"*C'est bien!*" the driver shouted back. "I'm going as far as Angers. Climb up!"

We took off in a roar of noise and exhaust, and I sat between the two men, gazing out the windshield as the countryside flashed by. Silently I bid farewell to the cathedral diminishing on the horizon behind us, and to the girl I had been until two days ago.

"From where are you traveling?" the driver asked, changing gears.

"Me, I'm from America," I replied. He hit the steering wheel with both hands.

"You know Davy Crockett?" he asked enthusiastically. "Day-wis, Day-wis Crockett, za kink off za vild fron—tier!' he sang out of tune. A small smile played on Dani's face, but he continued to stare out the window on his side.

"Your friend is American too?" our driver asked at the end of his impromptu song. I shook my head.

"Not really," I mumbled, letting Dani answer a question that did not have a simple answer.

"Canadian," was Dani's unlikely response before he turned back to the window.

The day wore on as we jounced our way across the west country of France, passing through fertile fields and windbreaks and quaint old villages. I had no idea where we were except that I was exactly where I wished to be, my thigh pressed warmly against Danilo's and my shoulder touching his. We gazed out at the same world flashing by and we moved under the same sky, more aware of where our bodies met than of the road we were on. The focus of our attention made us very quiet.

Although our driver chatted happily the whole time, we said almost nothing during the last two hours of the journey. Only when we pulled up for gas in Angers did we resume conversation as he pointed out the way to the youth hostel nearby, giving us one last, bawling rendition of Davy Crockett, and commenting that we looked like Gypsies.

"That's right!" Dani shouted up to him as the engine revved up, slamming the cab door closed. "We are!"

We sat apart from the others at the long table in the farmhouse kitchen of the youth hostel, eating our artichokes slowly, irresistibly gazing into each other's eyes. Petal by petal, we plucked the artichokes down to the delicious heart, scooping out each petal with our teeth and discarding the leaves in a common bowl between us. Then we scraped off the spiny thistles, slathered the hearts with cream, and gobbled them down in four bites, sucking the cream off our fingers. Then Dani leaned towards me, his eyes beseeching.

"What you said before," he began quietly, "about looking for home…?"

"Um-hm."

"That squeezed my heart." His eyes glistened and I reached for his hand. "It's true, I have no home."

"Your family in Zurich…?" I began. He shook his head slowly.

"That is my family, and I will always belong to them—just as you will when you learn to forgive your parents," he added slyly, "but I am a man now and have to make my life somewhere. Zurich is not my home—not now, not ever." He sighed and picked at the discarded artichoke leaves. "You came right into my blood when you said that this morning."

"I'm sorry. I shouldn't have," I almost cried. "I'm so sorry I hurt you…" He shook his head slowly, hushing me.

"No, it was good what you said, even if I don't like to face hard things." With one finger he stroked my chin, and when he stopped I could still feel his finger there. "I am just surprised how fast you found your way to my heart."

After a restless night, we found a ride with a local farmer who was going to a village near Nantes—Carquefou—just at the gateway to Bretagne. Tossing our backpacks alongside the cabbages and leeks in the bed of his truck, we took off into the sunshiny day through green fields dotted with bright red poppies. Fluffy clouds, like a child's drawings, hung in a blue sky, and the road we traveled could have been the road to the kingdom of Oz.

Dani and I sat pressed together in the front seat, hands clasped tight, learning Breton songs from the farmer. Then we swapped songs, Dani teaching us a Czech folksong, followed by my rendition of Row, Row, Row Your Boat. By the time we arrived at the crossroads at Carquefou, the three of us could sing it as a round, and before he would leave us off, the farmer insisted upon teaching us the dance to a Breton *galliard*.

"Now bend and bow," he instructed, his truck idling and his two disciples skipping nimbly on the tarmac at the *carrefours*. We all applauded.

"See over there—that line of trees?" he pointed. "There's a lovely stream there. You can swim to your pleasure and then when you're ready to get back on the road, come back to this crossroads. Many cars pass by here on their way to Nantes."

We waved until his truck disappeared over the hill, and then we stood in the cricket-chirping silence on the verge of the road, suddenly alone together in the middle of nowhere. I was with someone I had known for only four days, I realized, and for a moment I wondered if I should be scared. But I wasn't.

"Hah! This is what I live for!" Dani exclaimed, rubbing his hands together.

"Me too," I echoed, knowing that for me life was just starting.

"I love getting lost and having no idea what's coming down the road!" He chuckled happily. "Especially if I'm lost with a beautiful woman." He winked at me. I looked down.

He had said *belle femme*, not *belle fille*. That was the first time anyone had ever referred to me as a woman, not a girl. I wasn't sure how to respond.

"*Andiamo*," he grunted, hefting his pack to lead the way from the middle of the road toward the tree-lined stream. The only thing I could do was follow his lead.

A clear, bouldery stream spun a lazy course through a wildflower- and oak-studded meadow, and we could hear its gurgle before we could see it. It was a storybook brook with rills and clearwater pools, its banks trailing with wild honeysuckle and pink vervain, and flowering grasses that came right up to its edge. With each footstep we crushed fragrant mint and chamomile, and birdsong and running water was the music of the air.

"*Voilà!*" Dani exclaimed, shrugging off his backpack. "This is my church!" With a single motion he pulled his shirt over his head and shook out his arms, inviting me to do the same. I lowered my pack to the ground, trying not to stare at his smooth, muscled arms and the forest of dark hair massed on his chest. I wondered if his pants were going to come off next.

Suddenly shy, I froze up and couldn't feel a thing. What a hopeless oaf I was! What was a girl supposed to do now, especially if she had never seen a boy naked before? My heart was beating hard in my throat.

Dani probably had all kinds of experience, and since I had agreed to go hitchhiking with him he must have assumed that I did too. It was too embarrassing to admit to him that even though I was almost twenty I was still a virgin. He stood there half naked and took stock of the situation, and then gently opened his arms to me. Fully clothed, my heart in my mouth, I moved right into them.

Our hug must have lasted an hour. We held onto each other as if for dear life, swaying and rubbing and murmuring nonsensical words. When we finally parted, weak-kneed with desire, we walked hand-in-hand to a willow by the stream, took off our boots and sat dangling our feet in the cool running water. He raised a questioning eyebrow at me.

"I've never…" I confessed. *"Toi?"* He nodded, his face so full of longing that I lowered my eyes.

"Yes, but not recently. When I was in the refugee camp I was a wild man, but now I am—ahem—more discriminating. *Et, tu est une innocente, toi?"*

"Extremely innocent," I confessed with an embarrassed giggle. "Stupid, in fact."

"It's not so stupid to be a virtuous woman," he stated. "Anyhow, I happen to find virtue very attractive." We laughed, me rather uneasily.

For the next hour or more we sat and lay by the stream barely touching, talking about love and sex, our pasts, and his college girl-friend, Rosa, who had been his only real lover.

"She finally dumped me," he confessed with a grin. "She wanted babies and I was too much of a rogue for marriage." He gave me a playful leer and I pretended to shrink in fear—maybe more than pretended. In fact, I was scared out of my wits as my body yearned for him and then seized up in alternating currents.

I told him about my occasional boyfriends, and my crush on my high school gym teacher—a woman—and the boy I had said yes to before I had the guts to say no and hand him back his ring.

"And you never made love with him?"

"No—I didn't love him, so I couldn't," I tried to explain. "I knew it wasn't love because I didn't feel about him the way I had felt about my dog Dukie." Dani flopped onto his back and roared with laughter. I laughed too and added, "When I broke our engagement I told him that, and he was so insulted he stomped out of the house and never came back."

"Oh, deliciously delicious!" he cried. "Tell me all about Dukie right now!"

And so the day passed in stories and laughter, hugging and kissing. By the time he stood up, unzipped his pants and leapt into the water naked, I think I had told him everything about my love life there was to tell—which was not very much, after all. And he let me know that he was attracted to me but would never push me in any way. I nodded gratefully, too shy to do more than that.

For the rest of the day, he in his skin and me in my tank-top bathing suit, we played in and out of the stream. We floated on our backs with the current, paddling around rocks that jutted out of turbulent water; we treaded in deep pools where fish nibbled on our toes; we waded upstream, feeling the currents slip around us. He picked a bouquet of watery wildflowers from the bank—white and pink and yellow—and presented them to me with a bow. I plucked vervain and buttercups, tucking them into his wet hair like a crown of flowers. When we got waterlogged we sunbathed on the bank, and when we got overheated we jumped back into the stream.

It was hunger that finally forced us onto dry land. My towel became the tablecloth, and we set our table on the grassy verge with a *baguette* and Camembert, ripe tomatoes, and watercress gathered from the shallows of the stream. Tepid water from his canteen was our wine, and a bar of melted chocolate from my pack our ambrosia.

When nothing was left but crumbs and their attendant ants, we stretched out side by side on the grass and dozed, occasionally muttering to each other. The sun's heat smoothed our skins and relaxed our minds so that the senses in our bodies could feel their way unobstructed through the maze of our desire. I wanted him so much it hurt, and I had to brace against the twitching in my legs and the insistent throbbing in my groin. He rolled over in his half sleep, laying an arm across my belly and I moaned, turning towards him like lodestar responding to a magnet, but when he began to explore me with light caresses and a questing tongue I pulled back, scared.

"It's OK." he whispered, out of breath and lying still until his breathing settled down. I felt like an idiot girl—or only half a woman. To my helpless shame, I was not yet ready.

"I'm a hungry man," he admitted later as we washed our clothes by the edge of the stream. He scrubbed his dirty jeans against a stone, rinsing them out in the current. On the bank lay an assortment of our underwear drying in the sun; he wrung out his jeans hard, and spread them next to the rest on the grass.

"When you've come up so close to death as I have, you know there's only time for what is real, and there is only right now to live it." His voice was very matter-of-fact. He scrubbed away at his sweatshirt; downstream from his stone the water ran brown and then clear again.

"So what do you consider real?" I asked, spreading my cardigan out on the bank next to his jeans where they looked very homey together. I wanted to hear how he would describe himself—the off-beat intensity and kindness of the person I was coming to know. And sexiness, I had to admit, feeling the heat stir in my body. He looked up and regarded me thoughtfully, knee-deep in the running stream, his penis dangling frankly from a bush of black hair and his laundry draped over his hand. His green eyes held me in their gaze.

"This," he said simply, indicating our surroundings. "A flowing river under a brilliant sun by a meadow with wildflowers, and that crow cawing away for all he's worth, and a man and a woman who desire each other madly. Right here, right now, us! This is real!"

"And the laundry," I reminded him.

"Always the laundry," he laughed, bending over to scrub away at his sweatshirt. Then he straightened again, serious. "Want to hear what wouldn't be real?"

"*Bien sûr,*" I replied, rubbing my socks together and rinsing them out, trying for an air of nonchalance.

"OK, what isn't real is denying attraction for any reason what-soever. Or thinking that bodies have to be hidden because they're sinful!" He spit this out with passion, making me painfully aware of my very proper bathing suit. But this still wasn't the right moment to take it off.

"Listen," he continued, his face beginning to collapse. I listened.

"In the refugee camp we had nothing—only each other and a bucket to shit in!" He grimaced painfully and the tears brimmed over. I slogged through the current to him and circled my arms around his slippery waist. "People were suffering!" he cried in a strangled voice, "old people, babies!" He broke down into tortured sobs and I held onto him as if both our lives depended on it.

"That's how you learn what's real," he gasped out. "It's being alive right now and not wasting a minute of life because tomorrow you may not have it! And it's loving whatever the hell is lovable— even the little bits of straw beneath your feet—because that's the only thing that matters. All the rest is shit!"

His body arched back and he wailed into the air like an air raid siren. The sound shook me to my core and I cried with him, both of us trembling in the water as it swirled against our legs, parted into tiny whirlpools around us, and flowed on downstream taking our muddy tears with it.

We did not need to make love that night. For now we were spent, content just to lie together on top of our sleeping bags, legs entangled and bodies quiet beneath the stars. A night heron burst out of the woods and took to the air, the flapping of her huge, slow wings audible over the burbling of the stream. A pair of crows squabbled in the trees and fireflies, searching for each other, lit up the darkness with their flashing bits of light.

Side by side, we seemed to have reached the edge of some deep intimacy that we were almost, but not quite, ready to plunge into. All afternoon, in and out of the water, we cried together and told each other the deeper and harder stories of our lives—the ones we could hardly tell even ourselves. And we had both listened. And received them with shared tears, finding each other all the more extraordinary, all the more beautiful because of our shames.

As I drifted toward sleep, Dani began humming the Breton tune we had learned that morning. I smiled to myself in the dark, turning toward him and rising onto an elbow to hum sleepily along with him. I found the harmony to his melody and we improvised around the rhythm. It was still the folksong we had learned, but embellished with our new sounds it became our own song. We teased the melody, sliding around each other's voices and finding new notes in the air, we grounded the song with new pulsing beats. One riff repeated itself over and over, leading us into a trance where the music came through us without any effort, singing us and merging us until we slid imperceptibly into sleep.

I awoke to wisps of morning mist, from a dream in which I was lost in the long hallway of an apartment house, unable to find the right apartment. One door stood ajar and I entered the nave of a vast, empty cathedral. At the altar, a choir of angelic voices beckoned me slowly forward. I had been waited for, it seems, and the singing was for me…

I slipped out of the dream, shifting gradually from the apartment-house cathedral to our camp beneath the oak tree, and the stream and fields beyond. Dani's place beside me lay empty, his sleeping bag rumpled with the impression of his body, and except for the twittering of birds out for their morning forage, the world was silent. For a moment I felt abandoned, but then I stretched and yawned deliberately before I looked around for him. After yesterday's revelations, maybe he felt shy. Certainly I did.

While I was brushing my hair I caught sight of him on a grassy hillside across the stream, a faraway figure striding unselfconsciously down the slope. He was like a kid, plucking wildflowers and blowing their fuzzy seed heads into the wind, squatting to examine insect colonies, leaping sideways over sheep fences. By the time he negotiated the rocks across the stream, his eyes looked excited to see me again, and I was breathless with wanting.

He greeted me with a chaste kiss and then took my hairbrush from my hand. Standing behind me, he hefted my hank of hair before running long strokes through it. I closed my eyes in pleasure, feeling his strong hands caressing my hair and smoothing it flat. When it was free of knots, he massed it in both hands and buried his nose into the nest he had created, luxuriously sniffing. I moaned helplessly and lifted my head, rubbing my neck against his lips, his cheeks, his ears, and turned in his embrace to melt into a hundred hungry kisses until we were both crazy out of our minds. My whole body throbbed, ached for completion, and he was trembling as he pulled away suddenly, his eyes dark and his breathing uneven.

"Not now," he said huskily. There was an edge of anger in his voice and I wobbled unsteadily, trying to catch my breath. We stood glaring at each other for a few moments of confusion, and then he broke the mood, grinning with mischief and clearing his throat.

"Hey, I have to check this out. Tell me the truth—do you love me as much as Dukie?" We both burst into laughter and it effectively shifted the moment. I realized I was but a novice in uncharted waters and that he, for better or for worse, would be my guide. There was nothing I could do but follow his lead.

The first car coming through the *carrefours* picked us up. It was a friendly couple on their way to Quiberon on the Golfe du Morbihan, with an hour or so stop in Nantes where they had some business. We were welcome to ride the whole way with them if we didn't mind the long stop. Happily we hopped in, looking forward to a steaming latte in Nantes and some shopping for provisions.

At the café we ordered passion-fruit ice cream cones along with our lattes, not bothering to conceal our smoldering gazes at each other. I kept drowning in the smoky green depths of his eyes, barely coming up for air before I was drawn back to drown again. Tiny smiles played on both our lips, and our ice cream cones sat unheeded in our hands.

And melted, of course, and dripped in a rivulet right down my arm. I took an absentminded lick, spilling even more over the cone's rim, but I hardly noticed. With a dreamy smile, Dani followed the line of the drip along my forearm with one finger, slipping it across my wrist and palm before lifting his sticky finger to my lips. I opened my mouth languidly to flick my tongue at his finger the way a cat would, and even though the day was hot we both shivered.

We were dropped off at the *quai* in Quiberon rather late in the day, just as a little ferry was ringing its last bells on the far side of the harbor.

"Let's take it!" Dani shouted, as we wished our kindly drivers thanks and Godspeed.

"Where's it going?" I called, waving good-bye and running across the cobblestoned wharf after him.

"We'll find out!" he called over his shoulder. We raced up the plank a moment before the ferryman revved up his motor, untied the ropes, and took off into the Baie de Quiberon.

We headed out into the mist towards who knew where, the water swelling and dropping beneath us, its wake cresting in two graceful arcs behind the boat. We learned that the ferryboat stopped at three islands: Belle Ile, which was fairly large and well populated; Ile d'Houet, which was much smaller with little population; and the tiny, wild Ile Hoëdic, which had a path but no roads. We opted for Ile Hoëdic, naturally, and settled down for the ride.

This was a two-person adventure, I realized, as the boat slapped in the troughs and shuddered on the crests. The seagulls were keening and coasting above us, and the air was briny with sea. I would never have had the courage or the know-how to do this alone and even though 'two' was only one more than 'one' it made all the difference. Together, we were a multitude that could make anything happen—even love. Especially love. Even more than grabbing a ferry to nowhere in a place you'd never been, love was the adventure. I looked up at Dani from where I sat in the runnel, his body leaning gracefully against the mast pole, his black hair ruffled by the wind, and his eyes, behind sunglasses, squinting and turning from where we had been to where we were going. And I smiled.

Ile Hoëdic is so small that from the path transecting the island you can hear surf booming on both sides simultaneously. When we disembarked at the stone landing, we felt like Adam and Eve dropped into a rock and wildflower garden. Red poppies dotted green seaside meadows, and giant standing stones—the mysterious megaliths from an era before known history—stood like sentinels guarding the spot. They reminded me of something I once must have known but had certainly forgotten.

Dani told me that standing stones could be found all over the world, but nobody knew who put them there—nor why, nor when. It was a great mystery, he said, but the people who had placed them had done so long before there was a cathedral at Chartres or even Roman walls. The megaliths were silent witnesses to a time when mysterious forces that linked the earth and the heavens were understood—forces that linked people to the cosmos and to each other through the agency of the stones.

I touched the rough granite of a tall stone on the path and felt it draw me in. Leaning against it I listened, and it seemed to hum just beyond hearing, a counterpoint to the crash of the surf.

The island's single path was easy to follow, although it was overgrown with gorse and rock rose in fragrant bloom. We met a few darting lizards, and in the air seagulls flew, but otherwise we were alone on the island. The path stretched before us, and we decided to camp at the first place that called to us as home.

"We will know it when we find it," Dani said confidently, slapping a hand companionably on a stout standing stone. We passed thickets of heather and copses thick with wild fennel, and through the green on either side we caught glimpses of wild blue sea. Humps of granite stuck out here and there along the path, indicating fallen *menhirs* and stone chambers long abandoned. At last, when we had reached the headland where the path petered out, we turned to each other, triumphant, and said at the same time, "This is home!"

The bluff jutted out like the prow of a ship, the edge thick with windblown bushes covered by a tangle of wild honeysuckle. What took our breaths away, however, was the *dolmen* with its back to the sea like a giant, aboveground cave. Supported by massive rock slabs, a single capstone of granite that must have weighed a dozen tons sat perched at an angle. A narrow entryway opened to a low passage that, from where we stood, looked dark as night, its ancient stone pitted by sea winds and covered with a layer of lichen. We stood gazing at it, silenced.

"What do you think it was used for?" I whispered.

"Don't know," Dani whispered back. "Or how they managed to move those stones here. Notice that they're not from the island."

"You're right!" I declared, looking around me at the flat contour of the land. Except for the deliberately placed stones, not a boulder marred the gradually tilting surface of the island. "That's incredible!"

"Don't I take you to nice places?" he teased. Nodding, I squirmed out of my pack and hunkered down at the musty opening to crawl inside. Two feet into the low, narrow tunnel I was in total darkness but I stayed low and kept crawling. The narrow walls opened suddenly into a pitch-black chamber of invisible proportions, and I shivered.

Dani crawled in after me and found me in the musty dark. We clasped hands and stared into nothing. He started to speak, then stopped, and I scooted closer to him. The lightless chamber subtly resonated with our breathing.

"Let's sing," he suggested bravely, clearing his throat before humming a note. The chamber hummed back and I began to feel dizzy. I lowered my head, slumping uncontrollably into his lap as my eyes, against my will, heavily closed. Above me, Dani shifted sideways against the stone wall and in moments was snoring.

There was no resisting that sudden sleep and for how long we gave into it, I do not know, but we awoke simultaneously and sat bolt upright, breathing shallowly and holding hands hard.

"What happened?" he blurted out, bewildered, in several languages. "Let's get out of here."

Dani shook his head groggily and pulled me toward the narrow crawlspace, and we felt our way out backwards. Our eyes saw only the dark interior until we emerged again into the light.

"What just happened?" we both cried, burrowing into each other's arms at a safe distance from the stone chamber. We gulped in fresh sea air, briny and alive. "I don't even remember falling asleep!"

"One minute I was humming and the next minute I was waking out of a drugged sleep," he gasped, shaken. "It's said that mysterious things have happened around these stones."

"I believe it," I breathed. Thoughtfully we turned to each other, knowing that we were both feeling the same thing.

"I love it," he drawled, a slow grin creasing his whole face.

"Me too," I admitted. He shook his finger at me.

"You really fell asleep, didn't you?" he observed.

"Out like a light," I confirmed. "You too!" He nodded slowly and we stared into each other's eyes.

"Still want to camp here?"

"You bet I do," I declared without hesitation.

"That's my girl," he chuckled. I knew at that moment that I had found my very own perfect friend, and I snuggled into his arm. He squeezed me warmly and added, "But let's sleep outside, OK?"

We set up our camp inland from the *dolmen*, where we could watch the sun go down—in this season not until ten o'clock—and watch it rise again early in the east. We lay out our ponchos as a ground cloth and battened down the four corners with our packs.

"It didn't really feel so bad," I observed, untying my sleeping bag and rolling it out across the ponchos. "It was scary, but actually sort of peaceful."

"I didn't even know anything was happening until I woke up from it," Dani confessed. "All I remember is waking up and not seeing you."

"Not seeing anything," I reminded him, laughing shakily. "It was so dark…" We crawled across the ponchos and hugged. We started kissing, but then he sat back and regarded me with amusement.

"You love to be spooked, don't you?" There was a tone of mock accusation in his voice. I admitted that I did.

"But so do you, right?"

"Already, she knows me like a book," he teased, planting a chaste kiss on my forehead and rolling over to retrieve his backpack.

The trail to the beach was barely visible, wending its sandy way down the bluff through spiny dune grass and wild fennel. We wended with it, our arms laden with provisions and utensils for a supper on the beach. Dani was convinced he would catch us a fish, but not counting on it I had brought along a *baguette* and cheese and a small sack of oranges. He, more the optimist than I, carried his cooking pot, spoons, and a bottle of wine.

The cove at the base of the bluff was deserted; we were the only people in the world. Only the megaliths scattered on the island indicated the long-ago presence of others—longer ago than we had history for. Otherwise, we might have felt that we were the first humans to press our footprints onto this stretch of virgin sand. We heard it squeak beneath our feet.

The waves came again and again, rhythmically cresting and crashing in a rush of foam against the shore, and sea stacks, just beyond the lines of surf, jutted black above the water, catching white spray with each surge of the waves.

As the trail emerged onto the beach, Dani stopped and took it all in. His eyes gleamed with pleasure and his whole body radiated his delight.

"Look!" he exclaimed, turning me this way and that. "Look at the color of those waves! See that seal? Oh, my God!"

He dropped his bundle on the sand and ran, whooping, down to the tideline where land and sea met in a shifting embrace. He rolled up his jeans, riffled his arms in the surf and ran back to me, dripping. I stood at the top of the cove, my arms crossed, and just watched him. When he came spurting back, he dribbled seawater all over me, breathless with excitement.

"The first time I saw the ocean I was sixteen," he exclaimed. "It was in Israel, after the camp. It was my first taste of freedom." My eyes filled with tears.

"You are so amazing," I muttered wonderingly, plunking down on the sand to untie my boots.

"They had to finally carry me off the beach," he continued, unzipping his jeans and hopping on one foot as he tried to extricate his pants from his boots. "It took my two uncles..." He couldn't get his pant leg over his boot so he bent over, bare-assed, to untie his bootlace first. I dissolved in hysterics.

"Yah—it was funny. Two strong guys it took to carry me off that beach!"

I laughed helplessly and took off my shoes and clothes, still a bit nervous, but with a little more decorum than he. My bathing suit was still up at our camp, left there deliberately, and I tried to act cool on this day of many firsts with more to come. Dani was so excited I don't think he even noticed.

The sun warmed parts of me that had never before been exposed to the air, and the breeze on my breasts gave me a tickle of deep pleasure. Dani raced down to the surf, arms and legs flying, and galloped over low breakers into the water.

"Oh, you beautiful male person," I heard myself exclaim, my eyes bursting with the sight of him bright-skinned and muscular, his hair flying and his penis bobbing, his limbs agile and powerful as he went headfirst into a curling wedge of water before being engulfed by the sea.

I followed him in, waiting in the shallows until I saw him surface and then wading through the first spurt of surf to join him in the waves. Neptune himself with bubbles and seaweed dripping from his hair, he caught me in his arms and spun me weightlessly round and round in the swells.

We played like kids, splashing and diving around each other, rising and falling with the waves. He swam under me and lifted me onto his back. I wrapped my legs around his waist, and he gave me a piggyback ride until he dumped me unceremoniously into an oncoming breaker and then rescued me with a fat wet kiss. Then he wrapped himself around my back and let me carry him, his arms holding my shoulders and his penis nestled comfortably into the small of my back.

We cavorted until we ached with laughter, and then he pointed to one of the sea stacks.

"There's our dinner, I do believe!" Swimming closer, we found that the rock surface was teeming with barnacles and mussels. "We'll need a bag to put them in, and a knife," he shouted above the breakers, treading water and spitting. "We brought my pocket knife, no?"

"In the bag with the oranges!" I shouted back.

"And a towel?"

"*Oui.*"

"OK, I'll go get them. Watch out you don't scrape against the rock. I'll be right back." And in a flurry of tumult and foam he rode the surf with strong, steady strokes, back to the beach.

It wasn't easy maintaining contact with a rock covered with living shells in a sea that constantly surged and sucked us back and forth, but we found handholds and footholds next to each other and hung on, prying the biggest mussels we could find from their fellows and tucking them precariously into our towel-turned-bag. I held the bag while Dani worked at the mussels, attacking the adhesive side where their wings met and tugging them up and down until they let go into his hands. His face, while he worked, had the pure concentration of generations of hunter-gatherers, and I gazed at him insatiably.

While the sea tried to bash me into the rock and the mollusks gave subtle hisses as their stronghold was being breached, my heart knew this as a moment of perfect happiness. Even if I never had another such moment in my life, I could accept my fate because right here, right now, this was mine!

I memorized the way Dani's jaw tightened to his task, the feel of the waves rocking me against the sharp mollusk beds by his side, the touch of his slippery fingers as he handed over two more mussels for the towel. In the spray of the next wave we exchanged a grin confirming that we both felt exactly the same way. He crowed like a rooster and bent again to his task.

"Last two for the pot!" he shouted, handing me two more mussels and pulling a strand of seaweed from the sea stack before pushing off back into the waves.

"Let go!" he hollered, immediately getting swept away. Releasing my hold from the rock, I reached out for him, gasping and spitting, but he was already being carried towards the shore. I kicked off after him.

We found each other again in the shallows and sat at the tideline panting from our efforts. He still had the seaweed dangling from his fingers.

"Here," he said, taking my hand and delicately wrapping the strand of seaweed around my ring finger.

"Wilt thou be my wife?" he asked in English. It sounded more like *Vilt zow pee ma vife*, and I burst into a fresh gale of laughter that welled up from somewhere deep in my body, and with hot tears on my cold cheeks I gave him my hand.

We came up the beach arm in arm, two innocents in Paradise with the towel full of mussels slung over Dani's shoulder. Late clouds scudded shadows across the sand and the sun, in a blaze of orange and blue-green light, dipped toward the west. Just opposite, in the darkening part of the sky, the glow of the coming moon began to seep up from the other side of the world. Embracing, we stopped to watch the sunset, swaying in time to the waves pounding and spurting on the shore. Through skin and muscle and bone, we felt each other's blood pulsing, and hungry, we reached for it with nibbles and tender bites.

But it was time to build a fire before there would be no light to see by. Like green wood we resisted parting, our thirst unslaked, but like the hunters and gatherers we had become we searched the beach for driftwood to burn.

Dani gathered five rounded stones for our firepit and placed them in a circle at the edge of the beach. Then we scoured the cove for driftwood—small sticks for kindling and bigger logs for burning. When two good piles of wood were stacked by the firepit, Dani taught me to construct a flimsy teepee to get the fire started and then to reinforce it with bigger sticks and branches.

"When this all gets hot," he told me, "then we throw on the big hunks." I tittered uncontrollably like a child, but so did he. He poked a playful finger at my bare midriff, and my belly lurched wildly. His eyes were smoky, and he grabbed a matchbook from his bag and took out the first match.

"Ready?" he asked with a sly grin, chuckles rumbling like effervescence in his throat. I could barely speak and nodded helplessly.

"Ready," I replied, as soon as I found my voice.

Our fire started as a wisp of smoke spiraling up the teepee, but as it caught it became a lively blaze of heat. Piece by piece we added driftwood to the flames, piling them vertically on the stones to keep the fire going strong.

"How about *Soupe de Moules a l'Orange et Feneuil?*" I suggested from the invisible cookbook in my hand. Mussel, orange and fennel soup.

"*C'est trés bien, ça,*" he said, pulling the cork from the wine and taking a swig. He passed the bottle to me and I took a taste, pouring some into the cooking pot for the broth. Then we sliced all three oranges, dropping the slices into the pot, peel and all, and balanced the pot on top of the hot stones. When the broth set to boil we dropped in the mussels one at a time, adding feathery fronds of fennel when the mussels began gently to open their shells.

Salivating with appetite, Dani rubbed his hands together and watched intensely as the last mussel yielded and revealed its brown-orange flesh. Then he tore off a hunk of bread, dipped it into the spicy stew and offered me the first taste.

"Mmmm." I licked my lips and dipped the bread into the pot for him in turn. His eyes closed with pleasure as he chewed and swallowed. Then he took the pot off the fire with the sandy towel, spooning mussel soup into each of our cups, and handed me mine.

I lifted a hot mussel gingerly to my mouth, sliding my tongue beneath its plump body and sucked it out, licking the salty sweet shell for every last bit of flavor. Dani then did the same thing, mirroring me. As we ate we never took our eyes from each other—even when we scooped the broth from the pot, even when the stew juice dripped down my arm and Dani bent his head to lick it up, his lips and moustache and tongue spreading glory up my arm all the way to my belly. He handed me the wine for another swallow and it went down warm. We dipped each other's last bits of bread in the spicy broth and fed each other, our arms linked.

The moon rose higher and the stars spun in their paths, and beneath them on the sand we were two pure flames burning.

"Now," he whispered, placing both cups beside the fire where our moon shadows swayed in firelight. I burned towards him.

The waves thundered on the shore and the moon embraced the world, and with a howling, shuddering force that broke through all the bounds of space we came together urgently, our bodies fusing with the energy of a thousand spiraling galaxies. On the trampled sand we matched the sounds of the universe as we took each other in ecstatically, singing and crying, and all the while the world whirled and whirled wildly into radiant vortices of Light.

The Force of Attraction

*Then a throb, a pulse, an urge, a flutter of love—
an impulse or desire in the ocean of consciousness
to create and enjoy. Unlike an ordinary desire or
impulse, it emanates from everywhere at once.
From that initial movement, the whole world
comes into being. This ocean of consciousness is
the Absolute; the throb is its creative power.*

From a creation hymn of the Kashmiri Hindu Shaivites

~~~~~~

*T*he attraction between Danilo and me was so strong that we couldn't have resisted it if we had tried to. Some force larger than we were pulled us inexorably together to seek union—the Essential Eros.

All of Creation was expressing itself through us: the universal urge for sex, the pull of gravity, electromagnetism, molecular attraction, chemical affinity—it was all of that and more. Everyone who has ever fallen in love will recognize the irresistibility of that raw, primal force which expresses itself so insistently, especially when the hormones are in youth's full flood.

What our bodies seemed to remember—Danilo's and mine—and our minds would still have to learn later, was that ever since the first throb that shook the Unified Field out of its perfect equilibrium, all the vibrating bits of the web have been yearning toward each other, longing to again merge in union. We were its expression, just as every act of love in the world is its expression.

~~~~~~

Imagine the Unified Field as an infinite, multidimensional web of fabric, permeated with intelligence, every strand of the weave held in perfect suspension. It appears still because all the strands are held in equilibrium, but actually every molecule of the web is bursting with energy.

And then from within comes the flutter of love, the throb of desire that jogs the Field out of its perfect equilibrium and sets it aquivering. (Big Bang is one way of expressing this initial throb; creative gasp could be another. I prefer imagining the world more as sexy than warlike.)

This creative gasp unbalances the Field and sets it into motion, unsettling the whole thing into a wild shimmy. What was one whole, its vibration so fast that it appeared to be still, has let go into a jiggling fandango with many levels of interacting vibrations, all inextricably connected to each other because they come from the same Source.

This dance of vibration is fast and slow, wild and sedate, and an infinitude of variations in between, and each frequency is another dimension, another aspect of our world. It is a cosmic dance of action and reaction, attraction and repulsion, rising and sinking, creation and destruction. Everything exists in relationship to everything else, and once it is set into motion, nothing ever rests. There is a rhythmic beat that, like our hearts, pulses continuously from birth to death. And like us, every created thing dissolves back into the Unified Field from which it arose. Nothing is ever lost.

During our idyll on the Ile Hoëdic, I picked up a long, pointy spiral shell on the beach one day and held it up for Dani to see. Both of us, at exactly the same moment and in the same intonation said, "Unicorn!"

It was a moment of union in which we were 'on the same wavelength.' In our intimacy and mutual pleasure at being together, our minds seemed to be in automatic communication; we were bonded by a shared frequency of vibration. To each other, we called it love.

I felt him in my mind—a sense of connection I will never forget, as if the attraction between us was the same force that held together all the things of the world, from particles and atoms to planets in their orbits.

I wonder if, as the Kashmir Shaivites describe it, the impulse that set the world in motion and emanated from everywhere at once does not also describe the attractive forces of gravity and magnetism. I wonder if desire and longing for union aren't built into the very structure of the universe, and we humans only act it out in our own way. I wonder if everything we do isn't in microcosm what the universe itself does. I wonder if our lives are not metaphors for the whole, and that if we want to understand what's going on out there, we'd do well to study ourselves.

I wonder...I wonder where Dani is now...

FIVE

Martine

It seems strange to me now that on that first morning of classes I hardly noticed her. Sixteen students were gathered at the Centre d'Études Médiévales, high in the tower of what, in the fifteenth century, had been a *chateau* by the river Clain. I was the last to arrive, out of breath from the climb up the spiral stone staircase, and I took my first look at the people who would be my classmates for the next year.

Our class consisted of college students like myself, and a few older scholars from universities in other parts of Europe. The younger students were mostly French, but I detected other accents: Dutch, Italian, Spanish. I appeared to be the only American in the class.

It was only later when we went around the room introducing ourselves that Martine Crozier came into focus for me. It might have been that her chestnut brown hair and buff trench coat simply blended into the old wooden beams of the room, or that her calm demeanor and slow smile caused me to overlook her. Whatever it was, when I walked in I noted the animated clusters of students in the room, but my eyes passed over the quiet girl by the mullioned casement windows. In my excitement, what I saw was motion, not stillness.

When the bells of Notre-Dame-La-Grande tolled nine times, our two professors were heard entering the courtyard gate below and toiling up the winding stone stairs to the library. M. Portejoie, a big bear of a man who entered red-faced and huffing, gave us a distracted smile and plunked his briefcase on the lectern in front of the big stone hearth. Wiping his steamy glasses with a crumpled handkerchief, he peered around the room to take the measure of his class, and he nodded twice in approval.

M. Renoud darted in behind him, quick and wiry, and looked us over with a delighted smile as if surprised to find us all in place and waiting. He laid his bulging book bag on the floor by the hearth, took off his black beret, and consulted a timepiece from his vest pocket.

"*Bon,*" he said, nodding to M. Portejoie, who was extracting papers from his briefcase and stacking them in haphazard piles all over the desk.

"*Bonjour, scholaires,*" M. Renoud greeted us warmly, acknowledging each of us in turn with a piercing look. He then clasped his hands behind his back, cleared his throat, and commenced a restless pacing back and forth in front of the blackened stone fireplace, a pacing we would follow with our eyes for the rest of the year.

"Are we all here?" M. Portejoie asked rhetorically, counting heads. One Bulgarian scholar was missing. His colleague informed us that he had not yet received his visa and would join us when he had. Except for him, the whole class was present.

"*Bon,*" said M. Renoud again, wasting no time. "Shall we start then?" His French was the most elegant French I had ever heard, clear and articulated. I would have no trouble understanding him.

"You all well know, having chosen to come to the Centre d'Études Supérieures Médiévales, that our school is extraordinarily unique."

He beamed at us, his chin tucked into his chest for emphasis.

"Here, we focus solely upon the period called Romanesque, from approximately the ninth to the twelfth centuries in Western Europe. Everything after that, we consider *moderne*." Everyone laughed.

"What distinguishes this from any other school is that here we bring all the strands of medieval culture together." He interlaced his fingers to illustrate the point. "Every aspect of the medieval world is seen in conjunction with every other aspect: the economy, the law, the social customs, the art, the music—everything! All are like spokes on a wheel, for which the hub is faith, and therefore everything is connected to everything else. Does everyone understand this?"

My eyes, which followed his pacing back and forth in front of the fireplace, began to sting. I was so excited I had to fold my arms across my chest to keep them still.

"I will teach all classes in art history, liturgical music, and iconography," he announced, "and M. Portejoie will be your professor of history, literature, and church law. Together, we shall engage in research on the pilgrimages to Compostella in Spain, for which some of you have specifically come to work with us, *n'est-ce pas?*"

By the time we received our class schedules, the rules and regulations of the Centre, and texts to be purchased, I felt overwhelmed but hoped I would find a friend in M. Renoud. As the bells from Notre-Dame-La-Grande tolled the hour of ten, he rubbed his hands together and said,

"*Trés bien.* You were asked to be prepared to speak on your thesis topics, *n'est-ce pas?*" Seated in a loose half circle around the fireplace, notebooks ready in our laps, our eyes followed him assiduously.

"Today we will listen to each of you tell us of the fine scholarship we can expect from you."

The more mature scholars took manuscripts from their sacks, eliciting uneasy glances from the rest of us. I began to wonder if I hadn't reached too high in applying here. I was not a scholar like the others—just an intense girl from New York who was here for her maiden adventure in the world. Other than what I had learned in Dr. Godwin's classes, most of what I knew about the Middle Ages was that a sculpture of a prophet on an obscure eleventh-century church in the middle of France had captured my heart.

Why had they even accepted me? My thesis topic was more an emotional stab at reality, than it was a scholarly subject. I was asking about fear, and the part it played in the psychology of religion, as evidenced in the Hell scenes on French Romanesque churches. I hardly could even say it in French! M. Renoud called on the first scholar.

Flinging his blue cape dramatically off his shoulders, Gabriel Fouchet removed his spectacles and spoke of his continuing work on the pilgrimage route to Compostella. Jean-Claude came next, describing his thesis on Romanesque church architecture, and after him was sweet-faced Dominique, on the early history of the Dominican order. My gaze strayed to the red-tiled rooftops beyond the leaded glass windows, and the open fields past the last streets of the town.

The Dutch girl, Han, went next and after her Marie-Therese, on troubadour love poetry. Drago Chernev, one of the three Bulgarian scholars, spoke in halting French about the Bulgarian collaboration to compile an inventory of twelfth-century churches in Eastern Europe. Under the Communist regime this was controversial, and for a while we sat in respectful silence.

"Mademoiselle Crozier, *s'il vous plait*." M. Portejoie indicated the quiet girl across the room. She shrugged off her trench coat and looked around before beginning.

"I want to study the resurrection of Lazarus because I am interested in the nature of the miracle." For two beats the room held its breath. I imagine we all wondered if we had heard her correctly. She looked up, and her lips parted in the sideways, gap-toothed smile I would soon be finding irresistible.

"The nature of *Le Miracle*, or the nature of Lazarus' miracle?" M. Renoud prodded, tilting his head with interest.

"*Le Miracle*," she replied softly. "That is to say, I wish to study the mystery of the universe through the story of the miracle of Lazarus."

I sat up and paid close attention.

"How will you maintain your objectivity?" M. Renoud asked. She took her time to reply.

"When I am addressing versions of the story itself, I will be quite objective and practice rigorous scholarship, but when I address the story as metaphor, I will allow myself a subjective approach, since that is the only way we can comprehend the Mystery." Again, there was a beat of silence before the two professors glanced over at each other, eyebrows raised. M. Portejoie spoke first.

"Well, Mademoiselle, as we have said, Le Centre is a place for unique scholarship. Yours shall indeed be unique scholarship and we wish you luck. *Merci.*"

I detected a blush of color returning to her cheeks.

A few offerings later it was my turn. M. Renoud rubbed blackboard chalk off his hands and faced me. I was nervous, and I found myself addressing my remarks to the girl across the room.

"I want to study the Last Judgment scenes on the tympanums of Romanesque churches," I began. "Especially, I am interested in the scenes of Hell."

My French was abysmal but everyone smiled encouragingly.

"I want to understand how fear and religion go together," I added, and then blurted out, "because I also wish to understand the mystery of the universe." From across the room Martine Crozier regarded me with frank interest.

"And can you also be objective and subjective while you are plunged in Hell?" M. Portejoie queried wryly, with raised eyebrows. My hands were cold and I took a deep breath. Martine's lips parted ever so slightly.

"If I can be, yes," I said, gaining courage from the girl by the leaded windows. "Objective in the scholarship, and subjective in the interpretation."

"So—this is good," M. Renoud asserted with a smile. "Our young American is plunged in hell, and you, Mademoiselle, are elevated in the miracle, so there is a balance."

When the session was over, most of the others left. Martine stood by the casement windows, her hands joined behind her back as she gazed out at the countryside. I waited and then joined her. Beyond the tile-roofed houses of the town, a stand of oak trees edged a road alongside fields where sheep grazed on stubbly autumn grass. Stone walls and hedgerows separated the patchwork of pastures, and the mist, giving way to blue-gray sky, was forming into flimsy white clouds. We stood side by side at the windows, our shoulders not quite touching.

"Have you been here for a while?" she asked quietly.

"In France, since June," I replied, "but here in Poitiers only since last week. And you?"

"My family lives in Lyons. I also came here a week ago. Where are you staying?"

"With a family on rue St. Denis, right near Notre-Dame-La-Grande. I have a room there in exchange for helping with the children."

"That's close to here, isn't it?" It was, and I described the narrow cobblestoned street I lived on, the old Roman walls behind the house, and the sounds—night and day—of the church bells.

"It must be very different from your country," she remarked.

"Very. I actually like it much better than my country," I admitted.

"I like your topic," she said abruptly. "It's very brave."

"So is yours."

She nodded and sighed. "It's a good thing not to be the only renegade in class." We both laughed.

"Normally you're the only one?" I asked.

"As you might imagine—just like you," she stated matter-of-factly.

We both turned and regarded each other with curiosity. A springy curl escaped her barrette and dangled over one of her hazel-gold eyes, but she looked through it and straight into mine until I sighed and said, "It's true, I've never been a very docile student."

"Nor have I," she admitted ruefully. Reaching forward, she unlatched a casement window and peered out. "How far are we above that roof, do you suppose?" she asked, pointing at the terracotta tiles on a small shed a few feet below us.

"I'd say about eight feet, not more," I judged, wondering why she wanted to know. Without a backward glance she leaned over the sill, took her weight on her hands, and neatly climbed out the window.

"What are you doing?" I cried in English, grabbing too late for her sweater as she jumped down and landed in a crouch on the clattering tiles. Her legs trembled, bracing precariously on either side of the ridgeline. Arms out to her sides, she slowly came to a tottery stand, adjusting her balance until she was stable. I was too stunned to say anything and I frantically looked around for help, but everyone had already gone.

"You should see it from here," she spoke in a careful voice, not turning her head.

"Please come back in," I said in a nervous undertone.

"I will," she said, "but first I've got to see the full horizon."

I leaned out the window to see what she was seeing, but my view was blocked by the round tower walls and casements.

"It's beautiful," she declared slowly, her voice tinged with humor. "Come on out." Twice I started to climb out the window, and twice I drew back.

"I think not," I finally said, not as brave as she.

Notre-Dame-La-Grande tolled the hour—twelve resounding bongs—and when the last echoes faded, Martine folded again into a crouch and crawled backwards until her feet were against the tower wall. Turning cautiously, she grasped the thick ivy and, like a mountain climber, hoisted herself up until she was framed by the casement. Then, with a single vault, she scrambled over the sill and was back in the room, brushing off her skirt and running fingers through her windblown curls.

"*Et voilà*," she exclaimed with panache, her eyes brimming with daring. Her quiet demeanor had evaporated like mist. "Shall we go get some lunch?" she suggested with studied nonchalance, pulling on her trench coat and slinging her book bag over one shoulder. Astonished, I followed her out the door and down the winding stone steps to the courtyard below.

The little café in the corner of the covered market, where working-class men sat over steaming bowls of onion soup, was our destination. Morning shoppers were thinning out as housewives hurried home for lunch, their string bags bulging with leeks, fat sausages, crusty baguettes, and tubs of smelly goat cheese.

We made our way through the aisles, stopping at a butcher's stall to stare at a whole sheep hanging on hooks from the rafters. A florid-faced butcher sliced at the glistening white fat covering the meat and deftly scooped out a pair of dark kidneys that gleamed in the overhead lights.

At the greengrocer's stall just opposite, a pyramid of green cabbages and orange carrots stood surrounded by yellow onions and deep red beets, creating a living work of art as if the vegetables were food not only for the belly, but also for the eyes. Ravenous, I went from stall to stall sniffing and examining the earthy roots and curly greens, the crackling breads, the pungent cheeses and spicy sausages, the pears and the pâtés, and the potatoes.

"I love this place," I exclaimed to Martine once we were seated at a small round table waiting for our onion soup. "It's so different from what I'm used to."

"Different how?" she asked, leaning across the table.

"Well, it's beautiful," I started thoughtfully. "It feels 'right,' like everything should be beautiful like this. No, that's not quite it—it feels to me like it's got *soul*. Where I grew up, there was no soul."

She regarded me curiously for a moment. "What do you mean when you say *soul?*"

What did I mean? It was a feeling of aliveness, as if everything was worth looking at. It was a sense of things belonging to each other and of me belonging to them. I pointed to the beets piled at the greengrocer's across from where we sat, hairy rootlets sticking out like little mouse tails on one side and shining red and green leaves poking out on the other.

"See those beets?" I began. "Well, this may sound ridiculous, but they make me happy." She gave me a surprised and lovely grin. "What I mean is that I feel related to them…I mean…" I trailed off and stared down at my fingernails, embarrassed by the emotion in my voice and then added, "I mean, I've never seen beets with roots and leaves before, only round red things in a bag!"

If I expected her to laugh at me, she didn't. She only reached across the table, touched my fingers briefly and murmured, *"Sainte Françoise des legumes."*

St. Francis of the vegetables? I had no idea what she was talking about.

"So," I asked after an interval of silence, "when you say *soul*, what do you mean?" She stirred her soup thoughtfully before replying.

"Well, I guess for me it's about how we're part of the ineffable—the part that never dies. It's the essence of who we are." She regarded me with a hint of mischief and added, "It's sitting in a café with someone you just met and already talking about the *soul*."

"*Le miracle?*"

"Yes, the Miracle—what else?" she drawled. We sipped our soup, dipping hunks of bread into the cheese-rich broth. She rolled a string of *gruyère* around her finger and sucked it off noisily.

"To me *le miracle* is just what's around us—sitting here eating onion soup, those beets." She blinked at the vegetables. "But every once in a while we suddenly wake up—sometimes just for a moment—and it takes our breath away even though it's just so ordinary. That's when we know we're part of something sacred."

I was so touched to hear my own inarticulate longings come from her that I spilled soup onto my skirt. We both laughed as I mopped it up.

"It's the same as you were saying about the beets," she continued, handing me her napkin. "We're relatives with everything, and that makes me feel ecstatic!"

"That's it, yes," I agreed. "That's just what I'm looking for, too."

"It's what I live for every single day," she observed quietly.

"Do you know many people who understand what you're talking about?" I asked hopefully.

"Not very many," she acknowledged. Our eyes met and the tears rose. We reached across the table to grasp each other's hands, and when the moment passed we laughed self-consciously and let go, quickly spooning up our now-tepid soup. The sautéed onions tasted sweet and smooth, like caramel.

When the churchbells struck the hour of three, the marketplace had emptied out and we still sat bent over the table, talking. The peppery dregs of soup had gone cold in our bowls by the time I told her about what I had experienced in the Sacred Heart schoolyard as a child.

"You've known *le miracle* since you were eleven," she affirmed solemnly. "In fact, it happened for me at about the same age."

She told me about being thrown from a bicycle and landing on her head, and of waking up in the hospital to a world that looked different.

"I could see God in everything," she recalled, "my hand, the sheets, the tree outside the window. I didn't tell anybody, but I was filled with a joy that lasted for weeks. Maybe that's why I still take risks," she commented with a crafty smile, "to help me find my way back there."

"Like climbing out high tower windows?" I chided. "Do you do that often?" She leaned back and laughed. "I was really scared!" I insisted.

"I know you were," she admitted. "I guess I was showing off."

"Well, you certainly got my attention," I retorted. The look that passed between us made me blush. I uneasily caught myself flirting with her, but it had slipped out so naturally. I should write to Dani for advice on this.

"That's good," she responded good-naturedly. "That means I don't have to do it again."

It wasn't until the bells struck four, and we had been standing on the square saying good-bye since three-thirty, that Martine and I finally shook hands and took off in separate directions—she up the hill towards the Centre and me to *rue St. Denis* where three-year-old Michel, the youngest of my five charges, would be waiting for his afternoon walk.

The d'Alverny family was, in so many ways, the family I had always longed for. They were loving and clever, boisterous and kind. In their home I was part guest and part servant, and as established members of the upper class, the d'Alvernys knew instinctively how to maintain that balance. As a foreigner I was an exotic visitor; as an *au pair* girl I was a maid of all trades. The fact that I attended the prestigious Centre d'Études Médiévales made me a personage of pride for the household.

To the children, I was a new playmate. The two teenage boys, Hughes and Pierre, challenged me to ping-pong matches on the dining room table most evenings after supper, and the two younger girls, Monique and Celine, used every excuse to come into my room and explore my wardrobe.

The baby, Michel, was my special pet. For some reason none of us understood, his name for me was *Clara Verte*, Green Clara, and our times together each day—naps, bath, walks—rapidly assumed the importance of ritual for him. He listened, rapt, to my silly stories told in halting French, and without my improvised lullabies he refused to go to sleep. I had won a heart, it seemed, and, as Madame told me at the end of the first week, my fit in the family was perfect.

Madame was right, I did fit here. Everything seemed to fall in place with very little effort on my part, and I found myself loving my life: the family I lived with, my work at the Centre, and my daily walks with Michel exploring the parks and byways of this ancient town. Things felt easy for the first time in my life. It was like picking up a box expecting it to be heavy, but having it spring right into my hands, light as a feather.

And of course there was my growing friendship with Martine. With her, I breathed a different air than I breathed with anybody else, and I couldn't imagine ever living again without it. I missed

Dani's passion and verve, yes, but Martine quenched my thirst like deep, underground water—not visible on the surface but essential to every living thing around. She was the calmness of the deep pool, the common salt without which life would go dry. I think all the students were a little mesmerized by her—even the Bulgarians—as if she kept a secret we all wanted to be in on. In her undemonstrative way, she held us together.

As for me, I was the moth attracted to the proverbial flame. I longed to be around her, and she never turned me away. In the afternoons we would walk along the river talking animatedly, or we would meet in a café, sometimes with others but mostly by ourselves, until it was time for me to fetch Michel. When we were apart, I held imaginary conversations with her, telling her my every thought and imagining her response.

"Before the winter closes in," M. Renoud announced one day, "we suggest you make some little pilgrimages into the surrounding villages to visit Poitou's Romanesque churches, which dot this countryside like jewels." He paced before the fireplace with his hands clasped behind his back while M. Portejoie spread out a map of the region.

"You will find magnificent frescoes, sculptures, and architecture, mostly in excellent condition. Old, but not relics. The faith in this part of France is a living thing."

I could think of nothing that would please me more—except, perhaps, to go to the eleventh-century church in Moissac where the sculpture of the Old Testament prophet stood.

Dr. Godwin had shown our class a slide of this sculpture—a beautiful, soulful prophet in flowing robes. Jeremiah, she had named him, artist unknown. He went straight to my heart and, with a certainty stronger than I had ever before felt about anything, I had decided to travel to France and find him. To Moissac, wherever that was. Now, a year later and only about two hours away, I knew the time had come to make my way to Moissac. With Martine.

After class I proposed a weekend trip to Martine and told her about 'my' prophet. She not only agreed, but said she had cousins on a farm in Auvillar, a village only three kilometers south of Moissac where we would no doubt be invited to stay.

"It will be an adventure," she said. And indeed, before the day was out we had both been warmly invited to come. "Luc has offered to fetch us at the train station and lend us bicycles, so long as we don't mind sleeping in the barn," she told me as we grasped hands in glee.

The d'Alvernys agreed reluctantly to my request for a four-day absence, our professors loaded us down with instructions and advice, and the following Thursday we packed our rucksacks with notebooks and cameras and boarded the evening train for Bordeaux.

Luc picked us up at the station at midnight, driving us through nighttime fields and hamlets, while he and Martine caught up on family news. I gazed out into the darkness, thrilled to be actually here, closer to him. On pilgrimage. This was how I wanted to live—always! Tomorrow I would be able to touch him. I'd send Dr. Godwin a postcard from Moissac in the morning.

It was very late when we arrived at the farm, and Martine and I were bone tired. Luc brought us directly to the barn where our sleeping places were arranged in the hayloft above the cows. They eyed us curiously while we climbed the steps over their stalls, but after huffling a bit they went back to their grumbling and chewing. Two fluffy comforters on side-by-side goose-down mattresses on the loft floor welcomed us, and I sank down gratefully, slipped out of my jeans, and immediately fell asleep half dressed. And dreamed.

I am walking down a gray concrete street with buildings so tall there is no sky. The people are also gray, and they return my greetings with harsh stares. This is the world I live in.

I turn the corner and see a fine crack in the side of a building. The hole is just large enough for me to squeeze through, and I slip in, following a steep path downward.

It is dark and I'm afraid, but I keep going until the path opens onto a different world, green and fragrant. The earth feels springy, and people greet me and smile. I hear snatches of song as I walk along, and laughter. I don't recognize anybody. Do they live here all the time, or have they found their way here as I have? I don't even know what language they speak.

I want to stay, to start my life over. And then Martine is there. I know her from the gray world—does she live here as well? Maybe it's her secret. I ought to hide, but she reaches out her hand and I grab it like a lifeline.

When the cock set to crowing at dawn, I awoke to find our hands lightly touching across the straw-strewn boards between our beds. For a while I watched her sleep, wondering if I had been in her dream as she had been in mine. I could almost smell the air of the green world, and the harsh glare of the gray world still prickled my eyes, but Martine's hand seemed to cross out of my dream into the barn loft, our fingers still touching.

Her eyes opened, closed, and then opened again when the cock renewed his crowing. Sighing, she turned over, softly disengaged our hands and tucked hers beneath her head. Through cracks in the barn's old boards, the early light entered the loft in slivers. I found my socks alongside my mattress and, holding the covers around me, sat up and pulled them on.

Martine stretched her legs. "Mmm," she mumbled, still holding onto sleep, *"Bonjour, Clara."*

"Bonjour, Martine." We spoke in whispers. A smile passed between us.

"It's so peaceful here," she said, yawning sleepily. Beneath us the cows mumbled in their stalls. "Shall we sit quietly for a while?"

Wrapping her comforter around her like a giant shawl, she crossed her legs, breathed in, and closed her eyes in meditation. I let my eyes close too and, hearing our breaths wash in and out together, relaxed into the stillness. The sounds of doves purling in the eaves deepened the silence, and after a while of random thoughts I settled into the intimacy of our being quiet together.

For how long we sat, I don't know. When the cock crowed again and the sounds of people at their morning chores reached us up in the hayloft, Martine sighed, yawned, and lifted her arms over her head.

"*Bonjour, Clara,*" she whispered again, bending over to stretch. I did the same, and my spine gave a loud crack.

"*Bonjour, Martine.*" I smiled back, reaching for my jeans and wriggling into them beneath the covers. We hoisted ourselves out of bed at the same time and met in the middle, hesitating only a moment before opening our arms for an embrace. Her touch lingered on my skin for the rest of the morning.

We laced up our boots and brushed our hair quickly, our breaths fairly steaming in the frosty air, and then we clattered down the steps to where Luc was milking the cows below.

"*Bonjour,*" he greeted us as he ducked out from beneath a cow, hefting a steaming pail of milk with him. "*Avez vous bien dormis?*" You've slept well? I shook his hand, which was still warm from the cow.

"*Trés bien, merci.* It felt like sleeping on clouds," I replied.

"All those goose feathers," he laughed. We followed him, chatting, to the henhouse, where he gathered clutches of eggs from each little nest, wading through the burbling chickens as if they were feathered water. Luc handed me the full wire basket to carry back to the house, and Martine got the milk pail.

"It should be clear today," he remarked, squinting across the fields where the haze was already beginning to burn off. "You'll be able to take the bikes to Moissac—it's a nice ride, about three kilometers. We'll draw you a map so you won't get lost. Are you hungry?"

We followed him across the barnyard to the house, where two urchin boys waited expectantly at the kitchen door to greet Martine and "the lady who came all the way from America to visit Moissac."

"That's just about right," I laughed, kneeling down to greet them at their level. "I came all the way from America to meet a stone man at your church, because, I have to confess, I'm in love with him." The boys tittered behind their hands.

"I know just the one you mean," Luc's wife Marie-Claire declared. "*Le Prophète*. Some call him Isaiah, some say he's Jeremiah, but whoever he is, he is truly beautiful." She greeted me with a firm handshake before kissing Martine on both cheeks, and then she swirled around to snatch up burning toast from the woodstove.

"Unfortunately for you," Luc teased me, "he's made of stone and won't be able to return your passion."

"But miracles have been known to occur," I shot back. "Look at Martine here—she makes miracles happen all the time!"

"Our Martine," he said fondly, laying a work-roughened hand on her shoulder, "*is* a miracle."

Breakfast was a jolly affair in the warm kitchen. We drank fresh milk out of bowls and slathered slice after slice of crusty bread with sweet butter and honey. The boys wanted to know if I was a cowgirl, if I drank Pepsi Cola for breakfast, if I knew any Red Indians. When I tried to describe New York City to them, my words sounded so improbable I might have been talking about the moon. Not only to them, I realized, but also to myself.

Martine and I set out later in the morning, the *panniers* on our borrowed bikes filled with guidebooks and provisions for the day. The family waved us off at the gate, assuring us that after the long, steep climb out of the valley the road would descend the rest of the way to Moissac.

We started off slowly, pedaling hard up the demanding hill and occasionally dismounting to walk our bikes. By the time we reached the crest, we were both flushed and winded.

"You're red as an apple," Martine teased.

"You too," I countered, leaning over to touch her flaming cheek. For a brief moment I held my hand there.

Thoughtfully she observed, "Have you noticed that whenever it's hard to get up a hill you wish the road was flat, but then when you're coasting down the other side you figure it was worth the struggle up?"

I knew just what she meant. "So let's go!" I shouted, pushing off. We started into the wind, allowing gravity to pull us down the steep slope, our hair whipping around our faces. Fields of grazing sheep sped by, along with the golden stubble of harvested wheat. Rows of grapevines shorn of their harvest marched across the rolling hills, and large vats of sun-ripened grapes stood frothy and ready for pressing. We breathed in great gulps of winy air as we whizzed past, getting happily drunk on the day.

"Look!" Martine shouted, pointing to an armada of white clouds backlit by sun raying behind it. We lifted our faces toward the sun as it emerged warm from the cloud bank.

"There's the river!" I cried, spying a glint of silver beyond a copse of red-leafed trees in the valley below.

"Wheee!" we both sang exuberantly, standing up on our pedals and shouting into the wind. It thrummed its song past our ears and we leaned into it, speeding around curves and waving rakishly to farmers working in their fields.

We were forced to slow down and come to a stop only when we reached the stone bridge at the bottom of the hill, and we needed to consult our map. The town began on the other side of the river, but I felt a phantom tug on my right arm, as if I were sensing the location of the church and my prophet.

"I think it's that way," I pointed out, "across the bridge and a little further on." She continued to scrutinize the map. Finding it on the map, she held her finger on the spot and looked up to where I was pointing. She observed that I was pointing directly toward it, and she squinted at me quizzically.

"How'd you know that?"

"I have no idea," I replied with a shrug, but then added, "maybe the same way you had relatives in the one remote little place I came across the ocean to find." I grinned and our eyes met.

"We're both extraordinary, that's all," she announced after a while. "I guess there's still a lot we have to talk about." With that she pushed off, flinging her leg over the bike seat, and we took off down the alley to our right.

The grand *portail* of the church was on the same general plan as the one at Chartres, but considerably smaller. Moissac's Christ in the center of the tympanum was a rather uninspiring fellow with blank eyes and big ears, but he was surrounded by a multitude of intricately carved apostles and *seraphim* and fantastical beasts. Every square inch of the porch's adjoining walls were covered with New Testament scenes: the Annunciation, the flight into Egypt, the birth of Jesus, the Crucifixion.

Still straddling our bikes, we stood and stared up at the elaborate doorway. The prophet, I knew, stood half hidden on the side of the *trumeau*, the central pillar, but, nervous as a girl on a first date, I refrained from rushing over to where he was.

Instead, I wheeled my bike over to the iron railing, lowered the kickstand slowly, and waited for Martine to lean her bike against mine and join me on the porch. Together we gazed up at the tympanum before I took a deep breath and stepped through the right-hand doorway to see my prophet. Only when I had found him did she come up softly behind me.

There he was, so familiar it was like greeting an old friend. I reached out and touched his robe, and the old stone felt almost soft to my fingers. His long, slender body spiraled up from dancing feet, his hair flowed like water around his face, and his hand gracefully held a scroll. His head was tilted, and calm eyes gazed out at us with wisdom and compassion.

This man had sorrowed, had yearned, and had loved deeply, and he no longer judged the world harshly. It was his look of profound acceptance that had spoken so strongly to me that day in Dr. Godwin's class. Every gesture of his body, exquisitely twisting around his strong center, expressed this. I would have given a lot for him to be flesh and blood instead of carved stone. I *needed* him; tears rose precipitously into my throat. Martine came to stand alongside me.

"Do you see?" I murmured, grabbing her wrist.

"*Oui, je vois,*" she said quietly. I swallowed hard and together we gazed at him, our breaths intermingling. "You're right, he is extraordinary. Do you notice, though, how young he is?"

I took a step back to see him better. It was true. Although his eyes expressed the mature wisdom of an elder, he had the face of a young person.

"That's odd," I agreed. "He looks about our age."

"Early twenties at most," she speculated. "Too young for a prophet, I'd say. I'd guess the sculptor used his lover as a model. Notice that he's hidden away in the shadows where you've got to find him. I'll bet that's significant."

I started to object, not understanding her reasoning. The sculptors of the Middle Ages were undoubtedly all men, and this was definitely a male figure, so they couldn't very well be lovers—or could...they...? Martine saw my confusion and rubbed the back of her neck musingly. We stepped imperceptibly farther apart, our eyes fixed studiously on the *trumeau*. His stone lips seemed to soften ever so slightly into the beginnings of a smile.

"Well, artists have always..." she commented, "even though the church has never condoned it." The air between us pulsed with silence. "It's always been so. People love each other, that's all. You know."

Actually, I didn't know. Even in school, nobody had ever talked about these things. I found myself unsteady on my feet, my shoulder swaying into hers. Jeremiah, or whoever he was, regarded us with gentle compassion, and I stared back in confusion, not quite sure what I thought.

For the rest of the day we wandered in and out of the church and cloister, returning always to the porch where this sculpted figure has been dancing since the eleventh century. The more time I spent in front of him, the more I felt a clear line of communication opening between us, as if he were a real flesh and blood person.

"He's known great suffering," I noted, gazing into his clear-seeing stone eyes. We sat across from him on a sill by the entry's wooden doors, munching on a lunch of carrots, bread, and crumbly cheese.

"Fear too, I expect," Martine remarked.

"Mm-hm. And yet he seems so calm and balanced."

"Wish I could do that," she murmured. "Can you say what scares you the most?" she asked after a while.

"The most..." I murmured, imagining my personal inventory of fears. "I think what scares me most of all is to think that when I die I'll totally disappear," I replied at last. Martine nodded, her eyes intent on the ground. "I've tried, but I can't imagine the idea of just not being anymore—you know?" My body, despite myself, began to tremble.

"*Oui*," was her whispered response. We both sat with our arms around our knees, silent. Jeremiah watched us, inscrutable and calm.

"That's what scares me the most, too," she said after a while. "I think about death a lot." Lowering her chin to her knees, she stared into the middle distance.

"You do?"

"Ever since my little brother died," she said. "One day he was sick and the next day he was gone. I couldn't get over it; nobody in my family could. My uncle gave me a book about Buddhism then, and it helped a bit."

"How?" I asked, knowing nothing about Buddhism.

"Well, the Buddhists say that death is just part of the life cycle—life, death, life—and after you die you're still *you*, but then you come back in another form so it's no big deal."

I wasn't sure what that meant, so I looked up again at Jeremiah, whose eyes seemed to soften with tenderness as if the earnest attempts of two modern young women to contemplate the questions of life and death right there at his feet were touching his heart.

Luc had suggested we take an alternate route for the return trip, which was somewhat longer but much more level a ride. So we left Moissac by the road on the other side of town and cycled back to the farm with the sun grazing the hills and the blue of the sky giving way to greens and soft mauves. The light grew shadowy and then dim as we rode peaceably side by side, occasionally commenting on something we saw, sometimes turning to each other for no other reason than to smile.

"Moon's almost full," Martine observed, gesturing towards a faraway saddle in the hills where brightness was subtly gathering beyond our view.

"What luck!" I called back, referring to more than the moon. Luminosity just out of sight and about to be revealed.

And indeed, by the time we reached the farm in the deepening twilight, the moon had risen huge and orange above the surrounding hills, spreading shadows on the ground as if it were a sun.

At dinner, the boys kept us all in hysterics. I had to repeat every tongue-twister and riddle they recited while they giggled over my American accent. They taught us a naughty song about the good King Dagobert who put his underpants on backwards, and another song about an elephant on a seesaw, for which we all had to yell out the refrain. By the time the coffee was served and they were scooted, protestingly, off to bed, my sides ached from laughing. We talked a while longer with Luc and Marie-Claire, and after that the adults were ready to call it a day as well.

In the growing chill outside, Martine and I gazed up at the round moon in its immensity of star-filled space. The two cats followed us out, prowling around our feet and pouncing on the moving moon shadows.

"I wonder if there's an end to space," I mused.

"Or even a beginning," she responded, wrapping her arms around herself in the evening chill. "Maybe there's no beginning and no end—only a cycle that goes on and on."

"I could believe that," I assented, my eyes scanning the sky crowded with stars. "Ooh look, a shooting star!"

"And there's another! Whenever I look up at the night sky I think the Sufis must be right."

"Sufis?"

"That's the mystical branch of Islam," she explained. "To them the world is essentially Nothing, but it's a Nothing that contains Everything, and the Everything is Love. Get it?"

"No," I laughed, striking a match to light the oil lamp Marie-Claire had given us. It sent a warm pool of light into the surrounding barnyard. …nothing that contains everything but the everything is love… "So everything's always been here?"

"…cycling," she continued for me, "always cycling."

I remembered the kids in Brooklyn skating in circles beneath the gaze of Jesus. Round and round.

"Another wonderful paradox," she sighed. "I do love paradoxes."

"Me too," I said, picking up the lamp and, deliciously lost in the intricacies of the indescribable, we followed the moon-shadowed path to the barn.

We stopped to pat the warm, snuffling cows in their stalls and then mounted the stairs to the loft. The barn was fragrant with hay and manure, and in the shifting shadows of lamp-lit darkness, the four golden eyes of two cats gleamed at us as they stalked amongst the hay bales and followed us up the steps to our beds.

We slipped off our backpacks and the cats came to investigate, sniffing and rubbing up against our legs until we squatted down to pet them. The tabby came and nestled right into my lap, lifting a velvet paw to my lips. I sang him a little nonsense song,

"Petit chat, petit chat, comment tu t'appel?" What's your name, little cat?

"I think that one's Igor," Martine answered for him. "One of them is Igor and one is Stravinsky—I think Igor's the orange one." I stroked his soft fur while Martine rumpled the gray cat's ears, and for a while the loudest sound in the loft was of two cats purring. "They are quite musical, as you can hear," she joked. Igor's eyes closed in bliss as I scratched the white bib of his throat.

"I think cats are the most beautiful creatures in the world," I declared, regarding Igor with admiration. "If the world can create a cat, it has got to be a place of miracles." Igor rolled over, offering me his belly in response, and I raked my fingers through his fur.

"Cats and flamingos and banana trees, too," Martine laughed. "What's *not* a miracle?"

"That's what your thesis is all about, right?"

"*Bien sûr*," she replied, "and of course Lazarus is only an excuse to spend two years thinking about miracles." Her eyes glinted in the lamplight as she stroked Stravinsky's gray fur. Regarding me steadily, she then added, "And the Hell scenes are your excuse to deal with your fears, right?"

I jerked my head sharply, and Igor leapt off my lap. For a moment I stared past Martine, and then I sighed. Igor crept back and holding him against me, I confessed she was right.

She stroked Stravinsky's head with her thumb. I ran my hand along Igor's back. Shadows played on the rafters, the oil lamp hissed, and the cows below whuffled in their sleep.

"We're both imposters, let's face it," she said with gentle irony. I nodded ruefully. "And you came to France to find me because you searched for a friend who was a seed from your same pod, *n'est-ce pas?*"

Curled under the comforter with my cat, I petted the perfect curve of his body, fingering each bump on his flexible spine as his purrs and my breaths came into union. Random shadows played on the cobwebbed beams of the barn like wild dancers backlit on a stage. Martine crawled into her bed, and Stravinsky took his place on her chest and curled into a tight ball. She sighed deeply and gazed up at the rafters, the flickering lamp creating a light show on her face. All at once my dream of the night before came back to me as if it had rested on my pillow until I returned to reclaim it.

"Last night I had a strange dream," I told her quietly. I could feel again the stark contrast of the gray and green worlds, and the sensation of Martine's hand touching mine.

"Tell me?"

"It was very weird. I was in this gray, sterile place—all concrete and bare. I hated it, but it was where I lived. Then I'm walking along some street and there's a crack in the sidewalk, so I follow it and it goes down into the earth." The purrs of the cat vibrated under my hand, warm and alive. "And at the end of this descent there's another world—a green world. And the people there look happy, but I don't know anyone from there until…" Here I stopped short, hesitant to say what came next.

"Then *you* were there," I finally spoke it. "You, my friend from the gray world, was also there in the green world." She breathed in sharply. "I was scared and you took my hand," I told her in a small voice. My voice cracked and I cleared my throat while Martine's eyes met mine. In the candlelight they were gold flecked. Tentatively she reached out and touched my fingertips lightly. For a while neither of us spoke.

Then she said, "I am glad I was your friend there, Clara. I think your dream is a true dream, because I believe there really are two worlds, like layers in a cake. We both live in both of them, don't you think?"

"Sometimes it feels like I live in two places," I agreed.

"For me," she began, "it's like I have one home here but another, more real home somewhere else." There was a shining of tears on her eyelashes, and I reached out my hand to her. I had never before spoken of this with anyone. "So we meet each other in your green world," she continued.

"And have each other as friends in the gray world as well." I sighed with relief. "Does your family accept you the way you are?" I asked.

"Perhaps yes, perhaps no," she replied pensively. "Oh, they are good, dear people—like Luc and Marie-Claire, you know—but still I am the renegade of the clan, the odd one out."

"What was it like growing up?" I asked, settling down to hear her tell about her five siblings, the long years when her father was at war, her mother's courage, the closeness of the children through times of fear and deprivation. I stroked the cat's silky paw with my thumb, feeling the rhythmic bite of his razor-sharp nails on my hand, and asked question after question as I tried to imagine this family holding together through the horrors of such a war, and still managing to emerge from it loving and sane. Patiently, she replied to my every query.

"It was never easy for us," she explained, "but we were lucky—except for my little brother, we all survived. Other families weren't so fortunate." Igor stood up to stretch and then meticulously curled himself back up on my knees.

"*Et toi?*" she whispered. "You've never mentioned your family to me." I drooped, suddenly very weary.

"It's because I try not to think of them," I admitted in a hoarse voice.

"Why?"

"Because I feel helpless and sad when I think of them. And ashamed," I confessed. My throat jammed and I couldn't have said more if I tried. With Dani it had been easier to speak freely, because his people were my people and we both understood what it meant to be refugees and Jews in a Christian world. But Martine came from settled people with a mainstream belief system—the very people I had been taught to fear.

"It's that bad, eh?" she confirmed. My tears welled, and in the dim light I nodded. For a while there were only the sounds of the cows breathing below and the cats' rough tongues rasping themselves clean. She took a deep breath.

"*Ah, mon amie,* you can tell me if you wish, and I will hear you without judgment, or if you choose to not say a word, I still will not judge you."

It was the 'my friend' that broke me down, I think, and after a big breath I started to speak in a bare whisper that grew stronger and faster as I told my story. It gushed out of me like water breaching a dam. I told her of terrified refugees who felt unsafe everywhere, of poverty and ignorance and an implacable will to stay ignorant, of unkindness and prejudice and suspicion, of debilitating shame.

"My father has an uncanny ability to trust crooks who invariably betray him, of course," I gave a harsh laugh that surprised me by its bitterness, "and to mistrust people who are genuinely good." I threw up my hands despairingly and Igor jumped in alarm. I patted him steadily, stroke by stroke, until he lay down again.

"My mother is pathologically passive," I complained, "and so afraid, she's basically paralyzed. I was born when they were teenagers themselves, so it's like having disturbed adolescents as parents. It has always felt safer to be out on the streets than in our house."

My hands were balled into fists, and my teeth were so tightly clenched they hurt. I gave a rueful laugh and apologized for sounding so negative.

"But you left," she observed quietly. I slammed my hand against my knees.

"Sure, I left after nineteen years," I spit out, "but I left my younger sister and brother behind, and that nearly killed me!"

"Why?"

"Because they're not safe there either, especially my little sister. Martine, you come from a different world—you can't possibly know what I'm talking about." Her eyes never left my face, but they held no censure. I couldn't stop now.

"I thought I'd stay at home until they were old enough to leave too, but then I saw that picture from Moissac and I had to go find him. I couldn't wait around anymore."

"She went on pilgrimage…" Martine whispered, her cheeks glistening wet in the firelight.

"So here I am," I concluded breathlessly, burying my face in Igor's fur.

"Wait," she said, "your bother and sister—how old are they?"

"Eighteen and thirteen," I replied.

"You know," she began, "many traditions say we choose our birth family in order to do our soul work. If it's true for you and me, it's true for your sister and brother. You don't really know what they are supposed to learn from your parents."

Or what I was supposed to learn, I thought. This was a new perspective for me.

"Maybe all this has been testing you to have the courage to live your own life and do what you needed to do."

"You think so?"

"Where would you rather be, here or there—quick, what's your answer?"

"What a question!" I exclaimed. "I'm happier here than I've ever been in my life."

"That should tell you something. Anyhow," she said, clearing her throat, "I'm glad you're here, *ma soeur*." Our eyes met and she held out her hands. I reached across the divide between our beds and, just like in the dream, grasped them as if they were a lifeline.

Both of us spent a fitful night, waking each time the other restlessly turned over, until even the cats gave up on us and left. I felt mortified after my confession, wishing I could take at least some of it back. Our friendship was much too new for that level of intimacy; she would certainly back off. Damn, I never knew when to stop! Again I tossed onto my other side, and again I heard her turn over also.

The next morning we were both groggy and studiously careful with each other, avoiding each other's eyes as we helped get breakfast on the table before the trip to Moissac for the Sunday Mass. Nor did we have much to say when we piled into the back of the family Citroën, with a child on each lap. Luc drove, Marie-Claire and the boys did all the talking, and Martine and I stared out of separate windows.

The pealing of churchbells filled the air as we crossed the stone bridge over the River Tarn, where Martine and I had stopped yesterday to consult our maps. The bells sounded louder and stronger as we approached the church, and by the time we stepped beneath the bell tower they were resounding right into my bones.

Jeremiah—if that's who he was—was there waiting. The bells resonated into his bones, too, as they had been doing for centuries, apparently never jarring him out of his calm equanimity. In my agitated state, I wanted to hide in shame. I wished I could kneel before the real Jeremiah to ask for wise counsel, but this Jeremiah was a man of stone and chisel, not flesh and blood, so all he could do was acknowledge me with his inscrutable half smile as I passed through the *portail* on his side.

Numbly I followed Martine, the boys, Luc, and Marie-Claire into the church, kneeling when they knelt and standing when they stood. I sat on the aisle, painfully aware of Martine next to me—so close but so far away—and when the congregation stood to profess the faith and take communion I could bear it no longer and stood abruptly to go outside. If I had to take communion anyway, I might as well take it with Jeremiah. Out on the porch I stared up into his patient stone eyes, trying to let him know how foolish I felt, how frightened, and how disappointed. My eyes blurred with tears, and I could swear I heard him speak to me in my mind. "Why?"

"Because I've made such a fool of myself," I told him silently. "I don't know why I can't keep my mouth shut—I've probably scared her off for good."

"Is that all of it?" I seemed to hear him asking, his lips all but parting expectantly.

"N-no, it's not." I wanted to sink to my knees to make my confession. "No, there's more. Oh, God, I'm in love with her and we're both girls. What do I do now?"

"Don't you think it is alright to love her?"

"What?"

His eyes never blinked, but I felt something warm and alive emanating from his figure, as if the stone itself was breathing. He continued to gaze down at me.

"Trust love," was what I heard. I actually heard the words. In English. "Feel love and it will efface the shame. Have the courage to love, and then have the courage to be loved in return."

"How?" I was trembling now.

"By entering the fear." Those were the words I heard in my mind as the churchbells signaled the end of the Mass. People began emerging from the church one by one and then in groups, talking, greeting one another, and blinking in the full sunlight of the day. Martine found me there on the porch and joined me in front of Jeremiah.

"*Ça va?*" she whispered. When I nodded, she took my arm and we turned together, not saying a word, across the square to where the family was walking toward the car.

My work was cut out for me, and it was not only about medieval art history. Back again in Poitiers we dove back into our studies, the episode in Moissac having run its course without too much disaster. Martine and I were still a bit cautious with one another, but it was less about my indiscretions than about our growing mutual attraction. So when we were together we played it safe, being careful and polite and attending assiduously to our studies—she to the miracle of Lazarus and me to the Hell scenes of the Last Judgment.

Day after day we pored over images filed in the photo archive at the Centre, comparing and compiling them, keeping our discussions focused on matters iconographical and avoiding our personal drama, so that the intense intimacy of our time in Moissac had a chance to simmer down.

One evening after Michel was bathed and put to sleep, and the boys had beat me in a game of ping-pong, I sat on my bed cozily wrapped in a quilt and opened my copy of the Old Testament to the Book of Jeremiah. The French government poster of him, bought in the gift shop of the church in Moissac, looked down on me from the wall, and I greeted him with a secret smile.

By page two I wondered if I had the right prophet. Here was a coarse, vindictive diatribe instead of the precious, hard-won wisdom I had expected to find. By page five I was revolted by his whining. Whatever breathed with life, he despised. He denounced women as harlots and called the pains of childbirth well deserved. Nobody escaped his wrath. What was this?

"The heart is treacherous above all things," I read with dismay, *"and desperately sick...Let them be put to shame, but not me. With double destruction, destroy them!"*

"No!" I exclaimed aloud to the image on my wall. "No and no! I don't believe you would say these things!" Long after midnight I was still reading his ugly tirades, finally closing the Bible to stare in shock at the Jeremiah on the wall, who offered not one word of reassurance.

Martine was in the photo archive the next morning, and I plunked myself down across the table from her, slapping open my Old Testament to the next two pages. I thought that this ranting had to stop eventually, but after another ten minutes it only got worse. Here was all desolation and doom, grief and despair and vengeance. When I got to his lament about the day he was born, everything came into wretched focus for me.

> Cursed be my father who did not let me die in the womb,
> That my mother might have been my grave
> And her womb have remained pregnant forever.
> Why came I out of the womb to see trouble and sorrow,
> That my days might be spent in shame?

Oh, I knew the sound of shallow self-hatred only too well! Slamming the Bible shut, I shoved back my chair, grabbed my coat, and stomped out of the room. That self-righteous complaining was the sound I had grown up with; it was the angry cry of fearful people blaming everyone and everything for their misery. That voice had permeated my life since I was born, and I was gagging on it. Pulling on my coat, I rushed out of the courtyard and onto the narrow streets of Poitiers to try and walk it off.

With my hands crammed in my pockets and my head down to the wind, I strode through the back alleys of the town muttering to myself and wiping my nose on my sleeve. My bones felt stiff as the familiar shame and dread surged through me. The blood in my body remembered years of heart-stopping terror that *this* time I would finally be pulled under for good.

I knew in my cells the feeling of bracing against a shame so primal I considered myself unworthy to even eat breakfast. "No, Jeremiah," I heard myself mutter out loud, taking aggressive strides in the direction of the river. "You're wrong here and too cowardly to face your own fear."

I was tripping over cobblestones now. "The Jeremiah I trust—
'my' Jeremiah—told me to face my fear and I believe he's right. I
don't know who the hell you are, but I don't believe you, and if
a whole civilization has been built on your so-called wisdom, well
then, more's the pity. But not me, buddy, not me!"

I stalked the streets wildly, my head on fire as I tried to escape the
confines of my own skin. The Romanesque images of Hell with its
vats of boiling oil and grimacing devils were silly cartoons next to
this. True hell wasn't a place of weird-looking monsters, it was a
down-in-the-marrow-of-the-bones stink of self-hate; it was a humiliation of the soul so profound that one's very breath was not convinced it had the right to breathe. Oh, I knew that humiliation well,
but no fake prophet was going to drag me there again!

I stopped only when I reached the river. Leaning over the bridge
railing, I peered down into the swirling waters, my breaths gradually slowing down until they washed in and out with the flow of the
current, always changing, always the same. Here between earth and
sky I could breathe. With the winds in my face and my feet balanced
on the bridge, I remembered that I belonged to the world and had
my place here. Inhaling breath after breath of river-brine air, I finally
calmed down enough to turn around and head back to the Centre.
Hopefully, Martine would still be there.

The others had left for lunch but she was there, her expression
wondering and receptive. I began to sob and she met me in the middle of the room, taking me into her arms and holding me close. Her
smell was clean and leathery and I breathed it in, clinging to her like a
boat moored in safe harbor. After a while she said quietly, *"Dîtes moi."*
Tell me. For just a moment I hesitated, but then spilled it out like
dirty water, choking with anger and grief at the betrayal by all the
fearful ones of the world, especially those with the power to harm.

"How could they?" I repeated over and over. "They don't have to remain scared! They choose to stay ignorant!" I was thinking of abusive parents, government bullies—all those who masked fear with aggression. "It makes me want to scream!" I did scream, in fact, right into her ear. She ducked her head but kept holding me, her hands strong on my back.

"What I can't understand," I choked out at last, drying my tears on her shoulder, "is how some artist in the eleven-hundreds was able to turn that creepy Jeremiah from the Bible into such a soulful sculpture."

"I doubt he could even read the text," she reminded me. "Anyhow, his model was probably his lover—remember, we decided it was?" I nodded tearfully. "Furthermore," she teased, wiping a tear from my cheek with her thumb, "they must have had a wonderful time in the studio. That sculpture isn't about guilt, it's about Love."

An unexpected *frisson* rippled up my spine, and I reluctantly pulled away from her embrace, giving the Bible on the table a shove hard enough to send it flying. Martine caught it before it fell to the floor, wrinkling her nose at me and grinning her heart-melting grin.

On those days Martine and I weren't together during that winter, I found myself jealous of the rest of her life. And when we were together, studying side by side or taking walks by the river, we were acutely aware of the forbidden territory of each other's bodies.

In my letters to Dani I hinted at the dilemma and, free spirit that he was, he encouraged me to trust what was happening. Still, during those long, cold months, when Martine and I were more intimate than ever, we did not cross the invisible line we had tacitly agreed to draw in the sand. Strained we might be, but we were impeccable.

Meanwhile, we chewed closer and closer to the philosophical

bone, tearing the obscuring meat away from the question of fear and reaching for what might actually constitute a miracle.

"Do you suppose," I speculated one day in the library, regarding a grotesque Hell scene that showed a naked woman being plunged mercilessly into a cauldron of boiling oil, "that there might be a method to this madness? Maybe the guys in charge wanted to keep people terrified."

"Terrified and guilty," she added. "Jesus died for our sins, after all."

"Hardly an improvement on the Old Testament prophets," I muttered, "except that here you actually crucify someone and then get everyone to pray to him."

"If you grow up with that, though, you learn to feel compassion and it doesn't occur to you to question it," she explained. "But it's too bad that the image of Jesus as a victim rather than the Christ in glory is the one that lives on."

"It seems strange also," I persisted, "that we grow up not questioning so many things—inquisitions, holy wars, chosen people…" I counted them off on my fingers.

"Witch burnings, anathemas…" she added sadly. "I agree they are hardly ways to spread a message of love." We both sighed.

"And look at the Last Judgment, Martine," I observed. "Someone gets to be judge, but who chooses the judge? So some of us go to Heaven and some go to Hell, but on what grounds? What if I don't agree with the grounds?" I stared out at snow-covered rooftops and smoke spiraling lazily out of chimney pots.

"Go on."

"OK," I continued, "so there's this group in power and they want to stay in power, so they create a system that controls people by keeping them frightened of their own shadows. That way, the ones in power get to call all the shots, starting with defining what's real, and when people don't agree it's 'off with their heads.'"

"The saddest part," she interrupted, bright spots of color appearing in her cheeks, "is that what they call "real" defines the ordinary miracles of life as sinful—like nature and pleasure and females, for example."

"And only stuff like loaves and fishes and resurrections get called "miracles!" We stared at each other, aghast. "I'm wondering if our whole civilization isn't based on some serious misinformation," I offered archly. "I can't believe this was what the real Jesus had in mind."

"Let's walk," she suggested in a choked whisper, and reaching for our coats with trembling hands we left the library, our minds on fire and our hearts tentatively opening to the possibility that if we were right about this, then maybe other teachings of the church ought to be questioned—such as what constituted natural and unnatural love, for example.

In April, as Chaucer tells us, the rains *"bathe every vine in such sweet liquor, that people long to go on pilgrimage."* And so it was for us. We longed to break out of the routine of books and classes, but even more, to be on our own together. By the time spring came, we were the center of each other's universe. Every day spent apart was a day of yearning, so we borrowed two motorbikes from the older d'Alverny boys—a red one and a green one—and with sleeping bags and backpacks tied to the fenders we took to the road.

"Nous sommes sur la route!" we bellowed, feeling like escapees from jail as we sped east out of town. We're on the road! Our plan was to make a wide arc around Poitiers and visit remote churches and ancient stoneworks, sleeping in the fields when it was warm and dry enough, and staying at *pensions* in the villages when it was not.

We would spend Easter Sunday at St. Savin-sur-Gartempes, a large abbey church in a tiny village that was renowned amongst medieval scholars for its magnificent frescoes, but unknown to the rest of the world except for the farming folk who made up its parish. After Easter we would follow the road wherever it led us.

We were giddy with freedom, dissolving into hysterics every time my motorbike stalled—which was often—and tossing jokes back and forth above the smelly putt-putt of the motors. After months of being shut up in stuffy rooms, we were ecstatic to be out. We took to the open air, tasting the freedom of the wind and high currents along a road we had never journeyed before.

"Smell the spring!" Martine cried happily, bouncing on her bicycle seat. The earth, saturated and popping from the recent rains, was fragrant with decaying winter mulch—"brown food," she called it—and the new spikes of tender grass were vivid with green life. On the trees tiny buds had swelled, here and there already giving way to new catkins—red and white and yellow-green—and birdsong twittered in the air. Winter was over and the reawakening had begun.

"By the time we come back," Martine called over her shoulder, "this will all be in bloom!"

I was swelling too, happy and in love. My cup runneth over. My friend was by my side, I had passed all my exams, and in the fields on either side of the road newborn lambs bleated like tin toys on spindly legs. We were witty and wise, the pair of us, adventurous and silly, and we couldn't stop laughing. I tossed Martine a nonsense riddle I had just made up about why cows had four wings, and when she at last gave up I told her, "They don't," and shrieking with laughter, we nearly fell off our bikes.

"Is that an American joke?" she shouted into the wind, wiping her tearing eyes.

"No," I shouted back. "Hebrew!"

For the next two days we bumped our way along marshland canals and through scraggly pine forests. Humming windmills whirled by the sides of the road, and little lines of ducklings waddled along the marshes, following their mothers, plop plop plop, into the gently flowing water.

We slept under the stars and watched the moon, each night a little fuller, rise over the trees. On the evening of the Passover, when the moon was a perfect circle—the night of the Last Supper when Jesus would be betrayed—we found ourselves outside the village of Montmorillon at the ruins of an early Christian monastery. Only a small octagonal funerary chapel, surrounded by the fallen stones of what had once been the monastery, was still intact.

The door of the chapel creaked open as we entered, flashlights in hand. Even the sounds of our breathing echoed in the small chamber, and when Martine gave an exploratory hum, the chapel hummed it back.

I sang a note and heard my sound sing back to me until it faded. A laugh created its own resonance and our whispers reverberated as if the shadows were peopled with copycat ghosts.

Martine did a joyous two-step and, pulling a flashlight out of her backpack, placed it in the center of the stone floor. Dancing shadows appeared on all eight walls, and the sounds of our movements resulted in a mysterious choir of voices that echoed hauntingly off the walls; our laughter came back to us like jovial company.

For an hour or more we "played with the ghosts," as Martine described it, chanting as the monks of this monastery must once have done. We were celebrating the Passover in a new ritual that transcended both our traditions. Our song went on until the moon rose high in the sky, and it was after midnight before we left, unrolling our sleeping bags and laying them close together inside the ruins of what may once have been a monk's cell.

"Aren't those overtones gorgeous?" Martine yawned as we prepared for bed. Cold and tired, I crawled into my sleeping bag and tucked my knees up to my chest. She went on, "You sort of have to not listen to hear them, and then they just ring out like bells."

"Umm," I mumbled, my eyes closing. I was too tired to ask her what she meant. She stood next to me in our ruined cell and gazed up at the moon.

"Did you notice how you could only hear them when you weren't paying attention?" she persisted.

"Mmm...?" I mumbled, drifting closer to sleep.

"Say!" she exclaimed, "let's go back into the chapel and I'll show you."

I turned over to protest, but Martine's spirit was irresistible, even in the middle of the night, and with a yawn I wriggled out of my sleeping bag and shook myself awake. She pulled me to my feet and excitedly led me back into the chamber.

"Hmmmnnmm," she hummed into the dark. I hummed with her. Our voices grew louder, bouncing off the walls and swelling into a fullness that rang all around us. When our breaths ran out the tones kept beating in the air. I could hear the chord our note created, and then way above, almost beyond hearing, a high bell tone. From our single note the chapel sang back a whole chorus.

"Oh, my," I breathed when the sounds faded. We sang another note, and another, and the hidden tones revealed themselves, subtly vibrating in our chests and our throats. It felt like doors were opening in my body, letting new music into rooms that had been shut tight before. This was the true Passover. Martine and I held hands and listened for the fading of the last sounds before we left the chapel to the moonlight, and then we found our way back to our camp amid the ancient ruins.

Spring was abuzz in the countryside around Montmorillon, and the next day we followed a back road in the direction of St. Savin-sur-Gartempes. In no hurry to arrive, we stopped to gaze at nest-building sparrows and waves of new grass rippling down a hillside like water in the wind. We watched birds swoop and chase, and frogs croak noisily at the edges of puddles. Sap was rising into every branch and the forces of life were spurting everywhere as vibrant green growth. It rose for us too, and our thoughts tumbled into speech almost faster than we could form them into words.

"This is how the singing felt to me," I told her, as we lay sprawled head to head in a field vivid with yellow mustard. I closed my eyes to retrieve the sense of last night's many-layered sound, feeling it again vibrate in my bones.

"My whole body seemed to be hearing it, not just my ears," I recalled. Her eyes glistened tawny gold in the sunshine. "The space was filled with it…" This was not easy to put into words, and I tried again. "I mean, it felt like the whole place was alive."

"I felt it too," she confirmed. "It tingled me all over. What I got was a sense of layers coming together—you know, like in your dream? Worlds within worlds…"

"…like all the notes are there even in one single sound—you just have to know to listen for them," I broke in excitedly. Closing my eyes I felt the warmth of the sun penetrating my skin, heard the buzzing of bugs, and smelled the earth beneath me and the sap of the grass. A moment ago I had hardly been aware of them.

Martine pensively plucked a blade of grass and bit off the sap-filled end.

"I wonder if everything is right here all the time," she speculated. I glanced around our meadow of green grass and wildflowers. Above, castles of clouds drifted lazily across the sky's blue.

"Like everything?" I wondered aloud, "every thought anybody in the world has ever had, every breath, every dream…?"

"…and every person who has ever lived," she finished for me. "So that means all the dead would be right here, right now, but we can't see them."

"Hi, Grandpa," I whispered to the air, shivering. Martine smiled and pulled a dried stalk from last year's wild fennel and snapped it into bits, blowing the crumbles into the breeze. Another brittle stalk came up easily when I tugged at the base, revealing moist green leaves sprouting from the plant's living roots. Last year's fennel was over, but this year's leaves were already growing, so where was last year's plant? Here but not here. I pointed it out to Martine.

"*Voilà le miracle*," she affirmed. "The grand cycle of everything—plants, animals, people, the whole earth." Her eyes were as speckled as the dry fennel stalks, green as its delicate new leaves.

"So if nothing ever really dies," I concluded, "then that means there's nothing to fear."

"There's nothing to fear," she repeated softly. Our hands met palm to palm and trembling, we interlaced fingers.

"I love you," I said to myself, and then out loud, "*je t'aime*."

"*Moi aussi, je t'aime*," she whispered.

During our winter of growing intimacy, our menstrual cycles had synchronized, so when we arrived at St. Savin-sur-Gartempes on the day before Easter, we were both bleeding. We decided not to camp, in the interests of comfort and hygiene, and took a room in a pension near the church square where we could have our first hot bath in a week.

The baths were heavenly and we both emerged purified—silky, renewed, and done up in skirts brought especially for the holy weekend. The sunrise service would begin before dawn, and our plan was to spend the afternoon sightseeing, sleep dressed in everything but our skirts, and roll out of bed when the bells began to ring.

The good Saint Savin, a ninth-century hermit who had spent most of his life in a nearby cave, now lay in the crypt beneath the altar. Around his bones, this tiny village of few more than a thousand souls had grown. Although the village was small, the abbey church was monumental and filled with frescoes depicting scenes from both the Old and New Testaments. In other times, pilgrims had arrived here from all over France, but nowadays it was only art historians and the occasional tourist who came to visit.

"You may be our only outsiders for Easter," our landlady confided. "You are the lucky ones." Smiling, she shook our hands, kissed us on both cheeks, and presented each of us with a hard-boiled egg for Easter.

We considered ourselves rather splendid in our Easter skirts—Martine in purple gingham and me in bright yellow—and with colorful beads around our necks and newly washed hair swinging wetly about our faces, we tucked the eggs into our pockets and found our way down to the river. Wildflower grass came right down to the light-dazzled water, which sang as it flowed turbulently past the village. Once we were out of sight of the houses, we skipped the rest of the way to the river's edge, nudging off our sandals and scrambling down the bank to wade into the shock of the icy current.

"Ye-iie!" Martine shrieked, dancing from foot to foot and holding her skirt above her thighs. I splashed in after her, shivering and laughing, and was soaked within moments. Anybody watching would have seen two crazy girls cavorting in the river, having hysterics as they chased each other in and out of the freezing current.

But nobody was watching; we were alone in a stream flowing through a lupine- and poppy-strewn meadow under the sun, with only birds and butterflies and early bees as witnesses. Our church was the air itself—the sky above and the earth beneath our feet. Not very far away, where the church steeple rose high above the trees, others were preparing for the dark hours of Christ's Passion inside the old sanctuary. Another church—right now, not ours.

"The world is such a wonder," Martine remarked later as we lay side by side on the bank watching a young snake stitch its way through the grass. It halted to test us with a flicking forked tongue and then slithered out of sight.

"It is," I agreed, feeling the earth throb into me. Shot through with sun, I merged with grass and moist soil as a gush of menstrual blood flowed out of my body. I wondered if women had ever bled directly into the earth, and I started to mention it to Martine but then hesitated.

"I wonder why the good saint shut himself away from the world when it's so beautiful here," I murmured instead.

"Maybe it was only in the winter," she conjectured. "I imagine he was really saintly, and people recognized it."

"Maybe he was a skin-and-bones ascetic type," I said, to be contrary. "What do you think of this business of self-mortification?" Lazily, I flopped onto my side and breathed in the fragrance of rich soil threaded with roots. Succulent grass tickled my bare feet, and the burbling of the river merged with the clicking and buzzing of tiny insects going about their business. "Why would anybody want give all this up?" I asked querulously.

"I suppose there was a different mind in those days," she suggested sleepily. For a while we both napped in the sun, our hips softly touching and our fingers entwined. The heat spread comfortingly into our cramping bellies, and I rolled over onto my back.

"But people still believe it!" I insisted just as I heard the hard-boiled egg in my pocket go *cr-runch-ch*.

We peeled our eggs slowly, ritually, placing fragments of eggshell in a pile between us, telling each other stories of other Easters and Passovers, and bringing our families into our little circle. Then we separated the pile into four equal parts so as to scatter the shells in the four directions, as pagans once did, and we sprinkled them with water from the stream.

Facing north, then south, then east, then west, we took turns improvising prayers for the year to come, casting bits of shell into the water with each supplication. The last bits bobbed on the surface until they disappeared into a whirlpool and around a downstream rock; then we held our eggs between thumb and forefinger and asked for the sun's blessings, smiling as we entwined arms and fed each other the egg we had peeled.

At first we tittered at our pretend pagan rituals, but by the time the eggs were a crumble of yolk and white in each other's palms, our eyes had locked with tender intention. With every bite the act had become truer for both of us, and now we found it hard to swallow.

My throat may have been closed, but my heart was wide open and brimming. I blessed the day, the moment, life itself. More than anything I blessed my friend, and the miracle that we had found each other. On Love's holy ground we gazed at each other, confirming the bond between us. Leaning toward me, she licked up the last bits of her egg from my palm; leaning toward her, I licked up the last bits of my egg from hers.

We marked the site of our ritual with a small cairn of stones, adding purple lupine and early red poppies to it, and a bedraggled crow's feather we found on the riverbank. Bowing to our stone altar, we sprinkled it with the stream's holy water and recited The Lord's Prayer, first in French and then in English. Then we made our way, arm in arm, back to the village and the frescoes in the church of St. Savin.

The basilica was cool and dark after the brightness of the day, and it took some moments for my eyes to adjust to the immensity of the nave. Soaring arches supported a high, barrel-vaulted ceiling still brilliant, after all these centuries, with painted scenes from the Bible. Moses was there, and men in tunics constructing the tower of Babylon. Robed evangelists danced with angels, and Noah's triple-decker ark was bursting with smiling beasts who sailed on a wavy sea. Even God Himself was there busily creating His earth and the starry skies.

"Hard to imagine how they ever did this," I commented, arching backward to squint up at the rounded ceiling. The artist would have had to lie on his back thirty meters in the air and paint upside down onto a curving vault.

"With difficulty, I imagine," Martine grinned. "Look, there are the two Marys," she pointed out, "and Cain and Abel."

Heads up, we prowled the nave and found the angel who ann-ouinced to Mary that she was pregnant, Mary and Joseph's flight into Egypt on a knobby-kneed ass, and Christ being carried tenderly from the cross. Adam and Eve, naked and sexless as smooth-groined dolls, looked so innocent it was hard to imagine them doing any-thing naughty enough to get them expelled from Paradise.

"Cute snake," I remarked at the grimacing green serpent that towered over Eve.

"He looks like a pussycat," she observed. "Wouldn't be so hard to resist his temptations, I think."

"I've always liked Eve," I said, "and I still don't understand what was so bad about eating an apple from the Tree of Knowledge. What's sinful about women knowing things?"

"I just love how determined you are to take on all of Western civilization," Martine teased.

"But what's wrong with her having knowledge?" I persisted.

"What's all this about original sin, and getting kicked out of the Garden for eating a piece of fruit? Whose rules are those?" Martine snorted with laughter. "It's whoever didn't want women to have power, that's who," I continued with heat. I always became vehement with my menses. "So it's her fault that Adam gets banished from Paradise, and then she takes the blame for the next two thousand years!"

Later, lounging on the crypt steps beneath the altar where the good Saint Savin lay buried, we continued whispering as, above us in the sanctuary, village women busily prepared the altar for the predawn Mass. We talked about relations between men and strong women; we spoke of marriage and motherhood and new ways of being women in the world.

"Do you suppose anything is going to change?" I remarked finally.

"Have you changed?" she countered. "Are you the same as your mother?" I shook my head.

"Well, I'm not either," she declared. "My mother would never be sitting here asking the kinds of questions we're asking, and she'd never allow herself to feel this way about another woman."

There, it was out in plain language.

We both got very quiet. I lowered my eyes to avoid hers and could hear both of our breaths moving in and out. There was little more to say; if the old rules were no longer valid, then it was up to us to create new ones.

Whatever that meant.

We were out of bed with the first bells, dressed and out the door of the *pension* before we fully knew we were awake. The dark square in front of the church was already crowded with people, and we joined the others who streamed toward the open portals and descended the steps into the sanctuary. Each person received an unlit candle at the door as the crowd shuffled forward into the dark basilica for the service.

Muffled chanting echoed from the altar, rising in volume as we got closer to the crypt where, only hours before, Martine and I had sat and talked. Following the crowd of local people, we felt our way in the darkness to a *prie dieuxv* and we knelt there on the cold stones, foreheads pressed on wooden railings, and breathed in the aroma of incense and the pungent odor of sheep's cheese and wine emanating from our neighbors.

Lulled by the chant, I slipped into a half sleep where serpents slithering up trees to branching vaults, and a naked Eve waited expectantly for their encircling coils. I must have snored because Martine tapped my arm as a procession of robed men, with a shrouded cross held high above their heads, made their way up the aisle toward the entryway, to ascend the steps we had just come down. They intoned a slow chant in sibilant whispers, repeating it hypnotically as they processed past us towards the open portals.

Mysterium. I melted into the darkness, slipping from time into no time, from here to nowhere. I was awake and asleep, real and ephemeral. Dizzy, I hovered above myself and wondered if I would faint. Martine placed a hand on my arm, which brought me back down to ground, and I heaved in a sigh and then coughed. My cough echoed throughout the church.

In solemn procession the men and boys walked the shrouded cross outside into the night, their muffled dirge all but disappearing as they circumambulated the abbey church and ancient churchyard. Inside, only our shared breathing, the murmur and clicking of rosaries, and the occasional whimper of a child could be heard. We waited, held in the suspense of this the darkest hour. For a timeless moment everyone seemed to stop breathing, and the silence in the sanctuary was absolute. I could hear my own heart beating in my ears.

The procession came full circle back to the porch, the men and boys gathering at the entryway, and suddenly into the stillness the low-voiced dirge swelled into full-bodied singing. The shock of sound jerked me full awake. The procession came down the steps and into the church, robes and handbells swinging and voices jubilant.

"*Hallelujah!* He is risen!"

One taper was lit and then others, sending flickering pinpoints of light into the congregation. Person by person, the flame was passed down each row until the sanctuary was glowing and each tear-stained face was illumined by candlelight.

"He is risen! Christ is risen! The Lord is risen! *Hallelujah!*"

The farmer kneeling beside me wept into his work-roughened hands and then gazed reverently toward the altar. Martine lifted her candle as the shroud was lifted off the gleaming cross, and everyone in the congregation gasped, holding their candles high so the dancing lights might illumine the colors of the ancient frescoes.

"The Light of the World has returned! He is risen! *Hallelujah!*"

I sang along with the others, my heart and voice full. "*Hallelujah!*" I was filled with grace, transported to where love took over and nothing else mattered. If this was the Mystery, I accepted it. If this was the Miracle, I accepted it. By whatever name, I accepted it. Martine lifted both arms into the air, singing ecstatically and spilling hot candle wax onto her skirt. I grabbed at her skirt and quenched the hot wax with my hand as it hardened, my laughter unstoppable, free.

I was in love with the darkness that always cycles back into light, with the intelligence of seeds that know how to grow. I blessed the loyalty of birds to the eggs in their nests, the rains and the rivers their wetness, and ourselves—my own kind—who are willing to struggle on generation after generation even when we are frozen with fear. *Hallelujah!*

We were a river in full spate, freed from the restrictions of the banks and flooding love like fertile silt all over the countryside. The congregation stood and greeted their neighbors, singing, everyone pressing together and swaying apart, ebbing and flowing even as candles burned down to nubs and the darkness of night began to soften into the first lights of dawn. Martine and I were carried along with the people towards the ambulatory and the growing light outside, always singing.

By the font of holy water, we stood aside from the crowd and waited until everyone filed past us and up the steps, and when all had left the basilica and we were alone in the empty church, we turned to each other and clasped hands. In her brilliant eyes I saw myself reflected, glowing and whole.

The bells pealed as we embraced. Right beneath the Mother and Child we came together thigh to thigh, belly to belly and breast to breast. Our union was blessed by the Virgin Mother and Holy Child and by all the powers of the world since the beginning of time.

Then, hand in hand, we walked up the steps to the porch and out the great doors of Saint Savin to catch the sun as it rose, triumphant and glorious, over the rim of the world.

THE SPINNING VORTEX

The Absolute together with the Creative Power equals the Divine Couple. He rests always in his eternal nature and She is eternally active, expanding to reveal and reabsorb the whole of the universe. She is His first stir, and also the infinite stirring. This pulsation exists continuously, and exists in all the different states of consciousness. It is the residual, foundational substratum of the manifested world.

From a creation hymn of the Kashmiri Hindu Shaivites

*M*artine and I, in our year-long conversation about miracles and fear, were earnestly searching, whether we knew it or not, for the primordial pattern that underlies the universe. This was no small order for two intense girls of nineteen. At the same time, though we certainly were not aware of it, we were inscribing that very pattern between us, circling around each other in our growing intimacy, never quite closing the loop but creating an ongoing spiral of mutual passion for our subject and for each other.

The pattern we inscribed between us was actually hidden in plain sight on every surface of our world: it was in the errant curl escaping from Martine's barrette; it was in the swirling smoke from votive candles in the abbey of St. Savin. It was in the unfolding of a rose and the cycle from winter to spring; it was in galaxies and electrons, seashells and cyclones, and the whorl on the top of baby Michel's head. Everywhere we looked, had we the eyes to see, the cosmic vortex was translated into the manifested forms of our world.

As Martine and I continuously tossed ideas back and forth, we traced the path of this vortex, sparking each other's imagination and generating fresh insights and new directions of thought. We were expanding the dialogue from a closed circle to an open-ended call and response, creating a spiral of ideas that, once begun, was perpetually in motion. We were the stirrers and we were the stirred, as the Kashmiri Shaivites might say.

I remember sitting on the riverbank of the Gartempes just after the spring thaw, mesmerized by the icy waters whirlpooling around riverbed rocks in the river's impetuous rush back to the sea. The watery vortices formed and dissolved continuously—first here, then there, then bursting into spray before spinning again into a new series of whirlpools.

I imagine that if we could see beneath the forms of our physical world, on a subtler substratum where all of existence is connected, it might look something like this turbulent stream, with clusters of whirlpools in many dimensions spinning in and out of being.

After the dark of the night, the sun had come around to take its place in the sky the morning Martine and I set out on motorbikes through the Poitou countryside. The winter was turning to spring, our hearts were beating almost seventy beats a minute, and with each breath we recycled oxygen and carbon dioxide with the air around us. Our motorbikes traveled at about ten miles per hour, and the occasional car passed us at more than twice that speed.

That morning and every morning, linked cycles were taking place, each at its own pace and each in its own scale of space and time. The electrons spinning around the nuclei in our cells cycled at one frequency and the earth revolved around the sun at another, but the pattern was the same. If we could hear the buzz and beat of all the cycles together, it might sound like the polyrhythms of an African drumming circle—in which each drum holds its own beat and the ensemble entrains to one coherent rhythm implicit in all the individual parts.

I try to imagine the unimaginable—that moment when time began and the beat of the universe emerged out of the time-less stillness of the Unified Field. In a twinkling, unleashed by a 'flutter of love,' what had been energy in equilibrium became energy in motion. Everything was jumping! The dance was on!

The whole thing must have vibrated like mad—as, of course, it still does. Jiggling and shaking, every infinitesimal bit would have spun out of the Unified Field, the energetic pathways curving around, but never quite closing the loop. Thus would the spiral have been born, the shape of energy in motion that evolved order out of chaos.

Repeated cycles of creation and destruction—larger and smaller, faster and slower—these twirling *do-si-do's* would have appeared and disappeared, tumbling and clustering at a dizzying rate as they introduced Time, Space, and multiple frequencies onto the stage of the world.

In ancient Egypt, Hermes Trismegistus, 'the scribe of the gods,' is said to have spoken these words:

"That which is below is like that which is above; that which is above is like that which is below, for the miracles of the universe are part of one whole thing."

Martine, can you hear me? Here's the Miracle we were looking for—it's in the stir of the world itself. Really! It is spiraling energy that spins right out from the Unified Field!

If above corresponds to below, then there is intelligent life in the universe because the whole thing is intelligent and alive! Of course. The patterns match.

In every living thing, from bacteria to redwood trees, cells contain this stirring in the form of double helices coiled repeatedly around themselves to fit into the tiny space of their nuclei. DNA, we call it. Aside from the fact they are the chemical messengers of the molecules, the shape itself is in resonance with the Unified Field, receiving and transmitting information like minute umbilical cords connected to the lifeblood of the Mother. Intelligence is passed back and forth, informing us on every level we can receive. The molecules translate this code to our living systems, instructing its processes and maintaining its life—and death.

Here's a miracle, Martine: in my body and yours there are

about 125 billion miles of DNA, long enough to wrap around the earth five million times—and we are blithely unaware of it!

And get this, my friend: the two strands of the double helix wrap around each other six hundred million times inside each human cell!

Even in the smallest known unit of life—the bacterium—its genome contains 580,000 DNA 'letters' communicating back and forth with the all-embracing field of existence. I can hardly imagine how many 'letters' we humans must contain, but it is probably beyond counting, which means that at every moment of our lives, know it or not, we are linked up with the Unified Field and therefore with each other.

How could we ever have thought we were alone in the world? We're connected to the universe by every cell in our bodies, resonating to the various frequencies of the world like the resonant coils of a radio receiver tuning into one band on the dial after another. Every breath we breathe is recycled from the breaths of every being who has ever lived, and every synapse of our nerves comes from the inextinguishable Unified Field within which we exist and have our being.

I had a dream once—a dream of dancers. I was high in the rafters of a gymnasium, and below me colorfully costumed people were dancing in a circle, their colors flashing as they twirled in the dance. And then, still watching them from above, I was dancing amongst them! We laughed as we spun past each other, our two lines weaving in and out of each other. I skipped past green, then yellow, then purple, then red. I swirled around orange and grabbed the hand of blue. We leaped and we circled around each other.

Still watching from above, what I saw was a fabric—a cloth of many colors being woven before my eyes—with me dancing within the weave. I was inside and outside, above and below. I was a dancer, but from above I also watched the bright pattern of the gorgeous dance.

Then and now. There and everywhere. Myself and the ten thousand things.

SEVEN

Katsu

Kanzeon
namu butsu
Yo butsu U in
Yo butsu U en
Bu po so en Jo raku ga jo
Cho nen Kanzeon, Bo nen Kanzeon
Nen nen Ju shin Ki
Nen nen fu ri shin.

About a year before he died, Katsufumi Reiko taught me this Buddhist chant as his parting gift. We sat cross-legged on cushions in his darkened bedroom, copal incense swirling fragrant smoke into the air, a Sumi brushstroke painting of Kwan-Yin, the Goddess of Compassion, hanging over his altar. We recited the chant over and over until I had the words by heart.

"Cry, if you need to," he had said softly before we started the bedroom ritual. Moments later, meditating with this beloved man in the heart-ticking stillness of his sickroom, the tears flowed along with the words of the chant.

Kwan Yin, Goddess of Compassion, is also Myself.
She sees the sound of all suffering; bowing to her, I bow to
Myself.
I arise from the Buddha and I am the Buddha.
The Buddha holds me and I hold the Buddha.
The three treasures nurture me,
Buddha, Dharma, Sangha:
Buddha, the First Cause; Dharma, my life and acts;
And Sangha, the community of all Beings.
In the pure sky of Mind I exist in eternal joy.
At every moment, compassion;
Morning and evening, compassion.
Awareness arises from eternity,
Awareness arises from me, mind and heart.
Not separate—the same:
Kwan-Yin, Buddha, Myself.

We had met eight years earlier, Katsu and I, in the late 1970s when I took a class he was teaching on the Crazy Wisdom stories in the Zen Buddhist tradition. I was a beginning meditator, and now that all three of my children were in high school, I was free again to follow my own interests in spirituality and dance—twin passions since the days of skittering across the Sacred Heart schoolyard on borrowed skates. In fact, it was in preparation for choreographing a suite of Zen dances that I was taking Katsu Reiko's class at the Meditation Center.

My husband Ted and I had met in New York after my return from France, and we were married shortly after. He was a graduate student in physics, and since we were so mysterious to each other— he the pragmatic scientist and me the intuitive artist—we had fallen madly in love.

We moved to the San Francisco Bay Area after he was offered a teaching post, and we started our family right away, producing three children in the space of four years. I settled down to being his wife and their full-time mother for fifteen years until the children reached puberty, and for most of that time I barely looked up. But now that the children were all teenagers and claiming their independence, it was time for me to reclaim mine as well.

I was rusty at being a student, to be sure, but crazy wisdom seemed as good a place as any to start again. When I entered the quiet, wood-paneled room, fragrant with Japanese incense, and returned the bow of an exotic, brown gnome of a man in a purple silk *yukata*, I felt I had come to the right place.

Katsu looked like nobody I had ever seen before. Short and swarthy, with a long Mayan nose that came straight down from his thick, black eyebrows to sensuous lips, he looked like a remnant from some ancient people, long gone. His slanted eyes, one wide and open, the other smaller and watchful, seemed to peer inward and outward at the same time; his once-black hair was parted in the middle and hung to his shoulders, framing his wide cheekbones.

As I bowed to him, I tried not to stare. He welcomed me into the room with an easy smile of familiarity and showed me to a cushion at a low table, where I exchanged bows with the other students. I would later learn that he was part Mexican and part Japanese, spoke the languages of both cultures, and identified with the indigenous aspects of his two traditions. I smiled into piercing black eyes that seemed to be reading me down to my bones, and my heart shuddered in my chest. He looked curiously familiar to me, but I couldn't place where I might have met him before. "Where have you been?" I wanted to ask, as if I already knew him.

That first class passed for me in a haze of delicious fascination. He had read to us a conundrum from the *Blue Cliff Records*, classic

Zen teaching stories, in which nonsense sentences lead the student deeper and deeper into confusion.

"On the lone summit of the mystic peak, weeds grow in profusion."

His lithe body leapt around the small room; we could see the profusion of weeds high on the lonely peak. *"You lose your body, too."* I had no idea what to make of that, because the presence of his body was so strong it was hard to take my eyes off him. *"You've got your nostrils, but you've lost your mouth!"* he recited, lowering his voice mysteriously.

"So what do you all make of this?" he asked after he had mimed through the whole verse. I listened to several students' attempts to address the question logically, and it struck me that the story didn't have to do with the logic of individual body parts, but with the whole body. Hesitantly, I suggested that perhaps it was about the ability to see the body as a whole instead of piece by piece. He rose to his toes and then settled onto his heels. "More," he coaxed, his eyebrows lifted. I thought a while, and could think of nothing more.

"Umm, I think that's all," I said finally, shrugging.

"That's right," was his reply. "There is nothing more than seeing things whole and immediate. That's what every crazy wisdom story or riddle or koan is about—seeing things directly."

When the class was over I didn't want to leave. All the other students, residents of the building, went up to their rooms for the night until only he and I were left in the hall. On the steps outside I suggested, rather boldly, that we carpool to class together the following week

"No," he said in a tone that was neither deprecating nor apologetic, just informative. I must have expected that response, because I was neither embarrassed nor put off. I would suggest it again, that's all, which I did the following week, and then again the week after, when he finally agreed.

That's the way it was with us. Much later, when we were intimate friends and I asked him why he had turned me down that first time, he said that he knew it was inevitable we'd become involved, and involvement could be a disaster so he wanted to put it off for as long as possible.

"So?" I had asked.

"So, it's a disaster," he replied. But I get ahead of my story.

Through that fall and early winter, Katsu would pick me up each week for class and drive me home afterwards, never accepting my invitations to come inside and meet my family, never allowing me to return the favor of driving (and therefore knowing where he lived). But before he dropped me off we would always sit in his car talking. We thought alike, our temperaments were matched, and we shared fascinations for the same odd things.

Unlike Ted and me, who were models for the adage that opposites attract, Katsu and I were more like siblings separated at birth. I was continually delighted by how deeply we connected, by the scope of his imagination, and by the endless creativity of his mind. I felt sparked by him, challenged, as if he were presenting me with riddles to unravel, and I gladly took them on—took him on—excited by any assignment that put me into his stimulating presence. I wondered, always, about the details of the rest of his life, but on that subject he was mum; it would be several more months of guessing before I knew the reasons for his fastidious discretion.

I told him in the car one night about the Suite I was choreographing on Zen themes for a performance project. I was calling the suite *Finger Pointing at the Moon*, and the piece I was working on now was based on a series of *haiku* poems.

"I want to do dance improvisations of the *haiku*," I explained. "No set moves, but to feel the poems so clearly in my body that I can dance them differently in the moment each time." In the dimness of the car his strange eyes grew luminous with interest.

"When can you show me?"

"Tomorrow?" I responded boldly.

"Three in the afternoon?"

"That's a little late—the kids come home from school around then. How about one-thirty?" He nodded slowly, never taking his eyes from my face. I was jubilant but tried to act casual; Katsu was coming to my house, at last, and I didn't even have to beg.

All morning I was in an agitated state, cleaning and sweeping after the family left, trying to make every surface of our cozy clutter spotless for my Zen friend. Then I did warm-ups, one eye on the clock. Katsu arrived on the dot of one-thirty, bowed as he entered the house, and followed me out to my makeshift dancing space in the old garage. He sat on a cushion against the cinder-block wall, placing his scarf and bag neatly alongside him. I handed him my paper of ten printed *haiku* poems.

"Here are the *haikus*," I explained nervously. "Read each one aloud—you choose the order—and I'll take a few moments to get the feel of it, and then translate it into a quick dance. OK?"

Until I stood facing him in the center of the space I had stage fright, but then my eyes closed and I took a deep breath, feeling energy spread into my whole body. I waited until the space around me felt like a cushion of support. He seemed to know exactly when I was ready. He read,

April's air stirs in willow leaves,
a butterfly floats, and balances.

On my skin I felt the lightness of the spring breeze, the fragrance of early green, the ephemerality of the butterfly's life. I breathed in

Katsu's presence and his eyes upon me, and I felt myself soften deep down where my heart lived. I felt the April breeze move me, and I swayed to it until I was suspended on tiptoe, balancing, and then broke into silky turns that brought me back to the center of the space, where I rocked, almost imperceptibly, back and forth before coming to a perfect stillness. I heard his sharp intake of breath, and a smile came to my lips that I made part of the dance. Oh! The stillness seemed to pulse between us.

Up and down the barley rows,
stitching, stitching the butterfly goes.

I could feel the flicking of the butterfly's stitching flight, first in my abdomen and then in my arms, feel the quickness of its back and forth motion. The movement started in my toes, and then my body was all but lifted off the ground as I flitted across the room, weaving together the currents of air my movements had created. I gathered Katsu in with my stitches, laughing, hardly able to bring the dance to an end. At last I found myself perfectly balanced on one leg, still twitching, the laughter still ringing. He chuckled too, and that was the end of the dance. Again the stillness pulsed between us.

The peony in full bloom.
Look! A drunken bee staggers out.

It took me a while to shift from quick motion to the fullness of the peony and the buzzing satisfaction of the fat bee. Katsu waited. Then I felt the mutual seduction of the many-petaled flower and the hungry bee—the luscious sensuality between them. I could sense Katsu's anticipation, and with a huge breath, my chest swelling, I became the ripe red blossom harboring in my heart the sucking bee. My hips circled and my arms embraced, and by the time the bee staggered out, drunk and fulfilled, I was blushing. I detected a soft groan from Katsu, and he leaned against the wall and just stared at me.

"Where does she come from, this person?" he muttered, shaking his head. He liked it! He liked *me*.

"Wherever you come from," I dared mutter back. He looked again at the page sternly, and read,

The toad.
At the edge of the pond,
will it belch a cloud?

We went through each of the ten *haikus*, and with my rendition of the last one he collapsed into laughter.

The old dog,
his head bent listening.
The singing of the earthworms
must be getting to him.

"No more!" he begged. *"Dio mio!"* I stood in front of him breathing hard, my hands on my hips.

"Sit," he ordered, patting the mat by his side. I sat. For a long moment he said nothing, just studied my face. I had shown him my best and he had received it. There was nothing I wished for more in the world. He cleared his throat.

"You're good," he informed me seriously. "Tell me—tell me everything—how you work, what it feels like when you dance, why you do it this way…tell me!" His lips curled at the corners and he chortled deep in his throat. I loved him so much I felt like the blooming peony awaiting the bee.

"Well, I'm a faculty wife with three kids," I teased, suddenly too shy to respond with the intensity I was feeling.

"And…"

"And I'm looking for a peephole into the larger universe," I said in earnest, just as suddenly dropping the game. He nodded, his nostrils flaring. "And I'm hoping to find a way through dance," I added with my heart in my mouth. I had not spoken words like these to anyone since Martine. My voice turned up on the word 'dance' as if I were asking it as a question, but he nodded again, and said,

"You are."

When the children tromped into the house at three, we were still talking about the creative process, about stillness and motion, about beauty and the power of the breath. He articulated ideas I had not tried to put into words for twenty years.

He seemed to know my secret self, a person few others had evoked from me. He knew about fear and trembling, and the depth of art that could come from it. He understood the need to make beauty from things that hurt and the loneliness of seeing the world as vast and subtle and sacred. I felt that whatever I said to him, he could understand.

"I'd like you to see my work, too," he said when he stood up to leave. "Come to my house." He said this in a deep-voiced whisper, as if he were straining against his own resistance.

"When?" I whispered back. "Tomorrow?"

"No. In two days. One-thirty again?" I nodded. Then, with a sigh he reached into his shoulder-purse and handed me his card. "Here's my address," he said.

I plucked two ripe lemons from the bush on my way out of the house, to bring Katsu as an offering. Following his directions, I found myself in a warehouse district no more than a mile from home, but a world away. It was all gray concrete there, surrounded by chain-link fences. I was sure I had gotten lost until I noticed one patch of a green planter-box garden in the midst of all that grayness, vivid with rustling bamboo and climbing roses. Katsu emerged from a steel door and waved.

"Is this where you live?" I asked stupidly, stepping into a magical jungle world of tropical trees and ferns growing out of massive pots, with chirping birds tucked in amongst them in wire cages. It was the secret garden hidden behind a wall of stone, vines climbing across exposed piping and huge cacti surrounding a groomed bed of sand. The air was fragrant with flowers: gardenias and orange blossoms, datura and paperwhites. Gazing up, I saw a banana tree spreading its branches across the railing of the loft. "Oh!" I exclaimed.

"Yes," he said matter-of-factly, welcoming the two lemons into his cupped palms. We both bent over his hands to sniff them. "Newly picked," he observed. "Some tea?" I strolled after him, trying to take it all in. A whitewashed studio covered in drop cloths held an unfinished stone sculpture of a male nude, and just before the open kitchen was a simple shrine with a small stone Buddha, a burning candle, and a gong. Passing it, I bowed, and he struck the gong, which resonated through the room.

"So, you're a sculptor," I commented, glancing back at the figure emerging from the stone. He placed a kettle on a burner, took two earthen cups from a shelf, and spooned some green tea powder into a bowl.

"I'm a calligrapher," he corrected. "My partner is the sculptor." I looked up more sharply than I intended to, and found him gazing steadily at me.

"She's very good," I said, realizing my mistake as soon as the words were out. Suddenly everything I hadn't understood about Katsu came into focus. "He," I corrected myself, flustered. For a moment he just watched me, and then he came toward me, his arms open. We embraced softly until he let me go, taking the kettle off the stove and whisking the tea, smiling his inscrutable smile.

When it was ready he led me upstairs into the loft. Skylights gave light to apricot-painted walls that glowed, and one side of the room was taken up with an ink-splattered desk holding stacks of hand-made paper and jars of brushes. Behind a bead curtain a double bed, neatly made, waited for its occupants. I studiously avoided craning my neck and gave my full attention to the tea. We sipped in simple silence, draining our cups before we spoke.

"Yes," he said, indicating with his head the unfinished sculpture downstairs. "He's a genius."

"So you're a calligrapher?" I began. "I know nothing about calligraphy."

"Actually, it's Sumi painting that I do—a form of calligraphy." I gazed around at the brushstroke paintings on the walls—slashes of black ink on white paper indicating birds in flight, bamboo stalks, seated Buddhas. I turned to stand before a small altar and a brush painting of a robed figure, the tilt of her body expressing a depth of caring that brought unbidden tears to my eyes.

"That was done by my teacher in Japan," Katsu explained. "It's Kwan Yin, the Goddess of Compassion."

"She made me cry," I said in amazement, wiping my eyes.

"Good sign," he said quietly.

"Is it my imagination, or is it done with one single line?"

"One line. He was a master of single-stroke painting," Katsu confirmed. "It can take a lifetime to produce one perfect painting. I watched him do that one—it took about thirty seconds. He gave it to me as a parting gift when I left Japan, and now he's gone." We both gazed silently at her; she reminded me of the Moissac figure who still greeted me every day from our living-room wall. But thirty seconds! Like the Moissac sculpture, this Kwan Yin breathed.

"So, how do you work?" I asked, studying the brushes and papers on his desk.

He pointed to one of the cushions beneath Kwan Yin and replied, "Mostly on that *zafu*." He lit a stick of incense so its spicy smoke curled fragrance in the air, and he bowed to the altar. I bowed as well.

"The real art is in the living," he said enigmatically. "Every day you practice concentration, courage, compassion, joy…" He sighed and gazed for a while at the portrait, "…every brush stroke requires a lifetime of effort, and then when you put ink to paper—whoosh!— the whole universe draws the picture through you in a second."

"That's just how I improvise!" I exclaimed, recognizing why he was so interested in my *haiku* pieces. I wanted to reach out and touch him.

He turned around, his hair swinging, and he said emphatically, "Yes!"

"That's why…" I began, not knowing how to continue, but he interrupted me impatiently, cutting off words that had no need to be spoken.

"Yes," he said again, offering me a seat at his desk and taking out his mortar and pestle to grind some inkstone.

For the rest of the afternoon he demonstrated his craft to me, mixing the black ink powder with water and selecting the perfect brushes, including one made of cats' whiskers. His hands were small and sensitive, his fingers like delicate antennae feeling for what was essential enough to be expressed with a single stroke. His whole body was engaged in the making of each line, like a swift dance over the paper.

Later, we meditated together and he described to me the process of gathering the inner quiet, stilling the mind of its chatter, and breathing as if from the center of the earth. We breathed together and although my knees felt the strain, it relaxed me to feel his still presence by my side.

"And then," just as I drifted off, he whispered, "when I sense readiness, I pick up the brush, lift my hand just so, and then watch the image in my mind appear on the paper." In seconds, almost faster than my eye could follow, a face was drawn in a single stroke—my face. Two dabs later, my features were suggested by the slightest of squiggles, but I recognized myself immediately.

"How'd you do that?" On a sheet of paper that had been blank a moment earlier, I had appeared as if by magic. "How did you do that?" I repeated.

"I wait to feel the connection deep in here," he said, patting his abdomen, "and then I trust the universe to move my brush where it's supposed to go."

"Like a balance point," I observed.

"Like a point of balance with the whole universe, yes," he agreed, "and then the beauty comes pouring right on through." I yearned toward him, the odd beauty of him radiant in my eyes at that moment. I wanted to wriggle into his pocket, crawl onto his lap, live within smelling distance of him.

I'm sure it showed on my face, for very gently he touched my cheek and said, "It's all in the relationship," He paused and with a mischievous twinkle added, "with the world." His words thrilled me to my core.

We met frequently after that—mostly at his jungle home, sometimes in cafés, and of course each week for his class. He still avoided meeting Ted and the children, coming around only when they were not at home, and it was not until the third time I visited him that I met Michael.

Michael was the sculptor of the torso taking shape in their studio, but he also was a physician in San Francisco. He arrived home one day as I was leaving, tired at the end of a long day. He was without question the most handsome man I had ever seen in my life. In an instant I was jealous, as if with such a rival I didn't stand a chance with Katsu, but a moment later I had to laugh at the irony of the situation I had gotten myself into. Tall and dark, with jet-black curls and clear blue eyes, he greeted me warmly.

"Here you are!" he exclaimed, grasping my hand firmly. "I wondered if this guy would ever let me meet you." We laughed.

"I know you by your nude body," I jested, glancing at the stone taking shape in the studio.

"That's Katsu's, of course," he jested back. We eagerly exchanged information while Katsu folded his arms across his chest and watched us talk. Unlike his partner, Michael wanted to know about my children, my husband, and what the university community was like. In turn, he told me about his practice in the Tenderloin, the politics of medicine in the city, and the creation of their wild indoor jungle. In less than a half hour we covered a lot of ground—except what it was like to be gay in a straight world. That would come later.

"How about I walk you home instead of drive," Katsu suggested to me. "Give you some time to get home," he murmured to Michael, running a finger down his sleeve.

"I like Michael," I declared as we waited at the corner for the light to change. Giggling, I added, "I felt a lot more comfortable with him than I do with you."

Giving me a sidewise look, he retorted, "Because you and he aren't in love." My knees buckled and I all but tripped as we crossed the street. This unusual relationship of ours was getting more unpredictable with each passing minute, but perhaps that's what I found so appealing.

"Katsu?" I asked after a long pause while we each took in what he had said. Our reflections in store windows showed an odd couple: a dark-skinned pixie accompanied by a taller woman with long hair.

Who could have guessed at our bond? "Remember that first night, when I asked if you wanted to ride to class together?"

"And I said 'no'?"

"Why did you say 'no'?" He stopped and turned to me. In the storefront window were reflected two intense people, one gesticulating expressively and the other with her shoulders up to her ears. I released the tension with a deep breath.

"Because I knew you on sight," he said, noting my sharp intake of breath, "and I knew we'd love each other, and an entanglement could be a disaster so I wanted to hold it off for as long as possible." As he spoke this simple truth, his expressive hands and body began to dance, as if he were letting go of the postures of male restraint and becoming androgynous. I followed his moves with fascination, as did many of the other passersby. From the look on his face, it was clear he was used to attracting attention.

"So?" I asked provocatively as we began to walk again.

"So, it's a disaster," he replied with an inscrutable smile.

For the rest of the walk to my house, which took no time at all, we talked about ourselves and the outrageousness of our friendship. Since we both had a taste for the outlandish, we matched each other in cultivating opportunities for whimsy and fun.

"What makes us possible," he commented as we reached my neighborhood, "is that we're impossible."

"And I'm late making dinner," I laughed as the door to my house sprang open and three teenagers sprinted out, all talking at once, greeting me with waves, and staring unabashedly at Katsu.

"Daddy called and said he'd be home by eight," they told me, "and we're invited to Tony and Sarah's house for dinner. OK?"

"And I'm not late making dinner," I amended with a grin as they ran off.

"Then you get to walk me home," he said, nonplussed, starting back the way we had come. I left a note for Ted pinned on the door, chortling helplessly as I followed Katsu around the corner and down the street we had just come up, continuing our conversation about everything we could think of.

"What was it like growing up partly Mexican and partly Japanese?" I asked him. "There can't have been many others like you."

"True. Early on, the Mexican side claimed me. Mama's family is large and noisy and I was just one of the kids, but once I hit puberty and didn't go *macho* along with the other boys, I slithered over to my Japanese side, and instead of doing cars, I started doing art."

"How was it for your father living around all those Mexicans?" I asked, stopping to watch a child maneuver her new bike and training wheels down the block. "Good job!" I told her when she came reeling back.

"He was a fish out of water, of course. Mama was actually more at ease with the Japanese side of the family than he was with our Mexican mob, but then again he was also 'queer,' so after a while he slipped away into another life and only came back for holidays and to see us kids."

"My goodness, and I thought Russian Jews were complicated," I commented wryly. "When did you know you were gay?" We walked for a while without speaking. He petted a cat; I plucked a sprig of lavender from someone's garden; we nodded to a man passing by.

"Always," he replied at last. "That is, I always knew I was different. 'Gay' was hardly a category in our world—certainly, the word didn't even exist when I was growing up. But more than even my sisters and brothers, I carried the Mayan part of my mother's people: small build, indigenous soul. The people I felt safest with then were—interestingly enough—my Japanese grandparents, who nurtured the artist in me. It's probably because of them that I'm a Buddhist today."

"Your indigenous soul," I mused. "I think that's the part of you that I identify most with."

"No doubt," he responded with a smile. "It can get lonely for us indigenous ones." He stopped in mid-stride and faced me. For a long moment we took each other in. Then he laughed and began walking again.

"What's funny?" I asked.

"I was just thinking about the shamans of indigenous tribes, who tend to be chosen early from the children who are recognized as being different from the others—neither girl nor boy, but some combination of the two." I immediately thought of Martine.

"I loved someone who was one of those people, I think, when I was studying in France."

"Tell me," he demanded, taking my hand. While we walked I told him about Martine, starting with the moment I walked into the classroom and did not see her. "An invisible one," he breathed, apparently impressed. "They are rare."

"Oh, she was rare in every way," I agreed.

"And was she definitely female?" he asked. I pictured her standing in the moonlight, gazing up.

"Well, she definitely looked like a girl and she identified as a girl, but she didn't necessarily act like a girl—or like only a girl. Does that make sense?"

"Perfect sense," he grinned. "What would you say about me?" he challenged. "Am I more like a man or a woman?" I stopped and looked him up and down appraisingly.

"Mmmn," I replied as he strutted up and down for me, causing other passersby to stare at us. "I'd say you were unique in the history of the world, and acted like neither—or both. You're just Katsu

Reiko. Your own thing," I added.

"And you'd be quite right, of course, about everyone who they call 'gay.' We're just our own thing," he agreed, suddenly serious. "It seems obvious to me that there are more than just two genders. The world is really much more interesting than we're led to believe," he whispered in my ear. "Pass it on."

"No wonder I can't figure you out," I declared with admiration, taking his arm. "You don't fit into any category but your own. I love that about you," I said, adding wistfully, "but I imagine that being Mexican *and* Japanese *and* gay *and* Buddhist would make you an outsider just about everywhere you went."

"Not at all," he responded. "I'm so outside that I'm inside—the trick is to be a free spirit and define the boundaries. Then you can erase them when nobody's looking."

Michael was in the garden watering when we arrived back at the green oasis in front of their warehouse home. We were still deep in conversation, and Katsu had just begun telling me about his time in Japan studying Sumi painting. He was making sweeping gestures in the air as we came up to their entrance.

"I thought you were walking her home," Michael said when he saw me.

"He did," I laughed.

"Then she had to walk me home," Katsu explained with a straight face. Michael shook his head in dismay. "Now I've got to walk *her* home," Katsu added, taking my arm and turning me around the way we had come.

"No you don't!" cried Michael. "I'm hungry. I'll drive her and then pick up something for dinner."

"I'll come," Katsu declared.

"Why don't you both come to my house for dinner?" I suggested.

"The kids are eating with neighbors and Ted will be home late. Then you can finally meet him." A tick of hesitation ran around the room and then they both agreed. Michael turned off the hose, Katsu and I went inside to use the bathroom, and we all piled into their car to go back to my house.

If this had been a planned dinner party and we'd all had a chance to get nervous about our various complex relationships, it might have been a tense evening, but as it was everyone had a wonderful time. For starters, as soon as they walked in Michael recognized the Moissac poster on the wall.

"Eleventh-century, right?" he noted. "France."

I applauded. By the time Ted arrived home on his bicycle, he found me chopping vegetables in the kitchen with two strange men and excitedly discussing French Romanesque art. Bless him, he had the presence of mind to take it in stride and shake hands cordially with Michael and Katsu as if it were the most normal thing in the world to find a gay couple in our kitchen at dinnertime. I told him the kids were across the street and we'd have a stir-fry on the table in ten minutes.

"Katsu's the meditation teacher I've been telling you about," I informed him, "and Michael's a doctor in the Tenderloin." That started a conversation about the clinic's patients, while Katsu quietly mashed avocados for guacamole and squeezed lemons, and Michael warmed the room with professional charm and asked Ted about the university and the current state of science. All three men behaved exaggeratedly 'straight,' I noted—Michael and Katsu studiously avoiding extravagant gestures and Ted sprawling less than he normally did—but we were all basically comfortable, I think.

The children straggled in with homework to do, putting in an appearance at the table whenever the discussion, to which they each listened from wherever they were in the house, interested them. Mostly they came in to stare at Katsu, who, unlike anybody in our family, was calm as a Buddha and said little, listened much, and grounded us all. *Who is this new friend of Mom's?* was written all over their faces.

When he and Michael were leaving, with thanks all around, Katsu drew from the sleeve of his *yukata* a tiny carved gourd and handed it to me at the door. I leaned over and kissed him, right there in front of both of our partners, and held the gourd to my heart.

The belly of the gourd, I learned weeks later when a little hidden panel accidentally fell out, contained a note from Katsu saying, "I open if you know how."

That was the beginning of a playful exchange of gifts that continued for almost eight years. I responded to the gourd by giving him a beach stone containing a fossil shell; he came back, late one night, to leave a red Sumi painting on our sidewalk. My answer to that was to plant a trail of hawk feathers in their outdoor garden while they were both away at work.

After the class in Crazy Wisdom teachings was over, Katsu, without our ever discussing it, became my de facto Buddhist teacher. He taught by demonstration in the course of daily life, indigenous style. I would watch him engage a waitress in conversation until her face came alive; listen attentively to the story of a man begging in the street; water his plants with 100 percent of his concentration. When I asked him about it, he responded obscurely.

"Buddhism is only a finger pointing at the moon," he said, unwilling to discuss it further.

My Zen suite continued to develop, the newest piece based on a poem from a collection of Zen poems and riddles called *The Iron Flute*. I had decided to structure this section as an improvisation as well, feeling my way deeply into the Zen mind in order to explicate it in movement. Katsu came one day to watch my latest attempt and to give his feedback.

"Honest feedback," I insisted, "even if you can't stand it." He responded by shaking his head and shooing me out to the dance floor, where I launched right into the piece.

"No!" he shouted. I blinked in surprise. "Breathe in the world before you begin," he chastised, "and your out-breath should extend to the edges of the universe. You have to consciously include the whole world in your stage. Start again."

I started again, breathing in the whole world and then sending myself out with it when I exhaled. "That's it," he murmured. He let me finish the piece without interruption, afterwards staring into the corner of the garage for a long time before he offered his comments.

"Not bad," he said finally. I waited. He sighed.

"But not good," I offered in a small voice. His face was a mask.

"Recite the poem for me," he directed.

I took in a hesitant breath, suddenly feeling very exposed because this poem was about our relationship and was much easier for me to dance than to speak out loud. I closed my eyes so as not to have to see him.

"*True friendship,*" I began in a shaky voice, "*transcends alienation and intimacy; between meeting and not meeting, there is no difference. On the old plum tree, fully blossomed, the southern branch owns the whole spring. As also does the northern branch.*"

"What is the feeling?" he asked softly.

Love, love! I wanted to shout. My ribcage felt too narrow to hold my heart, my stomach was a nest of butterflies, and my arms longed to reach out and touch him. I couldn't seem to stand still, and my arm lifted to my side as I rotated to the right, my knee bending and my hips turning just as he whispered, "Dance."

This time the fullness came through and my whole being danced. I was the plum tree laden with sweet blossoms that held the promise of fruits; I was intimate with air and sun and rain, an all-embracing essence swelling with the longing for completion. We met in the middle, Katsu and I, where there was no difference between meeting and not meeting. I danced my dance for him with my whole heart held open. When I finished we were both embraced by the stillness in the old garage.

"Yes," he breathed simply. "You can feel the difference?"

"Of course," I murmured.

"OK, now do it again, but this time be even lighter. Cut your effort level in half," he suggested. "I'll read the poem.

"True friendship transcends alienation and intimacy…" His voice was rich cream pouring out and I rode it, letting the sounds of him carry me back into his heart. I went willingly, safely, trusting our collaboration—our friendship that transcended intimacy and alienation. The dance took on another dimension, which contained the depth of my gratitude to be in the same world he was, and by the time the dance ended my face was awash in tears. So was his, I saw when I finally opened my eyes and stood facing him. Our affection met and merged in the pure air between us.

One morning a week or so later, as Ted and the children were scattering for the day, the phone rang and it was Katsu in high spirits.

"Come quickly!" he cried. "The banana tree is having babies!" I was dressed, brushed, and there in a record twenty minutes. The door to his jungle home was open, and birdsong filled the air. I found him staring up into the broad leaves of the banana tree at a hanging purple, white, and red flower—huge—festooned with a bell-shaped blossom. On top, like a protective canopy, a large tawny petal was filled with the smooth green fingers of baby bananas, all pressed together.

"Oooh!" We both jumped up and down like excited kids. We stood on chairs and examined the bananas closely, touching the skins, smelling the blossom, and peering at every detail through a hand lens.

"Lookit this stalk!"

"Have you ever seen such a purple?"

"Feel how heavy it is."

Katsu gently rubbed his cheek against the pendulous indigo bulb and gave it a sweet kiss before he jumped off the chair and retreated into the kitchen to put the kettle on.

Over tea, I told him a troubling dream I had awoken with that morning—a dream of imprisonment and isolation.

"I was in a cell behind bars," I said in a raspy whisper, "all alone with nobody to even tell me why I was there." He leaned his elbows on the table and held his cup against his chin, eyes focused on me. "I thought I would die from loneliness, but then you and Michael came." Tears spurted to my eyes and impatiently I wiped them away. "I was so relieved to see you..." Despite myself, I began crying.

"I reached through the bars to touch you, but I could hardly reach you. All I wanted was to be close to you..." I sighed uneasily through my tears, "but there were bars between us, and anyhow the feeling was that it wasn't allowed. I woke up in a state I can't even describe—anguish, estrangement from the world—I don't know..."

"I knew I had to call you this morning," he said matter-of-factly, taking my hands in his. For a long while we just looked at each other, and then he sighed and nodded.

"It's time to tell the story," he murmured to himself pensively. "Ah, well, it's an old tale—my Mexican grandmother used to tell it. Actually most indigenous cultures have some version of it. Zia was part Zapoteca, you know, and a healer, a *curandera*, and according to this legend, in every age there exists a small, scattered tribe who are *in* the world, but not exactly *of* the world. They don't necessarily know they're part of a tribe, but they tend to feel they don't quite belong where they are. They're always looking for their own people and only very rarely do they meet one, but when they do they recognize each other instantly." I held my breath and we locked eyes.

"It's very lonely for them," he went on, his expression unreadable, "but they have a job to do, and that keeps them busy enough." He smiled wryly.

"What's the job?" I whispered. He squeezed my hands and let go.

"Oh, each one has to discover that alone," he said a bit sadly. "Sometimes it takes a whole lifetime. But I have a hint for you: the prison is an illusion. You yourself can take down those bars one by one—very carefully, mind you. Paint them out, as if they were lines on paper and you could erase them, because you can." He handed me his handkerchief and I wiped my eyes and handed it back to him. "Keep it," he said, "but your dream was right about Michael and me being there. Me, for sure."

"You really are, aren't you?" I sniffed, blowing my nose and leaning back in my chair.

"From the first moment of recognition," he replied softly. I slipped down off my seat to kneel by his side, my arms curling around his waist and my head in his lap. He stroked my hair and we both gave way to teary laughter.

He phoned later to see how I was, and we spent over an hour continuing our morning conversation. I was scrubbing the bathtub as we talked.

"I often wonder if it shows, this kind of set-apartness," I observed. "What do you do when people feel uncomfortable around you?"

"What do *I* do?" He laughed for a long time. "Well, because

I'm gay and I'm colored and I'm short, it comes with the territory. Nobody knows what to make of me. But you—you pass, honey. You have the advantage that you can hide in the crowd."

"Sometimes I hide so well I wonder if I'm invisible!" I sighed.

"Mmm," he hummed. "Yup, that's hard. It helps, though, if you can find the middle way and be neither invisible nor threatening."

"I don't think it's about being threatening," I muttered. I could hear his smile over the phone.

"Oh, I don't know about that," he taunted, adding more gently, "Please don't try and hide your light—especially from yourself." I listened in silence with the phone cradled in my neck, and shook a torrent of Bon Ami cleanser onto a stubborn stain in the tub.

"But the most important thing you need to do," he went on, "is to learn compassion. Compassion for everyone, no matter who they are, how they treat you, or whether you like them or not."

"What does that even mean?" I asked in a strained voice.

"Wait—I'm not finished," he interrupted. "Compassion for the others you'll find is easy. It's compassion for yourself that's the hard part."

"But what does it mean?" I asked again. But he refused to answer, and after telling me to come by soon and check on the bananas, he hung up.

During the next few years we lived as close friends do, attending each other's celebrations, gossiping on the phone, and sharing meals from time to time—often just the two of us, sometimes with Ted and Michael and the children, sometimes with friends. I continued on as a student at the Meditation Center, taking some of his classes and often meditating with him, both at the center and at his place. He was a cherished mentor and friend, and as artists we called forth ever more gutsy creativity from each other.

As the seasons passed, we watched my children grow into young adults and saw generations of songbirds hatch from the tiniest of eggs, while the banana plant sent up new shoots each year and, again and again, produced smooth, young bananas.

When the Dalai Lama made his first visit to the United States, we went together to hear him; when I performed my Zen suite, Katsu and Michael and Ted gave me a standing ovation, and when news of a mysterious disease, appearing to be limited to young men, began to surface, we watched its progress silently, but by each other's sides.

Michael was looking haggard and rushed, working day and night in the city and coming home only to sleep. He and Katsu became more involved in the epidemic as men—almost exclusively gay men—began dying. So while I phoned often to check in on them, and stopped by with little gifts of food and poems and stray whiskers from our cats, I saw Katsu less often and, of course, worried more.

"It's been too long," he said on the phone one day. "Let's get together for tea."

"My place or yours?"

"Why don't we go out to that new place on Telegraph Avenue? I understand they serve unlimited desserts." Katsu's familiar irreverent tone rang through the phone after weeks of sounding somber, and my heart warmed to hear it.

We met outside the café with a long hug, letting the crowds jostle us, and then we ducked inside arm in arm, squeezing through the narrow door at the same time. Katsu was done up in some wild garb that I had to study in order to understand how it came together. A rainbow-striped shawl was tucked into his *yukata*, an embroidered Guatemalan sash hung down to his knees, and on his head was a bright green beret with a tufted bobble.

"I wanted to make you laugh," he explained, and we both leaned back and laughed hard. When the waitress arrived with the dessert tray, we discussed the comparative merits of chocolate cake versus coconut custard, finally deciding on one of each—and then he ordered one of everything else on the tray. Oh, this man! We tasted each dessert in turn, spooning whipped cream with abandon and choking on crumbs until the table was a mess, getting overstimulated on more than just the sugar. Then Katsu wiped his mouth with a napkin, sat back, and fixed me with watchful eyes. I waited. My stomach knotted when I thought I understood.

"It's Michael," I said in an undertone, my fingers cold as ice. He regarded me closely, his eyes as deep as the ocean.

"No," he said finally. "It's me."

I was staring at him, frozen and speechless, when a blind woman with a tapping cane stopped at our table; a sign around her neck explained that the shoelaces she was selling were her only means of support. Blinded by my own grief, I hardly took her in. Katsu's eyes narrowed as he waited to see what I would do.

"Please, not now," I begged her, touching her arm carefully but never taking my eyes away from Katsu.

"Yes, now," he insisted, slipping a dollar bill across the table to me. I held it up to her with shaking hands and then fished in my purse for another dollar.

"May I have two pairs?" I choked out, placing the bills in her palm. She held the shoelaces in the direction of my voice and I took them from her hand, my heart pounding in my chest. Katsu sat still as a stone until she tap-tapped off to the next table.

"The heart has to awaken at each moment," he said gently. I nodded, too depressed to speak. He waited and then added, "If the world is yours, then its problems are yours, too."

"But I want you in it!" My lips spat cake crumbs all over the place.

He leaned across the table and with his napkin tenderly brushed the crumbs from my mouth. Looking at him, I felt a love so helpless it pierced me like burning arrows. I banged the table twice with my fist.

He took a slow sip of tea and nodded toward my cup. I picked up my cold tea and took a swallow. We gazed at each other above our cups, and his face slowly wrinkled into a smile. The green beret, still tilted on his head, was so ludicrous that I giggled.

"That's it," he breathed. "We'll have plenty of time to grieve. Shall I walk you to your car?"

He walked me the three blocks to my car, and we stood there another twenty minutes, talking.

"Shall I walk you to your car?" I suggested in as light a voice as I could muster. "Where are you parked?"

"Oh, not far from here," he responded, taking my arm and twinkling down to his toes. At his car we stood talking for another half hour, and then it was clear he had to walk me back to my car.

We must have gone back and forth half a dozen times, for by the time we parted it was getting on to dusk. Like clowns rehearsing an act, neither of us could stop grinning at the whimsy we were capable of dreaming up together, but the next day when he phoned we discovered that we both had blisters on our feet from all that walking.

A year later Katsu was still doing well, and I had almost forgotten to worry. He was working happily with an Iranian poet, translating a large body of poems from the Persian, of a thirteenth-century Sufi mystic, Rumi. He would phone every few days to read me especially beautiful tidbits from their collaboration.

"Listen to this!" he said excitedly one evening as soon as I answered the phone, reading me the poem they had just worked on.

Today, like every other day, we wake up empty and afraid. Don't just go through the door of the study and begin reading;

take down the dulcimer! Let the beauty we love be what we do. There are hundreds of ways to kneel and kiss the ground.

We both knew well that feeling of intense wonderment; once, during a walk on the beach on an Easter Sunday, we actually found ourselves kneeling amongst the dune grasses and kissing the ground as the windswept surf thundered in. We reminisced now, laughing as we recalled how Ted and the kids had taken off down the beach in embarrassment, and Michael had simply waited nearby for our transport to be over.

A few nights later Katsu was back on the phone, his voice a bit raw—he had caught a cold in the winter rains, and a persistent cough would not go away—with a new poem from Rumi.

"You'll love this," he said, turning away from the phone to clear his throat.

Between right and wrong, good and bad, there is a field.
I'll meet you there.
Our souls, sinking down in that fragrant grass,
will be too filled with ecstasy to even speak...

He stopped to cough, and it rang through the telephone wires raucously enough to hurt my eardrum. Another cough followed, and then another. It sounded like he was choking. "I'll have to call you later," he gasped, fumbling the phone onto the receiver several times before managing to hang up. I waited for an hour and was about to go over to his place, knowing this was a late night at the clinic for Michael, but just as I put on my coat to leave the phone rang and he was there.

"Sorry about that," he said hoarsely, breathing hard. He cleared his throat twice, and then read the poem again.

I hardly heard it this time, and when he had finished I said, "Katsu, I'm scared." For a while all I heard on the other end was somewhat labored breathing.

"Yes," was all he finally said. "Listen, can you come over in the morning? There's something I have for you."

The storm was severe enough to create running puddles on the slick cement walkways outside the warehouses, and I had to wade through ankle-deep water to get to their door. I let myself in to a dark green world and the birds were huddled in one corner of their cages, silenced by the thundering rain on the flat roof above.

In the dark kitchen, the kettle whistled on the stove and I turned it off just as Katsu emerged from the loft. He was wrapped in enough layers of wool to make him look roly-poly, and he shuffled in on feet encased in down booties.

"It's the Buddha with a cold," I joked as he blew his red-tipped nose and wiped his watering eyes.

"Not my finest hour," he commented with a snuffle.

"Not by a long shot," I agreed, "but you must feel properly humbled. Anyhow, I won't get close enough to catch it, I promise."

We kept the banter up—rather courageously, I thought—until the tea was steeping in the teapot and we had climbed the stairs to his loft-bedroom where the altar was alight with candles and copal incense burned on hot coals. The beauty and intimacy of the scene made my chest ache. I felt like I was entering sacred space; this was a room utterly familiar to me but transformed, by simple ritual, into a sanctuary.

We sat on two cushions placed in front of the altar, sipping our tea and saying little. Rain drummed on the skylights, creating a steady din that sounded like waves crashing against the shores of the world. There was nothing to do but listen.

"I've got something for you," he said once the tea had been drained from our cups. "It may be the most important gift you will ever receive from me." His face was serious; I noticed that his coughing had stopped. From his sleeve he pulled out a sheet of rice paper on which a poem was written in both Japanese calligraphy and in English. "It's the *sutra* to Kwan Yin, the Goddess of Compassion," he told me. "I'd like to teach it to you, but first let's just sit together."

While the rain kept up its steady thrumming, we meditated facing each other, eyes closed, until my legs began to cramp. Then he sighed—still not coughing—uncrossed his legs and twisted around his spine. I stretched out my legs until they touched his cushion and I bent over them, feeling my vertebrae crackle one by one.

"I'd like you to memorize the chant," he said, "and have it with you when you no longer have me."

I began to protest, but he put a gentle hand on my knee and shook his head. He gave me the rice-paper copy of the *sutra* and, tucking his knees beneath him, waited for me to do the same. The copal smoke swirled into the air, and the candles sputtered, flared, and burned brightly again.

> *Kanzeon namu butsu yo butsu u in yo butsu u en*
> *Bu po so en jo raku ga jo*
> *Cho nen Kanzeon Bo nen Kanzeon*
> *Nen nen fu shin ki*
> *Nen nen fu ri shin.*

We repeated the chant several times until I had it memorized. Then he translated it loosely, stressing the part that said, "Compassion in the morning, compassion in the evening..."

"Make it part of you," he said fiercely. "Put it in your heart, then deep in your abdomen, then all the way down to your toes. Learn it and repeat it over and over, all the time!" His words seemed to come from another place and pulsed in the air between us. For a few moments he was somebody I had never seen before; in Katsu's place was an ancient figure, wise and terrible.

"Remember," this deep, penetrating voice intoned, "that in a painting the blackest black always appears alongside the whitest white."

We sat in silence and inhabited holy time, the field of Rumi, where only ecstasy prevails. The rains thundered above us and the last of the tea had been drunk.

> *True friendship transcends alienation and intimacy.*
> *Between meeting and not meeting, there is no difference.*
> *On the old plum tree, fully blossomed,*
> *the southern branch owns the whole spring,*
> *as does the northern branch.*

He recited this in a warm voice, Katsu again. I felt his words ring in the air and I breathed them in, memorizing this moment, aware of every breath his body breathed by my side, every fragrance in the room, every magical point of candle flame spreading light.

"Between meeting and not meeting," I repeated finally with a tight throat, wishing I could truly believe it, "there is no difference." Again we sat in silence in a state of grace. He was still here!

"There is a field..." he recited after a while in almost a whisper. The rain slackened; below us the birds suddenly sang out and I started in surprise, feeling the sensation of their chirps like little electrical darts on my skin. Katsu chuckled and I laughed out loud.

"I'll meet you there," we chanted together in perfect unison. "Our souls, sinking onto that fragrant grass, will be too filled with ecstasy to even speak."

We opened our eyes to each other yet one more time, smiling, and Katsu whispered,

"I'll meet you there."

THE CREATIVE IMPULSE

*This throbbing vibration moves in the
atmosphere like a resonance. From this resonance
and the interplay of its vibrations, a symphony
of energies comes forth.*

From a creation hymn of the Kashmiri Hindu Shaivites

Katsu was every inch the artist, not only on paper but in the mundane round of everyday life. He cavorted around as if living was one huge game—from collecting cats' whiskers for his brushes to turning his final illness into a memorable event for his friends. He took everything in stride as inspiration and then transmitted it back out again as paintings, teachings, whimsy, and gifts, all transformed through his endlessly fertile imagination. Nothing was beneath his interest and everything was potentially raw material for his imagination to play with. We never knew what he might come up with next, and he never ceased to surprise us.

I would ask him about how he got his ideas, and his answer was always some variation of the same thing.

"By listening," he would say. "By tuning in and feeling the creative beat of the world. The Creation, you know, didn't just happen once and then—boom—it was over. Creation is happening every single moment of every single day, and if we want to be creative people, we have to listen for it and then boogie to its rhythms!" He jumped and writhed like a wild man, strumming on an imaginary guitar.

According to him, creativity was all about movement and change and our willingness to let go, moving and changing along with the universe.

Once the first impulse set the Unified Field into motion, patterns of energy would appear and disappear in the multilayered ocean of existence. The intelligence of the Source sent its imagination forth, its thoughts and longings shaping moving energy into a world.

The energies danced together in harmony, mixing and mingling and experimenting with new possibilities, new forms of beauty. Creative ways of cooperating were infinite in the 'multiverse,' and every improvisation on a theme was tested and embellished by a cosmic imagination that knew no bounds.

"What else could have dreamed up flamingoes?" he challenged me one day. "Big pink birds were God's joke, of course, but there they are. Did you know that the feathers in their armpits are hot fuchsia?" he whispered with a leer.

What Katsu seemed to be able to feel in his bones were the resonant frequencies in the air. He would close his eyes, listen for some subtle throbbing, and then, catching the rhythm, let it stream through him. Only when the resonance was clear to him would he express it on paper with a single stroke of his brush.

"There you are!" he would greet his drawing, regarding with

a critical eye what had just come through him. And sometimes, especially when the image that emerged took him by surprise, he would bow to his drawing with tender respect.

From him I learned that all creativity is reciprocal. Creating, we are in relationship with the life force that flows through the cosmos, which, Katsu claimed, is Divinity itself.

"Receiving and giving, learning and teaching—they go together," he would say. "Everything's a give and take, with creation happening on every level simultaneously. You never know what will spark a connection or what will light up a connection that already exists. Everything potentially can contribute to the miracle."

One time, to make his point, he bonelessly slid off his chair and landed in a comical heap on the floor. When I laughed at his antics, he rose to his feet, brushed himself off, and insisted that being as relaxed as a rag doll was essential for the making of fine art.

"Not asleep or lazy, mind you," he admonished, "but easy and focused. And trusting implicitly in your ability to bring forth the beauty."

He cupped his hands into a bowl. "Like this," he demonstrated. "Empty. Not knowing. Ready to receive whatever will come."

"I love that," I declared, knowing well the feeling of waiting to receive the first impulse that spun my body satisfyingly into a dance. "But it's scary, too. You never know but that maybe this time nothing will come forth." He had laughed.

"But it never works when you try to make it happen, right?" I had nodded. "Faith has to be part of the process, otherwise the alchemy isn't there. That's the adventure of it!"

Years later as he lay dying, he said it again in a new way. Reduced to skin and bones, a shrunken being under white sheets and exhausted from a bout of fresh coughing, he reminded me to keep the faith no matter what.

"Trust everything that happens," he commanded with an attempt at a rakish grin. "This may not look like much of an adventure, but it is. I'm still in the game, riding the waves and loving the excitement of it all. What a *hell* of an adventure!"

"Here's what I know for sure," he had panted, shrugging a bony shoulder and gasping out the words one by one, "Creation is...all...about...Love...That's the news. Pass...it...on."

NINE

Maud

It wasn't easy keeping up with her. Although she would soon be eighty, Maud Thomas set a vigorous pace up the steep trail that left me, twenty years her junior, panting in her wake. My thighs ached as I negotiated rocks and knotted roots, following her up to the ridge where, she had told me, a site not unlike the mysterious megalithic stones in Europe stood in partial ruin overlooking Saranac Lake and the Mount Marcy Range of the Adirondacks. "Eastern Lookout," she called the place.

She stopped to wait for me by a glistening white birch, its amber leaves brilliant on crown and sloping ground. Her arm was crooked companionably around the trunk, her cap of white hair tousled by the breeze, and her blue-gray eyes alight with pleasure. Around us, maple trees blazed like fire and the beeches were such a vivid yellow I had to squint. Small creatures poked and flitted through the bright leaf litter, foraging in the thickets before the coming of winter. I stood still, listening to their snaps and rustles, breathing in the musky spice of sun-warmed balsam in a forest that, at that moment, included me. And Maud.

A single red leaf let go of its branch and swirled lazily down in wide arcs until it sank silently onto the forest floor. We both watched its progress, and when it settled I glanced over at her. When your season is over you let go, her expression said.

Maud waited for me to rest a moment longer, then again she led the way. She climbed the trail with a relaxed, steady stride, her arms swinging by her sides and her boots kicking up layers of golden leaves, releasing their earthy mulch tang.

Happily, I breathed it all in; I was finally back in the Adirondacks.

I had met Maud almost a year earlier in California, when a friend had brought her to my house. Betsy had told me about an old friend of her mother's in upstate New York who, she claimed, she was sure I would like. What she actually said was, "You two are birds of a feather." She informed me that Maud still took daily hikes in the woods, and that her family had threatened to hide her skis from her as soon as she turned eighty.

She told the story again in my kitchen the day they came, and with a look of good-natured independence Maud retorted, "I shall be a tomboy for as long as I choose to be, thank you."

"A tomboy, indeed," Betsy had laughed. "I've always thought of you as the wise woman in the woods who gathers wild herbs and talks to the animals. I can't wait to hear what the two of you have to say to each other."

And she was right. As soon as Maud entered my house—a tall, angular woman with a generous smile that did not mask a cautious watchfulness in her blue-gray eyes—we both felt an intrinsic kinship. I wanted to reach for her, almost the way a lover reaches for a beloved, but a second later I got very busy with the teakettle, flustered by my passionate response to her.

Apparently familiar with people's confused reactions to her

presence, she smiled disarmingly to put me at ease. Her tanned face wrinkled into a roadmap of lines, and dressed in corduroy pants, a man's shirt, and embroidered vest, her eyes twinkled beneath her white bangs. I found her beautiful. I had been looking—forever, it seemed—for the friendship and counsel of a wise older woman. Perhaps she would be the one.

We wasted little time in small talk that day. In the course of our two and a half hours together, we confirmed that our lives, although a full generation apart, had several uncanny parallels. For both of us, the Adirondack Mountain region in upper New York State was home—for her it was actually home, as she and her husband had retired to her family's property on Saranac Lake; for me it was a memory of home.

Three summers I spent there as a teenager had imprinted me with the shapes and shades of those forested mountains, the sun-rippled lakes, the smell of mud after a rain. I could still call up at will the fragrance of balsam needles in the hot sun.

Maud and I had both married scientists, we each had three grown children—two even with the same name—and each of us was currently researching the subject of 'synchronicity.'

"What a synchronicity!" we declared in unison—but not surprise. Our eyes met and we knew a bond had been forged. It wasn't until the very end of our visit that she told me, at Betsy's urging, about the healing center she had founded.

"It's the Saranac Lake Forest Sanctuary," she said. "SYLVAS. It's on land that has been in my family since the 1920s, where I spent all my summers growing up. After my husband retired we came up to live there full time—we've been in the old lodge on the lake for almost nineteen years now—and recently we've opened the land to the public as a forest sanctuary. We recruit the local community to volunteer for work parties, cutting trails and such, to make the land accessible to the people who come. We've just built a small lakeside chapel, in fact, so bit by bit the place is taking shape."

She pulled a folded brochure from her pants pocket and handed it to me. I read:

The infinitely rich tapestry of the natural world is like a mirror; it becomes a metaphor for human life in all its diversity—whatever comes to our attention will find its counterpart in our own soul.

"Oh, yes," I breathed in appreciation. "You're saying the natural world is a macrocosm of the inner world."

When I gazed up from the brochure my eyes must have been shining, because hers reflected the shine, and when I returned the paper to her she held my hand in both of hers, saying with satisfaction, "Exactly."

"Tell me more about this place," I asked, hearing in my mind's ear the haunting cry of loons across a wide lake I once knew.

"Well, we have three hundred acres of forest on the western shore of Saranac Lake, and it includes a piece of the ridge. We've not logged, so it's very wild out there. We get bear and moose, and this particular area has a number of prehistoric sites. The locals call them Indian stone cellars, but I rather think they're even older. If you know anything about megalithic sites, I believe they date from the same era."

"I do know about megaliths!" I leapt out of my seat with excitement. "I've seen them. Do you know the ones in Brittany?"

"I do indeed," she affirmed, as Betsy nodded with delight. "Tell me what you know about them." So I told her about my adventures with Dani in Brittany when I was nineteen, and about returning twice more recently to explore the subtle energies there. Immediately we were in a discussion about healing, and the significance of the stones, and specific sites we each had visited.

"And you're saying they're in this country, too, in the Adirondacks?" I asked incredulously.

"Actually, they are all over New England," she replied. "Many were destroyed by the early settlers who used the stones for building, but out in the woods many are still intact. If you ask me, though," she confided, "I think some of the natural sites are even more powerful. I'll have to show you when you come." Not *if* I came, but *when* I came. It was that simple.

"When I come?" I repeated, pouring her a second cup of tea.

"Why, yes," she said frankly, "when you come. You will, won't you?" Betsy regarded Maud calculatingly.

"You've been looking for someone to work on outreach at SYLVAS, haven't you?" she asked. Maud sat back and laughed.

"Well, yes, but SYLVAS is three-thousand miles from here, dear."

"I know, but the season is short up there—three months, maybe." Betsy offered, a slow smile starting. She was grinning and so was I. The prospect of even one summer in the Adirondacks made my heart leap.

"We come east every summer to see family," I admitted. "So…"

Maud regarded me silently from across the table. Then she took a deep breath, leaned forward, and said, "Come."

By the time they left, we had discussed travel arrangements and set a provisional date in October for me to visit.

"When the fall colors are at their peak," she said.

I would spend a weekend at Saranac Lake with her, and she would introduce me to SYLVAS and SYLVAS to me, and together we would determine if there was, in fact, a match.

With one last hoist I joined Maud atop a rounded granite boulder that overlooked the long lake and mountain ranges beyond. Past the shining water stretched green-forested slopes, ridge after ridge, which melted into the blue haze of the far distance. Behind us, partly obscured by trees, was a pile of rocks surrounding what looked like the ruins of a prehistoric *dolmen*, much like the *dolmens* I had seen in France

"Oh!" I exclaimed with what little breath I had left. It was like standing at the edge of the world as it used to be. Maud chuckled softly and took my arm.

"And we look to the East," she announced, letting her eyes roam from one end of the horizon to the other. I followed her gaze over the expanse of shimmering lake and blue sky mirrored in its waters, and for a moment I was overcome with vertigo. I squatted and lowered my head; from the bare granite beneath me I seemed to be hearing voices whispering. I looked around quickly for whoever was there, but Maud was the only person on the ridge with me. She watched my reaction.

"Mysterious, isn't it?" she finally remarked, rubbing her hands on her thighs. I nodded slowly, still sensing the presence of others. "Tell me what you feel," she said. I closed my eyes and breathed in deeply, focusing on the feelings in my body: the stretched muscles, the pulsing of blood, the tingling of my fingertips, a sensation of subtle spreading. And beneath it, the whispering voices.

"It's as if we were not alone here. I feel my outlines sort of blurring and going soft," I reported, sensing effervescent energy rising into my belly, then through my chest, and up into my neck and head. "It's like being in warm mist," I told her, "inside and out." I felt as if the mist could expand right through my skin and spread out into the air. I told her that.

"Describe the air," she requested in a low voice. Forms and colors seemed to swirl and change behind my closed eyelids.

"There doesn't seem to be a beginning or an end. Everything keeps turning into something else." I said. When I opened my eyes, the real colors of trees and granite and sky seemed almost too vivid, and I blinked hard.

"Precisely," she announced with satisfaction, squatting down alongside me. "It's always been my sense that the 'old ones' are indeed still here, watching and waiting. What you felt is similar to how this site always makes me feel, too, as if everything connects up with everything else, even through their time and ours. This used to be one of my private places when I was a girl."

The granite felt rough beneath my legs.

"I used to come up here to daydream," she smiled. "With 'my other tribe' as I used to call them. When I'm troubled, I get reassurance here. When I'm confused, I receive hints and signs." She sighed and confessed that she rarely mentioned this to people. "I'm glad you felt them too. It's not many folks who do." We exchanged a grin and for a long while listened to the windy silence.

"I believe it was used as a doorway," she whispered after a while. I gazed out at green mountains ranging beneath a blue-and-cloud sky and the lake glinting below. In my mind's eye the clouds parted to reveal worlds beyond worlds—worlds too vast to comprehend, worlds too miniscule to see.

"Doorway to what?" I asked softly, running a thumb across a patch of velvety moss.

Her eyes twinkling, she replied, "Why, to the other dimensions, of course."

It was indeed an enchanted place. The ridge, rising a few feet above the tree line, gave a 180 degree view of the sun-dazzled lake and mountains, and the air smelled of sun-warmed granite, balsam, and wild blueberries, which grew out of fissures in the rock. The sky, rich with fleets of white clouds, came right down to the stony ridge on which we sat, penetrating the solid earth of the mountain with its airy winds. Right here where heaven met earth and where granite met forest floor, ancient people had enhanced a natural outcrop of rock and built their gateway to other realms. But who could they have been—these people who had muscled massive hunks of rock to form a hidden chamber high up on this mountain?

Now, a tumble of moss-covered stones surrounded what must have once been the entry, and an enormous slab of granite, perhaps the original capstone, now barred the way into the original chamber. Trees and ferns grew out of the rock pile, and the ruin was littered with leaves and fallen branches. I felt a surge of something whoosh through me, and for a moment I lost my balance. I blew out a shaky breath and Maud steadied me.

"You OK?" she asked. I nodded, still needing to take deep breaths to calm my pounding heart. It reminded me of what Danilo and I had experienced at the *dolmen* on the Ile Hoëdic those many years ago.

Even though the stones were in tumbled ruin, I recognized the familiar shape of a narrow entryway opening into a rounded chamber, the whole structure supported by gargantuan slabs of rock. I wondered again about megaliths and why they had been created. What had these people known that we have lost? The energies continued to throb in my chest until the tears welled and I wiped them away, trying to catch my breath. Maud watched me closely until my breathing returned to normal.

"Welcome," she said softly. She took my hand and we leaned into each other, my head resting for a moment on her shoulder. We stood there gazing across the lake, our hair whipping in the wind. I started laughing.

"Look at us—two aging ladies standing on a pile of rocks in league with prehistoric ghosts," I joked.

"You'd better believe it," she responded immediately. "And since we're disguised as little old ladies, we get to do the hard work of the world incognito." Sternly, she added, "And there's a lot to do and little time to waste!"

"I'm hearing the whispering again," I murmured, standing upon a large stone that shifted with my weight.

"Yes, they're here," she observed. Beneath me, a draft of dank air emanated from the long-covered chamber like a cold breath, and I knelt to peer through a crack in the rocks. Nothing to see—only the smell of untouched darkness and that subtle whispering. With a stick I probed until I touched water and the plunk echoed upward. Something jumped—a frog perhaps—and I fell back startled. Echoes faded around me.

"Was this once a well, do you think?" I asked, sitting on my heels.

"I think not—not here. We've had a lot of rain lately; it's probably standing water that has collected on the floor of the chamber."

For a long while we sat there listening to dropping twigs and buzzing flies, to leaves in the breeze and murmurs rising from the rocks. My mind quieted and Maud's outlines seemed to dissolve as she merged into the woods like one of its creatures. Still as stones, we breathed with the forest while a bird lit upon a branch and an orange salamander prowled the leaf litter for flies.

Gazing out at the open horizon, I settled into sunlight and rustling birds; beside me, Maud's rhythmic breaths washed in and out. My eyes began to close, my eyelids much too heavy to hold open. Just like in Brittany, I thought, as I sank into the warm rock. The last thing I noticed before drifting into sleep was a dreamy half smile on Maud's face.

I am standing at the edge of a lake, wavelets lapping at my feet. The water reflects sky to the ends of the earth. I sing into a glittering crystal suspended before me in the air, and my song churns the lapping waves into whirlpools. They swirl right, then left, then right, then left. As they change direction, a chaos of bubbles streams into foam. The crystal magnifies my song, and the chaos of bubbles opens to the sky above and the deep waters below like a mighty cataract.

I keep singing. My voice enters each bubble, releasing its energy and spinning it back to me. Sparked from above and below simultaneously, I feel the resonance in my chest. It is the vibration of the whole universe. I have access to it if I wish. All I have to do is sing.

I awoke with a start, sheepish to find I'd been so deeply asleep, and struggled to sit as the sounds of the song became identified again as wind and droning insects. Maud listened intently as I told her my dream, nodding with recognition.

"I expect they sang up here," I observed.

"Up here and also down at the lake. Sometimes both places simultaneously," she confirmed. "Certain times of the year, like solstices and equinoxes, I believe they used these sites to access cosmic energy. I like your image of whirlpools changing direction. I suspect that might correspond to solstice and equinox shifts. My guess is that it's just at those times that the potencies of both earth and heaven are accessible to us."

"Yes," I said slowly, remembering, "when the water was changing directions I could actually feel as if force was coming from above and below at the same time."

"There is an ancient farming practice in Germany," Maud explained, gazing thoughtfully into the middle distance, "in which barrels of water are stirred each spring while the farmer sings. When he stirs to the right, he sings up the scale, and to the left, he sings down the scale."

"Really?"

"Yes, and each time the direction reverses, there's this chaos of bubbles—just like in your dream. They apparently keep stirring for hours on end."

"Then I suppose they water the fields with it?" I asked.

"Exactly. According to what I've read, the water fertilizes the fields with both celestial and earthly energies."

"How extraordinary. I gather it works?"

"I imagine it does," she replied with a smile, "or we may never have heard about it."

"I wonder if it's still being practiced," I mused.

"For sure not in modern agriculture," she replied, "but others are bringing the old ways back."

"Like you," I teased gently, stroking her back with my knuckles.

"Absolutely," she responded seriously, "and like you, too."

A spider dropped down its silken thread to Maud's left ear and scurried onto her white hair. I leaned forward to brush it away, but then stopped.

"There's a spider in your hair," I whispered.

"It can stay," she said, sitting very still. The spider busily began weaving, suspending its web between Maud's hair and a low branch alongside, and the web grew, filament by filament, around its center. Drawing silk from its own body, the spider stitched industriously until the gossamer web was large enough to catch a flying insect.

Then, surprising me, it rapidly spun a thread to my knee and anchored the web onto me as well. Connected by the same tiny being, Maud and I sat as if in thrall.

"While you were asleep," she told me, careful not to disturb the line between us, "I received a message too."

"Mmm?" The spider scrambled across its web just as an unsuspecting gnat flew too close, and grabbed it out of the air. First meal on the web. "Tell me the message."

"Yes. I was told that there is a glittering stone nearby. Those were the exact words, 'glittering stone.'"

A glittering stone. I could see in my mind's eye the light-filled crystal of my dream. "Like a crystal?"

"What I saw looked less clear than crystal, and the shape was jagged, not regular, but it was a shiny stone and apparently yours to find. Not me, you. Anyhow," she speculated, "if it were for me, I would have stumbled upon it long ago."

"You sure you didn't plant it here?" I scolded.

She laughed. "It would have been cunning of me to set this all up, but I assure you I'm not that imaginative. Anyhow, why don't you have a go at it?"

Impulsively, I put my hands together to bow to her and broke the delicate web between us, leaving the spider hanging on tatters of silk. Maud shrugged and shook her hair free of spiderweb.

"Sorry, Madame Spider," she said, wrapping her arms around her knees. "I'll wait here while you go searching."

I rose rather stiffly, got my bearings, and staggered the first few steps before I found my balance. Standing atop the rock pile, I cast my eyes around the site for something that glittered. Shocked to see it immediately, I quickly turned my back to it—a sparkling bit of quartz on a patch of moss right above the capstone. Certainly Maud had placed it there. Deliberately ignoring it, I kept the capstone behind me, clambering around the rest of the site. Kneeling on ledges and peering between boulders, I searched through the expansive root system of a fallen tree and tromped through all the brush around it. I scoured every inch of the place and found no other piece of stone that glittered. Maud watched my progress patiently. When there was no other place to search, I went back to the moss above the capstone and stared at the glittering piece of quartz.

It was stuck fast and did not come easily out of its bed of moss. No, Maud couldn't have put it here—clearly it had lain in this spot longer than Maud had even known of my existence, as strands of lichen and moss held it firmly in place. Dislodging the quartz, I gripped it tightly in my hand and crouched down next to Maud to show it to her.

"It was right there. I wonder why you never found it before?"

"Amazingly enough, I've never noticed it," she declared simply. "Perhaps because it wasn't mine to find." She took the stone from my hand and held it up to the light, turning it every which way to catch its sparkle, and then she returned it to me, closing my fingers gently around it. For a long while we sat in silence, our heads bowed and our hands clasped together around the precious stone.

Meanwhile, several spiders busily bridged us again with their silk. In hushed tones we spoke of what had just happened, gazing in wonder at the piece of quartz in my palm. She told me about other messages she had received here over the years, always helpful. Like guides, she said. She spoke of her trials and many errors in her quest for authenticity as wife, mother, grandmother, and scholar. We exchanged stories about our husbands and their attitudes towards their "unlikely wives," in her words, and we learned that we had both sung at the stones, secretly, at night in Brittany when we thought we were alone.

This coincidence especially thrilled us and, laughing, we burst into song, making the hills around echo. We hooted and howled and the mountains hooted back. Our laughter rang back to us too, as if a band of giants on the opposite slope were playing a game with us.

"We're here!" she shouted.

"Here…here…here…" the valley sang back.

"Who's there?" I called.

"There…there…there…" the valley called back.

"I wonder what the songs of the old ones were like," I mused.

"Probably very simple, slow chants," Maud suggested. "Only one note at a time echoes back." She demonstrated, waiting for each echo to fade before she sang the next note. The effect was a harmonic wash of sound bouncing off the next ridge. "*Ave Maria* works well here."

"*A-ve Mar-i-a...*" We chanted each syllable separately, listening to multiple voices repeat the notes after us. We sang with delight to the hills, and the hills sang back to us. This kept us rapt until the sun began to dip toward the western horizon.

"We should start down," Maud declared, squinting at her watch, but we had started talking about the healing properties of music, which led to her telling me of her bout with cancer, and we were so absorbed we lost track of time again.

"It was eighteen years ago and I sang to my cancer," she told me frankly. "Twice a day, every day for months I would sing, and the hot spot gradually diminished until they couldn't find it anymore. I never went to the hospital."

"How did your husband take that?" I asked, imagining how Ted would have reacted to my refusal to see a doctor.

"I had to hold him off with a sword," she admitted wryly, and the conversation again went irresistibly back to our husbands, so that we barely noticed the sun's disappearance behind the trees. Dusk was already turning to night when we finally jumped up, and neither of us could see well enough to pick up the hardly used trail.

"We'll bushwhack," she said tersely. "Quick!" She tossed me a stick for balance, broke twigs off another for herself, and set out downhill at a swift pace. Crashing through the underbrush I followed her lead, keeping the only thing I could see in the darkness—her bobbing white head—in view as best I could. In the dark, the trees, shrubs, and boulders had no form, so I swerved when she swerved, slowed down when she slowed down, and tried to leap and hasten when she did. Alternately exhilarated and frightened, I was already imagining how I would describe this mad dash down the dark hillside to Ted, and by the time Maud and I reached the trailhead in one piece, both of us were breathless with laughter. We tromped the last quarter mile on relatively level ground by the light of a harvest moon, which rose, immense and orange, over the mountains, lighting a golden pathway across the darkening lake that seemed to lead straight toward us.

Maud and her husband Peter lived in the family's ancestral lodge atop a broad expanse of lawn that sloped down to the lake, but the small boathouse at the water's edge was her special refuge. She thought of it as her hermitage, and went there mostly to be alone: to write, to meditate, and occasionally to spend the night. Peter was away in the city for the weekend, so the boathouse on the lake, rather than the big house, was where we would both stay.

"It's almost *All Hallows*," she remarked as we sauntered down the dewy lawn toward the water. "Tomorrow the moon will be full. The veils between the worlds are very thin now."

Standing by the shore, the lake seemed like a sea stretching toward dark mountains that were faintly outlined by the moon. I breathed in newly mown grass and deep water, and zipping my windbreaker against the evening chill, I gazed up at a dark sky mobbed with stars. From somewhere a night bird *coo-ee'd* and both Maud and I *coo-ee'd* back. Smiling, she slipped her hand through my arm and I pressed it warmly against me. We stood still, listening to the rustle of the world's veils as they parted, before we tramped across the wooden ramp to the boathouse.

Eating a simple supper of grilled-cheese sandwiches and new apples, we snuggled on the windowseat overlooking the lake, wrapped up in a blue-and-orange quilt. Water slapped at the pilings beneath the floor, and in the eaves a family of squirrels scampered and chattered, stopping stock still when Maud rapped threateningly on the pinewood panels. The sparely-furnished room had a spiral staircase leading up to the sleeping loft; the boathouse indeed had the air of a hermitage, with its two rocking chairs, one low table, and a bookcase alongside the fireplace. A small sink and toaster oven constituted the kitchen, and the bathroom was a fern-filled outhouse in a copse of birches outside the door. The windowseat on which we sat and a single bedstead upstairs completed the snug little boathouse, where, Maud told me, her soul liked to live.

"This land is such a healing place," she said, taking a delicate bite of her dripping sandwich and wiping greasy fingers on the bandana in her lap, "that I had to make it accessible to others as well as just our family."

"Doesn't it get lonely out here in the winter?" I asked.

"Yes," she admitted after a while. "Especially when we first moved up here eighteen years ago—after my cancer—but solitude has been a great healer. In fact, I now look forward to winter when I can slow down and go deep into myself. And ski, of course," she added. "Also, the children come up with their families for the holidays, and friends drop by for skiing, so it can be very jolly."

"Does Ile Hoëdic function during the winter?"

"Some. The Board comes up for two working weekends to keep trails open and such, and we have one members' skiing day, but mostly Ile Hoëdic shuts down for six months. However, there's a lot of alcoholism and depression in this area during the winter, so I want to extend the program to include winter gatherings, especially now that we have the new sanctuary." She gazed thoughtfully out at the pathway of moonlight across the lake and went on, "That's why we're looking for a person to do outreach."

"From California?" I joked.

"Why not, if she's willing to come? So far, none of the locals have responded to the call, so I figure that if the two of us are able to contact the local spirits together, we ought to be able to reach the folks in town with a telephone and a fax machine!"

Bundling up in warm woolen shawls after supper, we walked out to view the lake by moonlight and to stroll along the shore to the edge of the woods where, Maud pointed out, the new sanctuary stood.

"This little bit of shoreline where the woods start was my favorite place when I was a child," she told me. "I've dowsed it many times through the years, and each time the dowsing rods all but fly out of my hands, the energy's that strong. I suspect there's an energetic connection with the site on the ridge, which is directly above us."

"I'm certainly feeling something," I affirmed, giving in to a subtle tugging on the right side of my body.

"Alright," she proposed, "I won't tell you where the sanctuary is and you see if you can lead the way." Following the pull to where the moonshadows of trees and brush striped the moonlit lawn, I left the dew-wet grass and ducked under birches into woods of fragrant leaf mulch. Maud followed, humming.

"On the nose," she commented a few moments later when we stood at the edge of the path leading to the sanctuary. "I'll bring us in." In a few steps, I felt I'd followed her through a veil and into a magical place of fairies and shadows. Everything was changed here, and in this realm Maud was no ordinary woman. She was a crone, a witch, a wise woman. Wrapping my shawl more tightly around my shoulders, I took my place by her side in front of the sanctuary.

Surrounded by forest on three sides and open to the lakeshore in front, the sanctuary was a six-sided *hogan*, or cabin, with clerestory windows and a domed roof, and its sides were faced with birch logs that glistened in the moonlight. Maud stepped onto the porch and waited for me to join her before she opened the door. She lit a candle in the small mudroom, and I followed her into the round chapel, where even our breaths echoed.

I stood by while she lit votive candles, placing them in a circle on the floor until the whole space glowed. In the flickering lights, sculpted tree trunks lining the walls cast long shadows, as if we were outside in the forest, instead of indoors under a roof. Maud placed one candle upon the simple, tree-stump altar and bowed, beckoning for me to join her there. I gazed around at the bark and heartwood and gracefully woven branches of the walls.

"You've made a sacred space in here," I breathed.

"Enhanced an already sacred space," she corrected me. In the stillness the room seemed to breathe with us, and we could hear the soft spurts of waves slipping over shoreline pebbles just outside the door.

"I love it!" I whispered.

"I know," she smiled.

The seasoned oak floor, inscribed with the spiraling circles of a labyrinth, Maud told me, was made of wood from a now-defunct military base. The walls were made from trees fallen on the property and the door had once been part of the icehouse. Every detail of the building was recycled, she said.

"The first thing I do when I enter is to walk the labyrinth. You're welcome to join me if you can see the lines well enough in this light." Indeed, the lines were barely visible in the flickering shadows, and I was reminded of that dark morning at Chartres, those many years ago, when I walked the labyrinth with Danilo.

"I've done it before in the half dark," I commented. "Someday I'll tell you the story. Just lead—I'll follow you." As I took my place behind her, an owl in the forest *hoot-hooted* twice.

"There's our sign," she declared. "The veils *are* thin tonight. Ready?"

"I'm ready," I replied as she took the first steps into the labyrinth. Slowly I paced behind her, following her around the spiral path toward the center, changing direction left, then right, then left again. Once, I felt dizzy enough to stop for a moment, but then my head cleared and I was able to continue. As I approached each turning place, I felt a moment of hesitation that released into a rush of energy as I shifted direction and with each successive shift, my body relaxed more and I moved with increasingly greater ease.

By the time Maud and I met in the middle, my head felt clearer than it had for months. I bowed to her and we stood facing each other in the silent space, breathing in quiet tandem with our eyes half closed. Then, when it was time, we slowly retraced our steps and walked the labyrinth back to where we had started.

"Did you know," she informed me later when we were lounging together on the floor by the pot-bellied stove, "that the English word 'church' comes from a Greek word meaning *circle*?" And from there our conversation circled for the next several hours and it was, indeed, like praying in church. The pine fire crackled and spat fragrantly in the stove, and the candles melted into hot wax as we talked about our childhoods in New York City, twenty years apart.

Maud had been a child of privilege—she was raised in Manhattan's best private schools and summered at the family estate on Saranac Lake—while I had been a child of Russian-Jewish refugees amongst working-class Catholics in Brooklyn. What we had in common was a sense of belonging neither to the worlds we inhabited, nor to our female bodies. Both of us had identified as tomboys, rather than the good girls our families felt they deserved, and we each had learned to stifle our natural exuberance while wishing, in our heart of hearts, that we had not been born girls.

"I'm still not much of a lady," she confided. I raised my eyebrows at that. "Much as I tried, I was never quite presentable enough for Peter's colleagues. Poor old Petey…"

"Well, too bad for them!" I countered with heat. "You were just too much woman for them." We laughed and I added more softly, "Just a little bit ahead of your time."

"Well, it's true," she sighed. "Times have changed. Your generation of women is demanding the freedom to be strong—and succeeding, I believe—but in those days we were expected to take a back seat and follow the rules, and most of us did. Certainly, I did."

"Hard to picture you ever following the rules," I observed wryly. She shrugged.

"And yet, for the most part I was good as gold. I was 'Lady Grin and Bear It.' I married the right kind of man, I had the requisite three children, I made little dinner parties…" she grimaced and went on, "and I did everything I was supposed to do, including going abysmally numb behind a cheerful façade. And there you have it."

My eyes smarted in the pine-and-tallow smoke of the remarkable space this woman had created. It was hard to believe she could ever have been anything less than her own woman.

"Well, thank goodness you outgrew that," I exclaimed, rapping my knuckles on the floor for emphasis.

"Well, yes indeed," she said mildly. "And how did you make it through?"

I told her the story of my meeting Ted after two years in Europe, and a bit about Danilo and Martine, which led to a discussion of the sexual mores of our times, which in turn led naturally to the question of gender. I told her about Katsu, and we wondered aloud about whether pure maleness and pure femaleness—or even pure homosexuality—were all there were.

"Actually, I think I'm all of the above," I conjectured.

"Or none of the above," she retorted. "I've long suspected there are more categories than we can imagine. I think the possibilities must be endless, and society has narrowed the playing field down to a paltry two. It's a shame…" Her eyes shone fiercely in the candlelight.

"So if you had to call yourself something," I asked her, "what might that be?" She rocked back and forth for a while, her arms about her knees. A small smile played lightly on her lips as she replied, "Why, an ecstatic, of course."

Well into the night we told each other our 'ecstasy' stories, starting with our coming-of-age adventures. Interestingly enough, we had both spent our early twenties in France—she as a canteen hostess during World War II and myself as a student there twenty years later.

"I ran a Red Cross club with another girl, where the soldiers gathered when they got back from the Front," she said. "We didn't do much more than hand out doughnuts and coffee, and be there to talk to, but it turned out to make all the difference to the boys, and it was the perfect work for me. I had no idea, until then, that I had the right instincts for helping people, but I did, and the experience awakened something deep in me, something I'm still working on."

"Which is…?" I asked.

She glanced up at the wooden beams crisscrossing the space. "Do you know about the Japanese tradition of 'tea ladies'?" she asked enigmatically, replying to my question with a question. I shook my head. "These are women who set up their little tea stalls at a crossroads and sell cups of tea to whoever comes by." She cocked her head at me. "That's all they do—they sell tea. But they have a secret agenda, of course. They pass the time of day with their customers, listen to their stories, offer encouragement and advice—very ordinary stuff."

"So you're a tea lady, you're saying?"

"Something like that," she answered. "Maybe I'm just a grandma."

"A rather fierce grandma," I noted. "And in disguise."

"Of course, the disguise is part of it," she smiled. "That way nobody gets intimidated—but let me continue with my story of what happened at the Front. You see, there was a fellow, a soldier, who I fell in love with. Jesse," she said softly. "Jesse was gay, as it turned out—gay at a time when 'gay' wasn't yet even a word, especially in the army. And most especially if you were a person of color. I think he may have been Native American, but he never would speak of it. We existed in that wartime world where neither the past nor the future has any meaning. There is only now." I scooted closer to her, lifting both her feet onto my lap.

"He was all but illiterate, but one of the wisest beings I have ever known. I loved him with all my heart but, of course, never with my body. In the year we were together we often slept on the same cot, but we were chaste."

A cloud of regret rippled over her features, but then softened into a nostalgic smile. "Anyhow, Jesse and I had a family. There were five orphans we had found wandering around in one of the bombed-out villages, and we took care of them in the tent we shared. They were like our children."

She sighed, and her creased cheek glistened with tears. "We were surrounded by all the horrors of war, but for me every day was ecstatic. I was in love with Jesse, in love with the children, in love with life. Perhaps the war gave everything a piquant edge it might not have had in peacetime; perhaps it was because Jesse was my first love—who knows? But I came of age in a state of bliss that lasted eight glorious months."

"Have you kept in contact with any of them?" I asked.

She shook her head sadly. "Jesse was sent off to the Front and I never saw him again. The children, one by one, disappeared into the melee and anyhow, I was soon transferred to England so I lost them also. I'd be surprised if any of my little family were still alive," she murmured.

I wrapped my arms around her and, laying my head on her warm shoulder, I wept quietly. She stroked and stroked my hair while outside a pack of coyotes bayed at the moon from high on the hill. Inside, the candles sent whorls of light into all the dark corners of the room.

"Compared to yours, my adventures were tame," I remarked after a while. "To begin with, we weren't fighting a war. I was just a student on the trail of a picture I had seen in an art book." I told her about Poitiers and the d'Alvernys and the burning questions I was asking about fear and religion. And I told her about Martine.

"She was my first real love," I admitted. "Even though she spoke French, which I spoke rather poorly, she and I shared a deeper language. We matched each other in intensity and sensibility in a way I've never been matched since. We were rather a wild pair."

"I would imagine so," Maud teased. "Were you indeed a pair?" Her straightforward question took me by surprise, and I considered it before responding.

"We were definitely in love, and we both acknowledged that," I said, "but we lived in a small Catholic town in France where everybody knew everybody else's business. And it wasn't wartime, so propriety was *de rigueur*—especially for an American living in a French household. So the answer to your question is that we behaved like best friends when we were in town, and occasionally took trips out of town."

"Whatever happened to her?" Maud asked.

"Ah, being Martine, she entered a convent after I left and became a nun."

"No!" Maud was genuinely shocked.

"Not because she was brokenhearted over us," I quickly assured her, "but because she had a kind of "visitation"—that's what she called it—and was told to spend the rest of her life in contemplation. So she gave up everything, said her good-byes to everyone, and entered a silent order. When she wrote me her last letter, she made it clear that it was farewell forever."

"You must have been rather upset," Maud said mildly.

"Devastated," I replied. "Devastated because I was losing her, which I couldn't bear, but also because I figured she knew something I didn't know, and I couldn't stand that! I wanted to fly back to France before she disappeared behind locked doors, just to see her one last time, but by then I was married and pregnant and living in California. Ted wouldn't hear of it. That was a hard time for me."

"How did you cope?" Maud asked.

"Well, once the baby was born I was distracted by daily life with a newborn, but in fact I didn't have to grieve for very long, because in a few months I got a long letter from her from Algiers." Maud's eyes grew round and I laughed.

"I tell you, there is only one Martine. She had escaped the convent at a run, she wrote me. She said it was a crazy place full of bickering women and not what she'd expected, so she took off for Algeria, where she got a job on the staff of a peace magazine. It was such a relief to get that letter—not only to know she was in my world again, but also to know that I hadn't missed out on something important." I confessed this with a sheepish grin.

"I think I would have liked this impetuous woman," Maud declared.

"You'd have loved her. She's very much like you, I think—that is, if she is still alive," I said.

"You don't know whether she is or not?" Maud asked.

"Actually, I don't. We corresponded for over twenty years, even after she returned to France and moved to the Pyrenees, to some remote mountain village where she set up a traveling library, but then I lost her. She had rejected all suitors by that time, wrote me after one break-up saying, *"Je ne suis pas comme des autres,"* I'm not like other people, and she kept moving further and further into the mountains until she finally disappeared from sight."

"This sounds so much like my Jesse," Maud said wistfully, hugging her shawl around her shoulders. "So interesting that both our first loves were unattainable and both vanished into thin air. Makes you wonder who they really were."

"And that each of *us* found one of *them*," I added.

"And both lost them," she whispered.

After the war Maud was married, gave birth to three children, and followed her husband to the various places his career led him.

Just as I had. Each of us had taken the role of wife and mother seriously, even as we had secretly pined for more.

"I went through all the proper motions," Maud said, "but in fact I was hardly ever present. Even at the births of my children, I'm embarrassed to admit, most of me was numb, except for that deep place inside where I loathed myself for being an imposter." Her voice was shaking and, cradling her feet, I gently massaged them.

"What made it so hard?" I asked. She took in a quavering breath and gazed at the floor.

"I wonder," she began, "I wonder… Of course it wasn't really an option at that time, but I wonder if I might have felt more fulfilled if I'd had relationships with women before I got married. Or even other men. But except for Jesse, Peter was the first lover in my life. Of course, I adore my children, and of course I have nothing whatever to complain about, but I'm still so curious."

"I know just what you're saying, Maud," I affirmed, massaging her toes with the heels of my hands. "It's kind of like living on a diet of only noodles when you're longing to taste sushi and enchiladas and fish soup as well. You want to eat the whole world, and not just in ladylike bites." She nodded, and her eyes took on a watery sheen. "I just got born when there was a little more opportunity to be voracious than you were," I added.

"Lucky for you," she commented.

"You're right, I have been lucky," I said. "The older I get and the more people I love, the more I wonder if monogamy is the smartest way to go."

"Have you acted on that?" she asked.

"Not really," I admitted wistfully. "I've had lots of passionate friendships—which had to be negotiated with Ted, believe me—but he and I have an agreement to be sexually faithful to each other even when we're tempted to be otherwise, and we have been."

"So am I to be one of your passionate friendships?" she asked, her eyes dancing with fun.

"I certainly hope so," I declared warmly, bending over to rub my cheek on her knees. She placed a hand on my back and petted me like a cat. I could hardly refrain from purring.

We went back to discussing the angsts of the past, trying to get to the seat of our restlessness. I told her about growing up with frightened Jewish refugees, and she talked about the strict proprieties of New York City Anglicans—"the frozen chosen," she called them. We talked about city living versus country living, about the East Coast versus the West Coast.

"These mountains are the only place I truly feel at home," she breathed, gazing out the window into the darkness, "and needless to say, Peter feels more comfortable in the city. Oh my. Conundrum. What to do?"

"So how *do* you do it?" I asked wonderingly. "How did he ever agree to retire here?"

Ted, I knew, would never have been willing to live in the country, no matter how I approached him. She toyed with the tassels on her shawl and let her breath out in a low whistle.

"By having a nervous breakdown," she declared finally, "a dark night of the soul which lasted several months. It frightened both of us enough so that it was he who finally suggested we move to the lake as a kind of last resort, pardon the pun."

Our eyes met, and I felt her gaze penetrate my bones.

"That period of deep despair," she continued, "was the hardest but finest, teacher I've ever had. When you hit bottom there's nowhere to go except up—or out. And if you don't choose to go out, then life stares you in the face in a whole new way. You realize there is only the present moment, and that life is finite and precious beyond reckoning. Living it authentically is all that really matters—everything else is secondary."

I carefully poked a sliver of wood into a candle-holder brimming with hot wax to rescue a drowning wick. "Did you come close to going out?" I asked cautiously.

"I certainly came close to wanting to," she replied. "Fortunately, through the haze of my depression I recognized the opportunity to do some serious soul work, and that pulled me through."

"How long did it take you?" I asked.

"Oh," she answered with a pursing of her lips, "this is an ongoing process that probably will take me the rest of my life."

"And still Peter has been willing to move up here for your benefit," I commented admiringly.

"Well, yes. He's a good man and wishes for me to be happy. Like Ted does for you," she said quietly. "We've also created a schedule that works for both of us. Peter goes down to the city at least one week a month and maintains his contacts there, and we do some traveling together—visiting the children and such. And otherwise, we're here and he's fairly content sitting and reading, and writing long letters to *The New York Times*."

"While you stride up mountains and ski across the lake," I grinned.

"Something like that," she allowed with a short laugh, "and also healing and meditating and doing the work of creating a sanctuary on this amazing land."

"What a journey you're on!" I acknowledged humbly. "Could you tell me more about the healing part?" She shifted her position thoughtfully, and tapped her fingers on the floor.

"You really want to know?" she challenged me. I nodded. "Ah, well, it's very catch-as-catch-can, involving years of struggling with more self-hate than you can imagine. Gobs of it—from hating being in a woman's body to despising myself for not having the courage speak my own mind!" She shuddered and stared into space before going on.

"I've spent whole weeks wailing on that mountain; I've swum in the lake until my arms couldn't take another stroke; I've sat on that ridge in anguish until I thought my heart would break. Months and years of effort have gone into finally coming into calm waters, and at last I feel I've begun to change the pattern." The room throbbed painfully as the echoes of her words faded out. We sat a while in silence.

"Thank you," I whispered, "for breaking trail for the rest of us and inviting us onto your healing land." I bowed to her and she bowed back.

"Do you know that couplet from *Corinthians*?" she asked quietly. "*'For now we see through a glass darkly, but then face to face'*?"

"I do, yes."

"I always thought I understood what that meant, but about twenty years ago when I was deep in depression it suddenly occurred to me one day that "face to face" means that you have to have a face. And I had no face. I was a blank in my own mirror. That's when I knew I needed these woods as I'd never needed anything before."

"It's your home place," I remarked, not without some envy.

"To my great fortune, yes, I had this home to return to," she agreed. "And you and everyone who longs for *home* are welcome to share it." She began to hum the old hymn of exile,

By the waters of Babylon
where we sat down
and there we wept
when we remembered Zion...

...How can we sing our song in a strange land?

I harmonized with her on the refrain, our voices ringing off the tree-trunk walls while the embers hissed in the stove. The moon, high above, reached the zenith and began its descent to the other side of the world.

We slept soundly until midmorning, Maud in the loft and I on the windowseat overlooking the lake, and might have slept longer had we not been awakened by a boom of thunder so loud it shook the boathouse. Another crash of thunder and the storm broke directly overhead, pelting the roof and windows with driving rain. I sat up and stared out at a roiling body of water, whitecapped and gray, which slapped hard at our fragile boathouse and obscured the distant mountains with dark mist. Maud, in purple pajamas and a sweatshirt, joined me sleepily downstairs and squinted appraisingly through the casement windows.

"Change of plans," she announced philosophically. "I guess we won't do the grand tour today. I'd been looking forward to showing you the lowlands by morning light—maybe even to see a moose."

I cranked the window open a crack, just enough to smell the rain pelting the lake, and glanced at her questioningly. I was certainly willing to brave the storm if she was. We exchanged a look of complicity, and with understanding she nodded her agreement.

"Let's take about an hour of quiet time first," she suggested. "Help yourself to breakfast if you want. I like to write in the morning, and later we can go out, rain or shine."

After she used the outhouse, she mounted the spiral staircase back up to the loft and climbed again into her creaky bed. I was glad to be alone after the intensity of the night before, with rain hitting the roof, waves thudding against the pilings, and only my own thoughts for company.

As the storm gusted, shaking walls and rattling windows, I felt like a small boat in a vast ocean pitching every which way at the whim of the waves. At intervals the lake was lit up with unearthly light and then torn apart with great claps of thunder. Gradually, the thunder moved westward over the mountains until it was barely audible, and the lake quieted as the storm moved on.

I lay awake listening to the voices of water beneath me and slipped back into my dream of the day before, hearing my singing voice meet the churning waves and enter its foaming chaos. I relaxed and let go into an irresistible vertigo, feeling the whirlpool gather force and sweep me through a narrow channel into open space where winds and clouds buoyed me. I was dreaming awake. I dozed on and off, rising in and out of sleep like a swimmer in a river run, and then I awoke properly when the rain started up again. Staring for a few moments out at the shrouded view, I then flung my feet out of the covers and onto the floor. I had to get outside into the rain.

I had pulled on a poncho over my nightgown, but the water sluicing down from the eaves caught my neck anyway, and within seconds I was drenched. Splashing barefoot through a cold puddle, I clambered down the bank to the lake's edge and lifted my face to the rain. Water was everywhere! It poured down on me, gusted against me, soaked my legs up to the calves, and broke into bubbles at my feet. Maud appeared at a loft window, shaking her head at the sight.

"You'll catch your death!" she called. "What are we going to do with you?" Wild laughter was my response as I scrambled back up the muddy bank and ducked beneath the roofline and through the door of the boathouse. Maud met me with a fleecy towel over her arm, and as I tore off my poncho and drenched nightgown she wrapped me warmly in it.

"I guess we should have some breakfast and get geared up to take on the storm," she declared. "Then we can tromp around to our hearts' content without coming down with pneumonia."

"And maybe see a moose?" I asked.

"And most likely see a moose," she confirmed, rummaging in the closet for two pairs of high boots, rain pants, oilskin ponchos, and long-necked fishermen's hats to keep us dry.

We never did see a moose that day, but it may have been one of those storms that the moose were too smart to stay out in. Not Maud and me, however. Keeping relatively dry in our layers of raingear, we trudged across a leaf-littered brook and clung onto each other against the powerful tug of its current. We slogged up to our boot tops through a squishy bog to a spruce-and-fir peninsula, and we talked about long-ago summers when, we calculated, we had probably been no more than twenty miles from each other.

"When I was sixteen, the Adirondacks literally saved my life," I told her. "I ran away from home to work as a kitchen girl at a music camp over on Schroon Lake, and I felt happier there than I had ever felt in my life."

We hiked through a dark grove of hemlocks that dropped tiny needles onto our heads, and then descended along a cascading stream.

"By the second summer, my parents were shamed into sending me there as a student rather than as kitchen help, and by the third summer I was counselor in a cabin of twelve-year-old girls. So these mountains gave me my start, and I'm eternally grateful to them."

"You've come full circle, you know," Maud said warmly as we huddled beneath a balsam tree to watch whitewater tumble over slick-wet boulders. "These mountains healed you, and now you've come back to them to help heal others."

"And it was *you* who brought me back here," I reminded her. The sound of a rushing brook was my favorite music in the world, the mulched earth the best of all perfumes, and the peeling bark of glistening birch the finest of all art. There was something about these Adirondacks that felt more like home to me than any other geography. It was healing balm, and I breathed and breathed it in.

"Ah, well," she said, as we hiked along the stream to the marshland at the bottom, "we know there are no accidents in this world, right?"

During a lull in the storm, Maud took me on a loop trail that led back through the hemlocks and waterfalls, across the boggy meadow, and onto a path that climbed to a low saddle in the hills. The upland trail divided and we took the lower path, eventually finding ourselves back at the lakeshore in the vicinity of the sanctuary. By this time, we were plastered with leaves and hemlock needles, our hair was in our faces, and sweat was pouring down inside our oilskins. Maud's eyes shone with the same high spirits I felt. Stomping water off my boots, I stood on the sandy shore and shouted to the lake,

"Who says you can't be outrageous after sixty?"

"Who says you can't *start* after sixty?" she hooted, throwing back her head and yodeling. We howled like happy maniacs, hitching elbows in a clumsy *do-si-do*. A new range of clouds boiled in above us, massing gray and then black before dropping a new shower on our heads, but we danced through it until the cloudburst scudded on and a patch of blue showed between moving clouds.

"By the waters of Babylon," Maud sang, clapping her gloved hands and rocking from one foot to the other. I joined her in a made-up Reggae version of the old hymn, *"where we sat down, dum da dum da dum, and there we wept dum da dum da dum when we remem-bered Zi-on doop doop dada..."*

I slapped the beat on my soaking knees and stamped on the sand in rhythm. *"How can we sing our song...in a straaange...land?"* We sang with our whole bodies, feeling the beat of waves and pelting rain and pacing clouds above our heads. We rocked in tandem, our voices coming out of the weather and bouncing off each other, and everything merging with everything.

"Baby-lon...Zi-on doop dadoo...Baby-lon...dum dadum...and de waters of de world dum dadum da dum...and I wept for de world dum dadum da dum...and I sing for Zi-on doop doop dadoo..."

Singing came as easily as breathing and we rocked at the edge of the lake, our eyes closed and our bodies loose and easy with the song. Maud lifted both arms to the bits of blue sky emerging from the mist, and her song slid into another pitch. I followed the riff, and then led until we were playing off each other like a couple of jazz musicians. As the song rose we evoked earth and sky, sun and rain, and all the powers of life and elemental forces that formed the world.

Laughing irresistibly, we sang to the cycles of change—day and night, summer and winter, birth and death—singing to time itself. Our bodies bowed to the plants and the animals, and to all beings alive on land and water and air. We prayed for everyplace on the earth, from this lake with its loons to the vast cosmos spreading beyond time and space.

A wind picked up in the tops of the highest trees, swaying them like massive wands against the sky, and we sang louder and prayed to the winds of change. And how the winds gusted! They roared across the lake and into the surrounding woods, lifting off every tree the multicolored leaves still clinging to their summertime branches.

Suddenly the air was filled with leaves! Rich reds and yellows and browns and purples took to the air in droves, spinning and flying like wild confetti. We stood, heads up and mouths open, gazing in astonishment as autumn gave way to winter in glorious display.

Tatters of color swirled above us, ecstatic to be free. The winds blew through once more, grabbing stubborn leaves from their branches and tumbling them through the air, and then with less strength pulling off the last few and dropping them onto the forest floor before moving on.

Maud and I stood silent on the shore as the last bright leaves settled to be food for next year's growth. The woods grew still as the branches dripped softly, and we were cloaked in soft mist, gray as warm velvet. The sucking earth popped as water percolated into leaf-rich soil, and twittering birds ventured out onto the now-bare branches of the trees to peck for insects at crevices in the bark.

I was crying. Maud held me against her and I sobbed into her slick-wet poncho as we shared the fullness of the moment. Together we had seen the forest's display of ending and beginning, had been part of a moment of inexorable change and saw that it was good. With our arms tightly around each other, we knew that we took our place in the earth's awesome round.

"All shall be well," she recited softly as we stood arm in arm on the shore, *"and all shall be well, and all manner of things shall be well."*

"Amen," I whispered, my chest filled with heart. Extracting a wadded-up tissue from my pocket, I blew my nose hard. We stood apart and gazed at the bare-branched trees; no longer filled in with leaves, the forest looked spacious. We could see between the trees into the distance, each tree distinct with it own shape like sculpture—living sculpture that twisted, branched, and reached. Winter trees. In a twinkling, all had been changed.

We were very quiet. And tired. It had been an exhilarating, but arduous day and we turned toward home, peeking into the sanctuary for a moment before walking out of the trees and onto the lawn, making our way along the shore to the boathouse. Way above us the sun, slipping out from scudding clouds, sent its warm yellow light down upon this place like a blessing.

"Look!" cried Maud, pointing toward the shallows where a great blue heron, intent on the hunt, stalked. It stood absolutely still, bill poised for the capture, and with a sudden downward jab it came up with its prey. The helpless frog was hefted once, twice, and then with a toss of its majestic head, the heron gulped it right down. On slow, stilted legs it continued to hunt.

The bright blue sky between billowing white clouds was reflected on the now-calm surface of the lake like a second sky. Looking down and looking up were the same. The great blue, like us, was taking advantage of the break in the weather to stalk slowly and to feed— the heron on hapless frogs and Maud and me on chocolate bars. The heron turned in our direction, stared at us for just a moment, and then opened its enormous blue-gray wings and lifted lazily off the ground. Flapping past us, it flew along the shoreline right above the water. So two great blue herons, perfectly synchronized, appeared to be flying along the lake: one in the air right-side-up, and the other in the water upside-down, and the cloud-layered sky reflected beneath its wings down, down as far as the eye could see.

We were good and cold now. Maud took six split logs from the woodpile and dumped them inside the boathouse door. Shivering, we pulled off our muddy Wellingtons and wriggled out of our raingear until we were down to wet underwear.

"Let's get that fire going," she chattered, scurrying up to the loft for dry clothes. "And put up water for tea."

I changed quickly into a pair of dry jeans and a red flannel shirt, and pulling on a pair of Maud's goosedown booties, I placed a kettle on the hot plate and brought in an armload of twigs and pinecones for kindling. While Maud got dressed, I dropped the kindling and logs by the hearth and filled a teapot with dried rosehips I found in the cupboard.

Surrounding a crumpled wad of newspaper with four pinecones and a teepee of twigs, I struck a match and lit it. Immediately the paper caught and roared through the firebox, igniting the skinny twigs and sending a draught of smoke up the chimney. When the stouter sticks and pinecones began to crackle and the teepee had disintegrated into glowing embers, I added the logs, and by the time Maud came down the fire was blazing merrily and adding the spice of woodsmoke to the smell of rosehips coming out of the galley.

Maud, wrapped in an old brown bathrobe, her hair wet around the edges and her feet encased in woolly slippers, brought in the teapot on a wooden tray, cups and saucers jangling. She placed the tray on a low table by the fire, standing back a moment to admire the scene before returning to the galley.

"I'm not much of a cook," she admitted, "but the local grocery is known for its scones. Hope you like scones."

"Love 'em," I returned, giving the fire a poke. Outside, the skies rumbled again and the clouds darkened across the lake for the next burst of rain. When it came, drumming against the eaves and running in rivulets down the shrouded windows, we were glad to be snuggled cozy and dry in front of a blazing fire. When the tea had steeped, Maud tilted the teapot and poured some into each of our cups; I bent my head to sniff its fragrant steam before I took a burning sip. Maud blew on hers, thoughtfully gazing into the fire.

"Chop wood, carry water," she said enigmatically. I thought of Katsu, who often had used the Zen phrase when he talked about simplicity and integrity. "When you chop wood, chop wood," he would say. "When you carry water, carry water," and I would always smile because both of us lived with furnaces and faucets, and had never chopped wood or carried water in our lives.

"It all seems so simple," Maud mused. "For two years I've scoured our area to find the right person for this job, and when I wasn't looking—when I was three thousand miles away, in fact—you showed up." We both smiled. "Tell me, how will Ted feel about your being gone for three months?"

"Not great," I replied, "but he's prepared for me to do it. He knows how I feel about the Adirondacks and how much I want to do this. He's a generous guy, is my Ted."

"Yes, he is," she confirmed. "What does he make of all these synchronicities that led to your coming here?"

"As you'd expect," I replied. "He doesn't know what to make of them. He's not sure what to make of me altogther, for that matter."

"How much will you tell Ted of our adventures this weekend?" she chuckled, pouring fresh tea into both our cups.

"Pretty much everything," I said after a while. "I tend to tell him about what I'm thinking and doing, even when I figure it's not up his alley. If I don't, our lives slip apart too quickly. What about you?"

She regarded me with a thoughtful smile and then said slowly, "I tell Peter what has happened, but not what I feel about it. If I start with the deeper emotions he gets uncomfortable and I end up feeling wretched."

"So you went through all that agony alone?" I gasped.

"Not really, no. He was with me every step of the way—I think I might have died without him there—but the gut level stuff I didn't share with him. Not ever."

We reached for each other's hands and held on as the patter on the roof decreased in intensity. Darkness came on, and with the last of the rain spurting out we spoke of the difficulty of communicating soul to soul with people in general, starting, of course, with our men.

"I've been wondering for decades how to bridge the gap between Peter's intellect and my intuitive feel for things," Maud declared. "I've always been baffled by his literal-mindedness, but he's the successful one in the family, not me."

"Well, yes, by society's current standards," I noted, "but don't you think that's changing?"

"Perhaps in time for you," she said with a gentle smile, leaning back in her rocker and staring dreamily into the crackling flames.

As evening came on and only a drip-drip from the eaves remained of the rain, our conversation got deeper and wittier as we exchanged even more private stories, alternately laughing and crying in the firelit room. Bit by bit we exposed more of ourselves, and in the process the harder truths came out and we laughed until we cried, cried until we roared with laughter. When the pain was great we sat very still, and when we were plumb wrung out and scraping the jug of cream clean with our fingers, Maud said,

"We could have dinner, you know. I've got a butternut squash to bake, and there's salad makings and good bread."

I yawned my assent and heard my bones creak as I stood. Stretching, I followed Maud to the little galley, feeling lighter than I had for a long time. Low in the sky, a buttery yellow moon rose above the mountains and lit a narrow path onto the lake. Full tonight.

"Let's go for a moon walk while the squash is baking," Maud

suggested. She glanced out at the moon and added, "We'll give it another ten minutes to get a bit higher and then go out, OK?"

"Sounds good to me." Taking two plates from the shelf while Maud sliced a butternut squash, I placed them on the table. I quartered two tomatoes—the last from the garden, Maud said—and rinsed lettuce leaves until all the grit was gone. Mixing the greens and tomatoes with dried basil, lemon, and a dribble of olive oil, I tossed the salad, added salt and a little pepper, and put the bowl aside until later. Maud set a wedge of Cheddar and crusty bread on a board and took them to the table, along with a bottle of white wine and two glasses. The first aromas of baking squash sizzled up from the oven, and outside the moon sent a broad pathway of light onto the lake.

"Baking squash and wood smoke are the smells of autumn to me," Maud said, sniffing contentedly as we crowded into the mudroom to get our boots. Wrapped up in woven shawls, we went out to where the moon was throwing moon shadows with abandon over the lawn, and the lake shone with twice-reflected light.

We walked in and out of moonbeams, stopping at an outcrop of rock where the horizon opened and we could gaze out into a night world of faraway mountains beyond starlit water, where mystery held sway beyond the seen, and the forms of the world lost their daytime shapes. We were very small beneath this sky, and we knew it. Each breath felt like a blessing, and every love a gift. And we knew it.

A bat fluttered close by, then swooped away, and an owl called from a nearby tree. Wavelets broke softly against the lakeshore, hissing back over sand and pebbles, and beneath our feet the rock was solid. As the moon climbed higher into the sky we walked across saturated ground that squelched muddily in our footsteps, our prints filling back up with groundwater as we returned slowly to the warm light of the boathouse.

Out on the dark lake a second full moon held sway, shivered with the low winds, and broke apart with the movement of the water. And the fragments, again and again, came back together for an instant of perfection—now and now—each time reflecting yet again the unbroken wholeness of the round, luminous moon.

MATTER, FORM, AND THE NATURAL WORLD

*Substance and form are created without
ever losing unity in consciousness.*

From a creation hymn of the Kashmiri Hindu Shaivites

*M*aud believed in fairies—angels, too. One summer evening after a long, hot day clearing trail on the ridge, we sat in canvas beach chairs on the shore watching the last lights of day fade from the darkening sky. Venus appeared overhead, and the haunting call of a loon echoed across the waters. At our feet wavelets broke softly against the beach, and the breeze picked up just enough to ruffle our hair.

"Not little people with gossamer wings," Maud clarified, "energies. Invisible forces that form the things of the world."

In the growing dark, the green of the leaves and grass had lost all color, and the woods seemed to merge with the night. Only the hissing of water sliding back and forth over beach stones, and the occasional call of a loon broke the stillness. I inhaled deeply, utterly content, one eye out for the errant fairy that just might materialize on the shore around us.

Beyond my toes the ceaseless action of the waves had left a light line of detritus—algae, snail shells, driftwood—marking the edge between the water and the land. A visible boundary between realms, it was constantly reinforced by the repeated motions of the lapping waves. Mesmerized in the dark, I listened to the water come softly to the shore in its own rhythm, as the first fireflies flashed their tiny lights on and off around us. I could no longer tell where the lake ended and the sky, studded with stars, began.

"I will not believe the universe is mindless," Maud remarked, as the dissonant cries of a pair of loons echoed across the water, dissolving into the night as they flew toward the reeds on the far shore. The earth released its nighttime musk, and high on the ridge a coyote barked twice and stopped. All was still until, from far away, we heard wild responding yelps in the valley that raised goosebumps on our arms. Maud sighed with pleasure.

How could such perfection emerge randomly from an unconscious source? How could we not feel gratitude for some 'something' out there? It was as if we humans had been given a gift of such staggering beauty that we had no choice but to try and match it and return the favor to the world—like the give-and-take games Katsu and I used to play, but on the grand scale.

I could imagine, at the beginning, the intelligent void of the Unified Field catching its first breath of longing and carrying an intention for beauty along with that breath. Even now, we are stll hearing an echo of that first pulse, which continues to vibrate, each beat creating a new moment of being.

I envision the spinning, infinitesimal vortices of energy in this vibrating field bumping into each other and coalescing into little clusters, like gaseous clouds. Bonding together, I imagine they would form a kind of subatomic structure, like tiny crossroads in the ether. We might think of these clusters as solid particles, but I imagine they are more like moving air that gathers into spinning clouds. We might also think of these clusters as inanimate, but I suspect that in this world there is no such thing. Ultimately I believe that everything is conscious and alive—*everything.*

As the clouds would accrete more girth, their structures would become more distinct, forming atoms and molecules and gas—the beginnings of matter. Each grouping would have its unique frequency of vibration, and each relationship would make possible one more area of unfoldment. And as each new form would emerge ultimately from the Unified Field, every minute particle would contain the inherent consciousness of the Field.

Possibility, itself, must have been a moving force of the new universe. Like a baby discovering its hands and toes, the universe would have explored itself—clumping here, fragmenting there, combining and recombining its elements until it learned what it could do.

For a long time—millennia in our reckoning—I would guess that the process gradually reached a level of stability, refining the ability to coalesce energy into what we call "matter," stable enough to sustain and replicate itself.

"How do fairies and angels fit into all of this?" I prompted Maud, smoothing a silky, rounded beach stone across my lips. The Seven Sisters of the Pleiades were clustered just above us, and the lake, by the pinprick lights of the stars, was sheer, dark satin. An owl hooted, night creatures foraged at the tideline, and the trees breathed in their sleep.

Maud thought for a while and then replied, "It's not easy to talk about subtle realms, because we have no language for it. Since our language has few words to express the invisible, it mostly misses the connections between things, and since we tend to presume that only what can be seen is real, then everything appears to exist in splendid isolation from everything else."

"Frustrating, isn't it?" I offered.

"Rather," she agreed mildly. "So—about fairies—if you accept that nothing is separate from anything else even though it appears that way, then what holds it all together? How do trees and lakes and grass come into being in the first place? I suspect that the energies we call "fairies" and "angels" are the universe's way of constructing the world as we know it. Each "fairy" has a specific frequency, a specific set of instructions and a specific job. We both laughed at the image of busy little fairies flitting invisibly about us.

She whimsically continued. "I suppose it's like building a house: first, there's an architect who designs the house, then carpenters put up a frame, then roofers put on the roof, then come the electricians and plumbers and plasterers...you know.

Everyone has his own expertise." She chuckled and added, "Then you call in the guy who hauls away the debris."

Our laughter mingled with an owl's call, and we hooted softly back. "I truly think that's how the elemental energies work; each corresponds to some aspect of form-building, from rocks and flowers to you and me. Without them, nothing would be here—certainly not ourselves."

Relaxed as we were after a long day of work, the fragrant night worked its magic on us and I could sense on my skin the presence of the birch tree nearby, and the sky. The 'birchy' energy of the tree reached all the way to the lifeblood flowing in my veins, just as the night sky filled my body with air. The fundamental force of the world held me connected to everything around me; the transient form of my human body separated me from the rest—or only seemed to. I breathed in tandem with everything that ever was or would be, and I jumped out of my beach chair.

"I'm going in," I announced impulsively, throwing off my work shirt and stepping out of my shorts. The lake was cold, and when I was in up to my knees I did a belly flop and swam out beyond the raft, treading in icy currents and gazing around me into the darkness. Only a thin sheaf of skin separated my body's water from the lake's, and nothing at all separated me from the immensity surrounding me.

The partnership between matter and spirit—mine and the surrounding lake and sky—was so seamless that there was no real distinction between them. The birch tree, the loons, Maud, and I were all physical forms of beauty informed by universal intelligence—spirit-infused matter.

I couldn't see the fairies, but I could feel them all around me: guiding intelligences envisioning forms, and forces building them; flashing energies flitting in and out of the wind. They were too quick and subtle for me to comprehend, but I could intuit their presences in every leaf and branch, and in the rill of foam at the water's edge. I knew them by their signs.

There is pre-Celtic Creation myth about the *faery* realm—a story of the Goddess Miria, who saw her reflection in space, and falling in love with herself, gave birth to the world.

Flashing her bright song, Miria spun back towards the bright reflection of herself in the curved mirror of space. Like droplets of light were the first beings of the world born.

The elements came first, Air wafting from the sylphs, gnomes setting down the Earth, nymphs flowing into Water and salamanders flaming into Fire.

The faeries turned sunlight into fern and leaf, undines flowed into living streams and the elves led forth the creatures. And every angel was hand-in-hand with a human child.

Miria's song rose to the heights of mist-clothed mountains and spread like mead across islands and lakes. And again she whirled towards the shining on the opposite shore and recognized it as love itself.

As Herself, Miria, who created the world out of Love. It was Love that spun the universe round on its orbit, Love that sustained life and drew us towards each other and towards the world.

In Love was where it all began, and back to Love all would seek to return.

Eleven

Marriage
The First Forty-five Years

I was getting ready for my second season at SYLVAS: summer clothes were washed, boots were broken in, and I had selected the reading matter to bring with me—books about sound healing, mostly. I was hoping to do a lot of singing at the land this year, especially on the ridge where we had found the glittering quartz. I wanted to experiment with sound and healing, and Maud had put the word out for volunteer 'patients.' She wrote to say people were already signing up, with symptoms ranging from migraine headaches and fibroids to chronic back pain and depression. It would be a busy summer.

The book I was reading when Ted got back from a checkup at the doctor's described an interesting collaboration between a musician and a biologist. This musician had sung to uterine-cancer cells in a Petri dish while the biologist had micro-photographed the cells at one-minute intervals for twenty minutes. The photographs showed cancer cells distending until, after twenty minutes of continuous sound, the cell walls dissolved and disintegrated. This was breathtaking news! I stood up to give Ted a kiss, eager to show him these remarkable pictures, but immediately I saw that something was wrong. He sat me back down.

"My PSA count has gone up," he said. "They want to do a biopsy next week, but the doctor says at my age there's little doubt it's prostate cancer. Early stages. The hope is that it's contained—then we decide if we want radiation or surgery. We're talking the next six months, more or less."

I put the book down, my mind blank. Ted and I held each other hard, not speaking, and then he murmured in my ear, "Nothing will happen here until November—you can still go to SYLVAS, you know."

For a few hours I clung to that possibility, but by the next morning I knew I wouldn't go—not even for part of the time. After several long-distance phone calls, I placed my boots ritually in the closet, and Ted and I climbed sadly back into bed. For the first hour we hugged, crying, and then until hunger drove us out, we talked. It was his idea that I not give up my plan to experiment with sound healing.

"Do it here instead," he suggested generously. "I'll be your guinea pig."

Ted normally never would have subjected himself to one of my odd experiments, skeptic that he was, but the situation we were in was hardly normal. The plan we agreed to was that I would sing to him in my studio every evening during the three months before radiation, and continue throughout the six-week radiation period—about five months altogether. He would sit or lie still on a mat, and I would improvise with sound for about an hour, letting the song take its own course. Afterwards, before we spoke, I would take notes on the session in my journal.

Our plan was not so different from what I would have been doing with people at SYLVAS—except it was with my own husband, my skeptical, science-professor husband, and not in the woods. Who would have ever thought of this scenario? Not me. Well, life was forever unpredictable, and despite the fact that I could hardly bear not to be at the lake with Maud for the summer, I decided that it just might be that this case of cancer had come to the right house.

The first day or so I was scared, but after that I was ready to start singing, although it wasn't clear how to begin. *Just start*, I seemed to hear in my head. Ted lay beside me one morning, so intimate after forty years of sharing a bed that we could read each other's moods in a breath. He placed a warm hand reassuringly on my thigh and I reached for it, twining my fingers through his.

"I'm going to sing right into your groin," I declared. "OK?"

"*Oy vey*," was his only comment as I scootched onto my knees, crouched over him, and toned right into his pubis. His pubic hair tickled my chin. Much as I tried to stay focused, my lips tingled with the unaccustomed sensation of sound against flesh, and our position was so outlandish we rocked the bed with our laughter. "Wish I could watch this," he remarked dryly while I sputtered into his belly.

"This is serious!" I scolded, coming up for air. But even then, self-consciously contorted over my husband's body, I could hear in my mind's ear a faint voice saying gently, *No need to do it on the body. Tomorrow, just sing.*

We had met the winter after I returned from Poitiers, on Christmas Eve in fact, at the Midnight Mass at St. Thomas Church in New York City—two Jews in a crowd of well-dressed Episcopalians. He stood out from the others, a tall, full-bearded guy with soulful brown eyes who reminded me of the Jeremiah at Moissac. We were introduced by a mutual friend, and Ted's handshake was immediate and strong. She whispered to me that he was the strong, silent type—a graduate student in biochemistry, a genius.

Dressed in an ill-fitting overcoat and scuffed shoes, he certainly did not strike me as a genius, but when we shook hands something electric passed between us, and the expression in his eyes made my chest ache. When he bent close to speak to me in the crowd, his beard brushed my ear and I could smell the maleness of him. I liked it. We sat next to each other during the choral Mass, arms barely touching, and exchanged stolen glances that were like unspoken conversations. Afterwards, he offered to take me home at three in the morning, and there in his father's battered old Ford, with our breaths misting the windows, we began the conversation that continues to this day.

On our first date, two days after Christmas, we walked across the Brooklyn Bridge and talked about our families. I expressed my ongoing sadness and dismay at the unhappiness in mine, and he spoke sadly but admiringly of his.

Like Danilo, he had been born in Europe just on the eve of the Holocaust, but unlike Danilo, his family had left when they could, making their way to New York to start a new life with their two small boys. For Ted, the hidden corners of his adopted city were an endless source of fascination, and he had been exploring its out-of-the-way treasures since he was old enough to use the subways: hillsides that had the best views of sunsets in every season; skyscrapers where you could take elevators to lookouts from the top floors; and the Hudson River garbage pier where seabirds congregated by the thousands in the mornings and evenings.

On our second date he took me to the garbage pier for a smelly, raucous, and utterly exciting time. He brought binoculars and we bird-watched for hours in the garbage until the sun went down. Afterwards, we walked arm-in-arm along the river and had a supper of duck soup and noodles in Chinatown, telling each other our stories.

We loved the same kind of adventures, it seemed, mostly

excursions into the undersides of the city. He took me to Harlem to hear music, to the Coney Island sideshows, to his lab at Columbia University. When, a week or so later, a blizzard was predicted he proposed we take the ferry to Staten Island and go to the beach. I accepted with delight.

"Cheap dates," said my father, still and always disparagingly off the mark. But I knew quality when I saw it, and I bundled up in many careful layers to go where angels, but not my new boyfriend, Ted, feared to tread.

We took the ferry in a blinding snowstorm, the only people out on the deck, and then we walked the wintertime beach hunched against the blowing snow. He told me that he loved science, with its clearly defined laws and neat proofs that you could count on. I told him I loved to choreograph dances that expressed the soft edges of things where many dimensions merged.

We were mystified by each other, but all the more intrigued. His reserve was a puzzle to me, and my intensity made him watchful. His mind was tough and careful, while I felt for patterns and could not keep track of hard facts. His sense of humor was dry; I had fits of the giggles. Our styles were completely different, but we kept probing each other, each flattered, I think, to be found interesting by the other. We were raw with wonder and ready for loving, so, shivering from more than the cold wind, we admitted we were both weird and kissed madly with frozen lips by the icy surf.

Hand in hand—or rather, mitten in mitten—we trod along the snowy shore and made up futures for ourselves: we would trek in the Arctic; we would both teach in India. We imagined we saw another couple way up the beach and went to meet them, only to discover they were two wooden poles of a jetty. Then we laughed at ourselves until we ached, and hugged for a long time in the driving snow.

Cold to the bones, we took the ferry back to Manhattan and

caught an uptown subway train to his furnished room near Columbia. Shy at first, we shed our wet clothes and draped them over the radiators to dry. Both of us were rosy with cold from the tips of our toes to the hair on our heads, and we gazed at each other's bodies in awe, embracing passionately before falling naked into his sagging bed and, in the time-honored manner of our species, generating enough body heat to raise the temperature of the whole room.

After finally accepting that I would be at home with Ted and not at SYLVAS with Maud, I gradually found my way into the healing process. I found that doing a dance warm-up for twenty minutes before Ted came into the studio helped me concentrate more deeply. Once he was settled across the room, I visualized a bell-shaped corona of light around me and imagined it spreading to include him. Then I invited in the whole universe and listened for the guiding voices I was becoming familiar with.

"Just sing," the voices kept saying. Day by day I gradually dropped my agendas for Ted's cancer and even my prayers—and just sang. The more simply the song came through me, the more powerful the information I received, and it seemed that Ted's illness was the least of what it was about.

During those first days, the song was a repeated primal chant. One tone, like the bass voice in an invisible chorus, sang itself over and over, a grounding beacon. I heard it as 'Ted's tone.' His parents appeared as intervals to his note, sometimes harmonious and sometimes not, and our children were there as grace notes. With each new song, more people from his family emerged: his grandparents and great-grandparents; relatives killed in pogroms and death camps; suicides and stillborn babies. Then my family arrived. Ancestor by ancestor these people came through the barriers of time to assist us, and welcoming them, I listened for their notes and sang them into our clan circle.

Feeling Ted's body through my own, I understood that his condition reflected the imbalance in our extended family system, and that my task was to try and restore harmony. High notes and low, slow and fast, I smoothed out the knots with sound, scouring our hurts with minute shifts of pitch up and down the scale.

Ted, by this time, often lay flat on the mat, sometimes snoring. I took his sleep as a good sign, and kept singing as presences unknown to me emerged from the song and joined the tribe of watchers—people from my bloodline and his, all singing soundlessly along with me.

We were married quietly in my parents' house the following spring, keeping the wedding very small so as to minimize the predictable family mishaps, but the day turned out to be a nightmare all the same. My mother and sister had a yelling fight, my brother hid out in the garage with his guitar, and my father held an unlit cigarette in his fingers throughout the ceremony. Ted stayed by my side, knowing not to underestimate my family's predilection for mischief, but even that did not help.

Just after the ceremony, a neighbor's child rang the doorbell and I opened the door, to my father's strong objection. When I invited her in, he slapped me across the face. I turned to stone, and Ted leapt between us, remaining there until escape was possible. When we could, we fled. We spent our wedding night pressed together on the sagging mattress in his room, with me sobbing inconsolably and wondering if, with my background, I could ever actually be somebody's wife.

Within six months we had left for a year in Oxford, to a drafty flat at the edge of the old Port Meadow, where the winter winds blew in through every crack in the walls. Being young and wildly in love, we didn't mind that the warmest place in the house was the bed, and we snuggled there tightly in the pair-bond for hours on end, telling each other the adventures of our day. And we giggled over the antics of the Irish couple downstairs, who squabbled continuously, he often retiring to the *loo* to sing Irish ballads at the top of his voice.

Ted was in Oxford for a postdoctoral year, and I had a part-time job at the Bodleian Library helping to catalogue the illuminations in their twelfth-century manuscript collection, but already my interest in the Middle Ages was waning. What intrigued me more were the lectures on Jewish history given by the great scholar Cecil Roth. Every Tuesday morning I took off with Ted by bike through misty rain, he to his lab and me to Magdalen College to hear about my roots. Later in the day I would arrive back at the flat pale and shaken by what I had learned, and I would wait for Ted to come home to hot soup in our cozy kitchen and later to our warm bed, where we would curl into the refuge of each other's arms.

During Christmas break we took a trip to Germany—to Aachen, where Ted had been born. Crossing the border during this trip was easy compared to when Ted, as a baby, had crossed it thirty years earlier. Then, his mother with the two babies had gotten safely to Holland, but his father had been apprehended and thrown into jail on the German side. Only the intervention and bribes of well-to-do relatives in England had sprung his father and reunited the family in London—from where, after two years, they emigrated to America. Now, the fateful border was simply another stop on the train. Only the presence of young men with fresh dueling scars on their cheeks—a badge of honor for Nazi youth during the war—made us wonder why we thought it was safe to come back.

For three days we walked the streets his ancestors had called "home," buying fruit at the market his mother had shopped in, peering at the house in which he had been born, and visiting his great-grandparents' graves in the Jewish cemetery on the outskirts of town. Until we went to the new synagogue, the only person who spoke to us was the keeper of the cemetery, who was touchingly protective of the souls in his care and proud of us outlanders who had come to visit their kin.

The synagogue—massive, opulent, and empty—had a fresh *swastika* scratched onto its entry doors, and corrugated iron shutters ready to clamp into place at a moment's notice. We were greeted by the president of the nonexistent congregation, a Polish Jew lured back by the promise of reparation money, who immediately mistook me for an Arab and asked us to leave.

That night I dreamed of being stalked by Nazi soldiers who chased me from one hiding place to another before they trapped me in a cellar. Shivering convulsively, I woke in the darkness and clung to Ted, begging him to take me away from this terrible place. We held each other hard through a sleepless night, and at dawn we caught the first train out to Paris.

The song came through as a lament in minor mode, all sobs and tremolos. The images were of Ted's parents escaping Germany, leaving their homeland, and of Ted, the baby, losing the land of his birth—losing land itself, the earth. The connection between his body and the body of the natural world was broken, as it was for all Jews who were chased from their ancestral lands. There was a tear in the fabric of his being, and my lament mended the tear with arpeggios, bridging the gap with sound.

Continuance. The notes flowed in quick chromatics, halftone after halftone. If a person has not bonded with the earth, how can he recognize that all things are intrinsically connected? My body pulsed with heat, and my hands rose into the air by themselves.

"Transmit the energy," I heard in my mind's ear. "Offer it to him and to everyone." I felt my body become like the wick of a candle, aligned and aflame, and my whole intention became a prayer for all of us.

"The song tonight had to do with fractals," I told Ted at dinner a week later, after that evening's session in the studio.

"Sounded like a Souza march," he commented, helping himself to a baked potato and spreading it open. I passed him the butter.

"That's what it felt like—boom, boom, boom—but then the beats started to fill in. Did you notice? First there were eighth notes, then sixteenths, and then the rhythm got too fast for me to sing. And then what I saw was a sea of energy with patterns in it. Like there was nothing solid in the world, only moving energy."

I expected him to be intrigued by this, but he had no response. A bit deflated, I went on,

"So what I'm getting is that I shouldn't just address the cancer cells; I need to sing to the pattern of the whole energy field." He helped himself to more salad, silent. "Don't you have anything to say?" I pleaded in frustration. He sighed.

"I don't know what to do with what you're saying," he confessed, putting his fork down. "You're using scientific language, but it's not Science." I could just about hear the capital *S* in Science.

"So what if it's not Science! Anyhow, who says you guys are the only ones who can study the world? I thought science was about having an open mind and asking pertinent questions about reality!" I was close to tears, and again wondering what could be so hard for him to understand.

"Well, I liked it," he admitted, placating me. "I feel much calmer now." His statement effectively ended the discussion. We ate the rest of our meal in silence.

In fact, his health had improved since we had begun the singing sessions. He was feeling more relaxed and some of the symptoms that had sent him to the doctor in the first place were gone. Encouraged, I had begun to fantasize quietly about the paper we would write together for a scientific journal on the meeting of science and sound healing in a case of prostate cancer. In my dream of dreams he would avoid the radiation treatment altogether.

So when the numbers from his next PSA test had dropped eight points and were, in fact, fairly close to normal, I was jubilant.

"I knew it! I knew it!" I cried, dancing around him and flinging my arms around his neck. "Did you tell the doctor about the singing?"

"No," he admitted. I was stung to the quick.

"You didn't?" I tried to keep the whine out of my voice. "Whyever not?"

He shrugged and fingered the newspaper on the table. Finally, he mumbled, "He's a surgeon, for God's sake."

"You mean you were embarrassed to tell it to another scientist," I spat out bitterly, "even though you're clearly feeling better than you have in months." I was trembling, and did *not* add, "and you feel fine enough to go happily off to work every day while I sit around the house twiddling my thumbs instead of being out in the Adirondack woods." As was his way, he said nothing.

"Maybe the surgeon would like to be informed that there are alternatives out there," I persisted. "Maybe he'd be open to what I was doing. Maybe…" I stalked out of the room with clenched fists, my heart tight in my throat. But the next day, hardly expecting him to come, I did the song anyway, too angry not to. He came, though, quietly sitting cross-legged in his place across the room. I sang an angry shout-song in which my voice banged against brick walls, like the walls of dark apartment houses in Brooklyn's Brighton Beach, where generations of Russian Jewish immigrants have lived since my childhood. I stamped and yelled and he sat through the whole song in calm meditation.

Beyond the buildings was the Atlantic Ocean, vast and deep. Above the buildings was sky, where seagulls flew. I sang darting consonants at those walls—Ds and Ts and Ps—arrows aimed at the bricks. Like Joshua, I sang at my own battle of Jericho until the walls came tumbling down. Brick by brick, I freed the refugees from their fortress until they could see the sky and sea and sand. Freed us from narrow, dark alleys blocking our sight, to the vast panorama of the world with all its winds and chances. Not rigid—flexible. Not confining—free.

We came home from Oxford by way of Poitiers, where I showed off my new husband—and pregnant belly—to the d'Alvernys and all my friends at the Centre except for Martine, who was no longer there. All the d'Alvernys were impressed that I had married a doctor of science from Oxford, and with his height and unusual looks, my Ted was a hit with everyone.

From there, we went home to New York for a week to gather up our things and say our farewells before we drove across the country to start a new life in California. That whole week in New York, my father stalked us.

"I'm coming out to the coast to be with you in the delivery room," he told me several times. We were mystified until he added, "so someone can get you a specialist if something goes wrong."

"I can do that," Ted informed my father in a quiet voice while I hid behind him. I was glad not to be the one to have to say it, but also doubly embarrassed both by the depth of my father's insult, and by the interference Ted had to run between my father and me. It felt like I had two fathers.

At the birth of our son five months later, however, I was glad to let Ted take over completely, because on the day Claude was born, Dad had a massive coronary. When we phoned home with the news of Claude's arrival, we learned that he was in intensive care.

Again, Dad stole the show. I went numb and hardly noticed when they took the baby out of my arms. Ted moved into action on all fronts, notifying everyone of everything quietly and effectively and taking care of me in between. If ever I needed a good, responsible father it was then. I accepted Ted's help despite myself.

The songs, these days, were coming out soft and lyrical, like lullabies. I got images of lost children—frightened children. They whimpered alone in desolate places and I sang to them, sang to Ted, the child in arms escaping in the night to strangeness and danger.

I saw him at two years old, afraid and uncomprehending. I saw him stranded in Holland with his mother and infant brother while their father, passports in pocket, got caught on the wrong side of the border and was taken away. I felt her terror as she waited for him at midnight on a street corner with nothing to her name but two sleeping babies.

The frightened children of every era, every cruelty, marched through my mind and I sang them comfort. Generations of boys followed their fathers to war, their young hearts closing before it could hurt too much. I saw it.

I saw Ted's father, good-natured but headstrong, crossing back into Germany to smuggle money out when just getting out wasn't good enough. I saw my father and his father before him, gentle at the core, but ashamed not to appear like "real" men. I saw the lineage of grandfathers, once boys, learning to be tough and passing down to their sons the legacy of emotional passivity. And I saw it manipulate the women into being overemotional to make up for the men.

My songs got stronger and took on rhythm. Ancestors came in to help: my mother's brother, killed in the war; my crippled grandmother; my fierce Russian great-aunt. Together we pulled on all the stuck men in the family—fathers, husbands, sons—urging them to wake up and grow. There was a family fabric to weave here, and emotional deadness was a weak strand. This healing was about more than cancer, it was about a close-knit weave of whole cloth, a family of men and women and children in balance.

My father had two more heart attacks, but he hung on for another five years. He wasn't yet fifty, after all. So he got to witness, from a safe distance, the births of our next two children, Eva and Abram.

For Eva's birth we had asked my mother to come and help, but she panicked when I went into labor, so we did not ask her again. For Abram's birth my sister Simone, who now lived nearby, offered to be on hand, so I spent my last few weeks of pregnancy calmly at home, preparing the house for the new baby and cooking rose petals from the neighbor's garden into rose-petal jam.

All was well except that Abram, characteristically, dawdled for two extra weeks before he made his appearance, and then without warning he gave us about twenty minutes to get to the hospital. Our bachelor friend Joe was at the house for dinner, and Simone wasn't home when we called her with the frantic news, so we left Joe in charge of two babies at bedtime while we dashed off to give birth to our third child.

Ted held my hand tight and ran to keep up with the gurney as I was rushed into the delivery room. I was already pushing when the doctor arrived to receive my precipitous baby. The birth seemed normal until the last minute, when it became clear that there was a knot in the umbilical cord; suddenly everyone at the working end got very busy.

"He did *loop-de-loops* in utero," the doctor told us once the baby was born. He carefully kept the knot from tightening. "You've got a gymnast here." Bloody legs spread wide, I gaped.

"Abram," Ted and I said in unison when we saw him, arms and legs flailing as if he couldn't wait to take off running, and a lovely, lopsided grin on his tiny face. We gazed with amazement at our new son, who already had quite a mind of his own, and when Ted cut the cord separating him, at last, from my body, we both cried. Less than an hour had gone by since we left the house.

Simone answered when we phoned with the news, in stitches.

Bedlam had indeed ensued there, but the kids were fine and Joe had survived his ordeal. He had finally reached her and she'd come right over, but while they were talking on the porch a wind had blown the door shut, locking them out and the children in. So Joe had hoisted her head-first through an open window, where she'd landed on a box of wooden blocks, much to the shrieking delight of the kids, whose aunt always did funny things to amuse them.

"So we're fine," she said after we told her all the details of Abram's birth, "but I've got one question: what the Hell do you want me to do with this pot of gloppy rose petals?"

We served the first jar of rose-petal jam at Abram's circumcision, and we opened the last one several years later in honor of Halloween.

We had lined three spooky jack-o'-lanterns up on the porch, and five of us sat around the kitchen table eating 'monster stew' and mashed pumpkin (called by Abram, "smashed pumpkins") before the kids went out trick-or-treating. They twittered like wrens in a birdbath, all excited about dressing up in their costumes and getting out there on the streets.

Claude was going as Batman in a black cape (*dunna dunna Batman!*), and Eva was an Indian princess in a *sari* with a *bindi* on her forehead and bangles on her wrists. Abram, the iconoclast of the family, was going as a haystack. With a grass hula skirt tied at the neck, he looked, indeed, like a grinning pile of hay. When they were all in their getups, eyes made up to resemble anything other than little kids, and shopping bags over their arms, we opened the door and said, "Go!"

All the parents on the block were out on their porches, candy at the ready, exclaiming with wonder as each pirate and princess clumped up their steps, each keeping one eye out for the progress of their own around the neighborhood. Ted distributed ropes of red licorice in a gorilla mask and talked politics with Dick next door, while Adrienne and Marty, across the street, lured the kids into the shadows of their porch where bowls of gummy bears, jelly beans, and…*raw fish*…awaited them. Each child in turn touched the fish and screeched before they ran away with the other loot, and we all spent the evening in hysterics.

This was our life. The children were growing up, and we along with them. Parenting took effort, especially when the children were little and life was a round of diapers and feedings, but we were in love with these little people who were in our care. Laughter rang in our house. We did the best we could as parents, and we tried to do better than our parents had done—but we also understood, by this time, that the job was tougher than it looked. We were luckier than they had been for a number of reasons, not the least of which was that we had each other and our love was true.

I was not in a good mood when I did that night's song. My mother had just phoned with an unhappy demand. Since my father's death, she had lived in California and was, more than ever, anxious and hard to please. The song reflected my disheartened state, and I saw images of dirty train windows, like lenses, and a sullied countryside fleeting past. I had to clean the windows if I wanted to see out, but I was incapable of it. The pathos of her condition had a power over me I could not resist and the song came out muddy, like gray water slopped over a filthy floor.

Then a tortured passage of wild sound emerged from my mouth and I stomped around the room hollering. Again I saw the escape from the Nazis and the helplessness and terror in Ted's mother. The baby in her arms was precisely the age when a child develops trust, and I saw through Ted's soul the betrayal of a mother who had no choice. I saw it imprint on his cells, on hers, tangling them together in a fear that neither had outlived. I began to groan in pitch, keening out a song that had no resolution.

Then the image of my own mother appeared, and then her crippled mother in a wheelchair at an institution for incurables, and then her mother being raped in a Russian pogrom. I was next in our line, daughter and then mother in turn. I sang sobbing microtones over and over, seeing all of us, myself included, passing on our disempowerment to our daughters. I began to feel compassion, rather than helpless pathos, for my own mother. I begged forgiveness from her and my daughter Eva, and the song lifted into the higher registers, ringing off the walls of the studio.

I cleared the air with clicks and shushes and felt it gradually reorganize from helpless chaos to a fine, complex pattern. I sang for every mother in the world, and everyone born of a mother, and every mother who had ever unwittingly betrayed the child she loved. And when the last tones faded into whispers, I brought my hands together and bowed deeply to Ted.

From his cushion across the room, having no idea what had just taken place, he bowed back to me. I went to him, sank down onto the mat, and curled, sobbing, into his lap.

My father went into congestive heart failure the year my brother Leonard started college in California. In fact, it was on the children's first day of school that we got the call to come home fast. Dad's negative timing was impeccable. We left that night, airline strike and all, distributing our three children to kind neighbors and sitting it out in the mobbed airport until we boarded a two-propeller plane. Ted, Lenny, Simone, and I got to New York in just under ten hours.

From outside the hospital room we heard my father's last cries. He was pleading with the code-blue team not to let him die, a sound none of us will ever forget. But we were already in shock by that time, because when we first arrived Dad had spoken his last words to us, which were considerably less than blessings, and Lenny had run out the door before he heard the entirety of his legacy. Only Death itself could stop my father.

By the time the medical team walked out of the room, faces turned away from us, Ted had searched every floor of the hospital and returned empty-handed, unable to find my brother.

Two decades later, when Simone was dying of pancreatic cancer, the same group of us—which now included Claude, Eva, and Abram—kept a similar vigil. She chose to die at home and she chose to refuse mother admittance to her sickbed. I understood her choice, but her decision made it torture for the rest of us.

Mother stood on Simone's porch and banged away at the door. Time and again Ted took her away and told her gently why it was better for Simone that she not go in. Eva tried. Claude tried. Abram tried. I did not try.

Time and again she sat and listened, and then came right back to pound helplessly on the door. I begged my sister to let her in just once, and finally Simone reneged, but then asked her neighbors, and their dogs, to be there at the same time. The mayhem in that house would have been funny had it not been tragic.

I was so unhinged by it all that while driving home, I ran over a woman on a bicycle. She survived only because she was wearing a hard helmet. As for me, I have never gotten over any of it.

I was singing my heart out these days, and receiving teachings, it seemed, from an invisible teacher. One day I learned about multidimensionality, and the next day I saw how everything in the world was ultimately energy. I learned about DNA being a step-down transformer of universal energy, and the significance of spirals. I longed to share this knowledge with Ted, but it was so counter to his notions of science that I knew we'd end up fighting. I was in a state of grace and would not sully it with arguments.

One evening, after I had received images of triangular lattices and nodal points of energy, I stood for a long time with my hands outstretched, ecstatic. The universe seemed to beat right through me, every subtle pulse like a dance of elemental intelligence.

I was shaking with the power of it all, and when Ted mis-read my state and scrambled to his feet to anxiously help me, I blew like an erupting volcano. Exploding into magma and fire, I threw myself out of the studio and up the stairs to our room. I was a million shards of lava sobbing helplessly into the pillow, my heart shattered in an unreasonable disappointment I could not have begun to name.

How could he be so thick? I didn't need rescue, I needed shared experience! Ted and I didn't speak the same language, and we never would! How could I stand another minute of not being able to share this wondrousness?

The eruption lasted for about an hour and then, somewhat calmed, I wrote out my notes for the song—so dry after the glory of the actual cascade—and started down the stairs to prepare dinner. Ted was on the phone with his brother—another scientist—and I overheard their conversation about Ted's treatment regime.

"I'll be going into radiation in about two weeks," he said, "and meanwhile I'm doing the hormone therapy and saw palmetto."

And? I waited for mention of the singing. Not even a hint. The volcano boiled dangerously again and the magma rose to my ears as, careless, I slipped on the next step and went down, hearing something tear. I lay on the stairs groaning, hot ashes in my eyes and my mouth and my head, and in my pelvis a fire that would take weeks to put out.

But I could be as stubborn as he; the next day I sang lying down in bed. He could be there if he wanted to be, otherwise I'd just as soon do it alone. I knew I was onto something remarkable, even if he did not. This wasn't for him anymore, it was for me. Hot tears crowded my throat, and I turned my head when he entered the bedroom and I sang to the opposite wall.

But the song came out choked and mournful. It held resentment and helpless love, and I broke down in tears more than once. Ted sat by the side of the bed unmoving, his head down and his hand on the quilt alongside *my knee. When the song was finished, I jerked my leg away from his hand, gasping at the flare of pain in my pelvis. He waited, silent. For a while our tense in-and-out breaths were the only sounds in the room.*

Then he said quietly, "It's my cancer, you know." For a moment I was too stunned to respond, but then I crumpled and he, careful not to touch my aching back, lay down beside me and waited until, with a great sobbing, I let him gather me tenderly into his embrace.

Each of us siblings had been interested in the distant past—my brother Leonard in ancient Egypt, myself in the megaliths, and Simone in the Anasazi ruins of the Southwest. So as she and I left the hospital with the prognosis that she had up to three months to live, she lit a cigarette, banged me in the arm, and declared, "Now I can tell you where you get to spread my ashes." I was struck dumb. "There's this *mesa* in Chaco Canyon I've always been too chicken to climb. You get to take me up there!" She was almost gleeful.

Little did either of us know at the time that during the week she died, Navajo elders would declare their lands off limits to white man's ashes. By that time, of course, it would be too late to consult with her about it, and the whole issue became a family debate.

In the end Eva, who was adamant about respecting her aunt's last wishes, carried Simone's ashes onto the mesa in a backpack in summer, and in the winter, on Simone's birthday, Ted and I made the trip without ashes to New Mexico to do our own ritual.

Except for the Anasazi ghosts, the snowy canyon was deserted. Even Ted balked when the trail up the steep-sided *mesa* was blocked by a series of snow-covered boulders jutting out over thin air, and I imagined Simone getting to this point more than once before turning back. For me, that was not an option. Ted held out his arms to catch me if I fell, and after I had safely negotiated the heart-stopping boulders, he went back to wait for me in the ruins below. We agreed to meet there in two hours, checked our watches, and waved good-bye as I continued up the trail to the top of the *mesa*.

"I'm here," I announced to my sister when I climbed out on top, gazing around at a huge sky and tablelands stretching, white with snow, farther than my eyes could see. A raven rode the wind and swooped down to perch on a boulder by my side, eyeing me with curiosity. My boots left the only footprints in the snow.

But the ghosts were there—I could feel them—and my sister Simone was amongst them. They followed me around the rim toward the high ruins. The silence was like a living thing surrounding me and the sky pressed down hard. I spoke to her out loud the whole time.

"I wish we could have done this together," I told her. "I'd always looked forward to how it could be for us after Mother was gone. Did you take off first to get her off your back?" A wind picked up and spun a flurry of snow into a mini white tornado in front of me. "Can't blame you," I muttered, entering the ruin. Framed by a doorway into what had once been a round *kiva* open to the sky, I searched the ground for her ash and the stone walls for her shadow.

"Lenny's going to take care of mother," I informed her. "He says it's his turn now, God bless him. There's a nice residential place in his town for dotty old folks…" My croak of a laugh echoed off the walls and spiraled out into space before it turned into quiet weeping.

"Oh, Simone," I choked out. "I'm so sorry. I would give anything to have you back, but who could blame you for leaving? Are the Navajo ghosts being nice to you? Have you made friends?"

The profound silence was my answer, and I hunkered down against the wall to gaze at the world she so loved. It let itself be seen, hiding nothing from my sight. I knew now why she wished to rest here.

From my backpack I took out my offerings one by one: a dry sage bundle, a spirit stone she had once taken from this very canyon and asked to have brought back, and a small canvas mat she had painted in the Hopi style. I lay out the mat and lit the sage, smudging the *kiva* in all the directions and offering prayers to the spirits there. And then I sang.

The chant rose up from my belly, and I stamped out its rhythm in the snow, puffs of steam coming from my lips.

"O hey-a hai-a! O hey-a hai-a!" I had no idea where this was coming from, but I sang it with all the breath I had. Throwing my head back, I shouted into the wind as the ravens circled above. *"O hey-a hai-a!"* I sang, tromping the snow and frozen grass in the *kiva*, singing for her and for myself and for our parents.

I sang until it was time to go back down into the canyon to meet up with Ted, having trampled the pristine snow within the *kiva* into a mess of footprints. But that was Simone's style; I couldn't imagine she would mind. As for the spirits here, I just hoped they welcomed her as one of their own.

As I took the trail down, I caught a glimpse of Ted waiting below at the trailhead, but when I reached the canyon floor he wasn't there. I meandered the perimeter of the lower ruins, assuming he had just taken a stroll. I still couldn't find him. I called as loudly as I could. No answer.

I circled the ruin again, calling, and checked and rechecked my watch. A half hour, then an hour went by. Ted was the most responsible person I knew; he would never be late for this appointment. The sun was sinking to dusk—soon the canyon would be in darkness and I was alone in this place, me and the ghosts.

"Simone, help!" I called silently.

Something had happened to Ted in the twenty minutes since I'd last seen him waiting for me right here. Perhaps he'd been kidnapped. Perhaps he'd been bitten by a poisonous snake…in the snow? I called again. No response.

I circled the ruin one more time, trying not to panic. The Rangers' Station at the head of the canyon was several miles away, and even though our car was still parked by the ruins, Ted had the keys. I would have to walk out and get help before nightfall. Already the canyon was in shadows, and cold. Shaking, I started running toward the road and there he was, as if he had materialized out of thin air.

"Where *were* you?" we both cried at once, clinging to each other with relief. "I saw you coming down the trail, and then you disappeared!" he accused.

"I saw you from up on the trail, and then when I got down you weren't here!" I argued.

"But I was!" he insisted.

"I looked everywhere," I insisted back. "I called, I walked around and around, and I waited where we agreed to meet!"

"I did too, and I didn't see you..."

For the next twenty-four hours we went over and over every detail of our story. What had happened was impossible, it seemed. I suggested that maybe we had entered an interdimensional time warp, or some subtle wrinkle of space known to the Anasazi but not to us.

Ted wouldn't buy that. He figured that since we had both circled the ruin several times, we had somehow managed to always keep the walls between us. "But I kept calling you!" I protested.

"Well, it was windy and I didn't hear you." We were at an impasse.

No doubt Simone was watching the whole comedy, shaking her head and rolling her eyes—not for the first time—at her sister and brother-in-law's ongoing, unresolved debate.

The song came through strong and throaty, like a Native American chant, and Ted visibly relaxed as the repetitive chant became hypnotic. I heard in my mind's ear, "Let the song sing through you."

I dropped my effort level in half, as Katsu had once taught me to do, and slipped into a state in which the song seemed to be coming from the whole room, not from me.

My voice reached higher than I thought I could sing and so low the sound was a growl. I could all but feel the cancer cells popping like champagne bubbles in Ted's body and dissolving harmlessly into the air of the room. When the song was over, I stood with my arms out for what must have been ten minutes until Ted opened his eyes and looked at me with a sweet smile on his face.

We bowed. Could it be that he didn't need radiation after all? Would he ever agree to that possibility? Of course not. As he had said, it was his cancer. But what if...? I went over to the mat and, kneeling, eased him down and lay beside him.

After three months of singing solo improvisations, I longed for harmony. It was mostly a lonely time altogether—the children far away and busy with their lives, our brothers on the other coast, and Simone gone. We chose to keep Ted's condition a secret from both our ailing mothers and so I was mostly alone with it all day, every day.

Ted was feeling fine, better than ever, and he went off every morning to the university. I didn't see him again until dinnertime. With 'cancer' in our midst, I had little impetus to return to the work I had put aside in anticipation of three months away, so I didn't have enough to do and I felt bored and isolated.

There were days when I stared at the four walls, restless and weary, waiting for Ted to come home. I would daydream about Maud and the Adirondacks, about leading a nature walk up to the ridge, or clearing a trail around the bog. The woods at sunset would be lit by that special golden light through green foliage, and the lake would feel like liquid silk after a day of work...

Why not fly back there for the last few weeks of the season?

Just until radiation started. Mentally I located my boots, raingear, and backpack. The leaves would just be starting to turn. And then I leaned back against the couch knowing that my place was right here, whether I liked it or not.

My friend Kaila struck a chord in the violin's low register and I followed her there with my voice. Dark tones emerged from both of us, slow and sustained, and their vibrations pounded in the air. I got images of bones and stones and earth, primal and dense.

We kept the song simple, listening for the beats between us. Overtones—like high, ringing whistles—hovered in the air as Kaila drew her bow long and low across the strings. I teased her notes with a run of vocal overtones that struck the walls and bounced back at us. I felt them as squiggly spirals spinning invisibly in my body.

"The sounds within the sounds can be made audible," I heard in my mind's ear. Kaila rose into her higher register and I grounded her, keeping my voice low and feeling it vibrate against the bones in my chest. "Use the cancer," came as a surprise. "Use it to provoke the spirit to speak through the physical body. Awareness can emerge through the experience of illness."

When the song was over, the whole room throbbed. Kaila was flushed, and Ted had fallen asleep sitting up. I felt like a glowing lightbulb.

"You guys are fantastic!" he exclaimed later, making room for us on the mat. "You could record that." We laughed, but it was also clear to me that from now on I should do this work with other people as much as possible.

Claudia, a friend from the Pacific Northwest, was my favorite singing partner in the world. I called her one evening and asked if she might be willing to come down for a few days and sing with me for Ted. We had helped each other through hard times before, and if ever I needed her, it was now.

I met her at the airport and we started warming up right there in the car. We were on the same musical beam, Claudia and I, and our song that night beat together like a heartbeat—lub dub, lub dub—grounding us in a basic rhythm.

"The pattern is fundamental," I heard as we sang. Ted relaxed into the music, nodding in time. "You are in league with genes and stars. Resonate to the same tune."

We did. Making minimal shifts of pitch and color, we made a kind of ancient music. It was magic, each phrase becoming the next without effort, and as always, the music left us breathless.

"Restore the pattern," I heard, "and you will find your true relation to one another." When the song ended we didn't want it to stop, and when Ted looked up he gazed at us with respect.

While Claudia was with us, the messages came thick and fast. We saw how the whirling spirals in our bodies reflected galaxies in space, and how our DNA connected them. We sang ourselves into astonishment, and we sang Ted into profound sleep. We talked late into the night about a world in which people would sing to each other as medicine.

Each time we sang, our song carried a variation of the same message: match the patterns of nature, feel for the beat of the world, get subtle enough to recognize what is universal and what is uniquely yours. The insights came through whispered elisions, tricky articulated rhythms, swift melodic turns. Our music, we thought, was stunning, and it awed us by the news it carried.

I went with Ted to his introductory radiation appointment, but after that he wanted to go alone. Each morning, five days a week, he drove an hour to a clinic in a nearby city, got zapped, and went directly from there to his laboratory at the university. Every evening I sang for him, and every evening he showed up for the song. When I mentioned to his doctor, during the introductory visit, that I was practicing healing sound every night, all I got was a bland, professional smile.

At the clinic a technician showed us around who told us that by the second week Ted would probably be feeling worn out, that he would become nauseated a few weeks into the procedure, and that after a while he would need to be driven to and from his appointments.

"We're unfortunately going to take out your good flora and fauna along with the bad," he explained. "If you can stomach it, eat yogurt."

By the time we left the sterile clinic that day, with its lethal life-saving machines, I was the one who felt nauseous.

On the weekend before the first radiation treatment, Ted and I took a pause. We drew a line in the sand between our lives thus far and everything that would come next; all debates were over. Calm and tender with each other, we had long breakfasts, took walks by the bay, and talked quietly. For two days we neither worked nor sang, and when Monday came, we were ready. On Monday night, after the first radiation treatment, I sang to him again.

The song came out like a clarion trumpet call, and I invited all my guides in to help. Again I was seeing Hitler's Germany—a time of steaming embers, the air smoking and still. And then I saw, through the haze, movement in another place, a different time. The culture, recognizable but transformed into a more durable version of itself, reappeared. As when a torn fabric is mended, the new texture was stronger, more interesting, as Ted would be after radiation. The fabric would be nubbly with scars, but altogether tougher—tested, its weave bright.

"Just sing," the voices kept saying. "Softly now. No trying. No ideas, no agenda." The tension in my shoulders let go and my throat opened. The sound flowed like water and I entered a half sleep, like singing in a dream.

During the next few weeks the songs emerged with sensations and pitches which I sang without vibrato. One night the images were all of water: surf and swirling streams and steaming kettles; another night I tasted metal on my tongue and felt the cling of metal filings to a magnet. Days later I had the sense of a white-sand beach littered with the bleaching bones of seabirds.

Water. Hemoglobin. Calcium. I was singing back into Ted the frequencies of the elements being leached from his body by the radiation! My voice had found the correct pitches without my knowing it. In awe, I covered my face with my hands and cried.

The next few days were hard on both of us. Ted's mood was foul, and therefore so was mine. He was scared. One night, I was trying too hard to reach him and he was resisting with all his might. I again saw the traumatized child on a street corner in Holland in the middle of the night. I saw the clenching of two-year-old muscles against an unimaginable fear, and I felt the radiation trigger the old terror, saw the muscles of his soul go into spasm. He was holding on for dear life.

I was no match for that level of fear. The sounds died in my throat and I just stood there, impotent. I didn't know what to do, so I did nothing. Feeling helpless, I just went through the motions. Ted loyally came to the studio even so, but I wondered if we shouldn't just give up. Then I remembered the quartz stone from SYLVAS and my dream of singing to the waves. I took it in hand and immediately heard, "Sing through the stone. Remember, it augments your intentions, good or bad, so be impeccable."

Ted was halfway through the course of radiation and, as the doctor had suggested, I began preparing blander meals for him— but he asked for more interesting fare. I offered to drive him to his appointments, but he insisted on driving himself. I looked for signs of fatigue, nausea, and the skin rashes we had been told to expect, but he had none of these; in fact, he looked as fit as he ever had. When I commented on this, he admitted that even the doctor found his condition remarkable.

"He says this sometimes happens, but not often," Ted told me.

"Did you mention the singing?" I murmured, pretending to be interested in the tassels at the edge of the tablecloth.

"No, I didn't," he replied, industriously scraping with his thumbnail at a dribble of candle wax.

Trace elements came through as delicate filigreed silver, and I trilled them in at the top of my voice. Globules of melody outlined the kidneys and adrenals and rounded bubbles of sound gurgled in to stabilize Ted's water balance. Holes in the web of connective tissue were fixed with clicks and whispers, like the sounds of knitting needles, purling one and casting off two.

And then, the day after the less-focused radiation was over, a skittery riff came out with notes all over the place, like a jumble of bugs in high spirits. They jostled each other, scrambling back into the intestines and rectum and bladder. Of course! The healthy flora and fauna, having been rudely decamped by the radiation, were going back home!

Through it all, a deeper healing was happening, and it was not about cancer. We were both being transformed by Ted's illness in ways still too subtle to name. It was as if we were being knit more closely together—bodies, minds, and souls.

Images appeared of the natural world: rippled sand at the edge of the sea, ponds reflecting moonlight, raging solar storms. And we were part of it somehow. In our trials together and the commitment of our bond we were step-down transformers, vehicles for the powers of the world. This cancer had not been for nothing.

Each night after I sang I bowed deeply to Ted, and each night he bowed deeply back to me.

It was Ted's last graduation after forty years as a professor on the campus, and I sat in the front of the hall to witness this passage.

Cancer had been, for many years, a concern of the past; Ted was well and strong and at his two-year checkup the doctor had given him a clean bill of health.

I stood as the strains of Pomp and Circumstance filled the auditorium, and I turned to watch the long procession of robed, jubilant students file in, with the tassels on their mortarboards swinging jauntily. The faculty in their colorful robes and hoods marched down the aisle more sedately, and Ted, as retiring senior professor, led the procession—a distinguished bearded scholar tall and erect, his gaze steady and warm. My man.

My throat crowded with tears right away to see him at the head of his community of students and faculty, which seemed to comprise everyone in the world: Africans and Slavs, Iraqis and Mexicans and Japanese. Burmese, Chinese, and Brazilian students waved to their families, who filled the hall in *saris* and turbans, headscarves and *kimonos*, sitting alongside each other and bursting with pride for their own. This was Ted's world.

One by one the professors handed out diplomas, and after the last diploma had been received the Dean asked Ted to come forward. Looking for all the world like a handsome elder statesman, Ted stepped to the front of the stage and faced his audience. He was lauded for his years of service and the quality of his work, and for how deeply he had affected generations of students with his clear, steady presence and his calm wisdom. Then he was presented with the university's highest award bestowed to a member of its faculty and the crowd rose to its feet, applauding. He accepted the award graciously, and then characteristically stopped to read it. Everybody laughed. I laughed along with them, and my hands kept on clapping until they were the last ones to finally stop.

The national election went badly that year—worse than anyone had anticipated—and armed with a new set of fears, Ted and I returned to the studio to continue our sessions. We didn't know what else to do. I sang while Ted meditated on the mat, and we listened for any guidance that might come through.

The songs were choppy and atonal, with images of fading leaves, stiffening rubber, and wheels slowing down. One night I heard myself singing the gospel tune of Ezekiel, and I saw the wheel right in the middle of the air, like a doughnut rotating from the inside out, and from the outside in. The top cycled around and the bottom came up through the center, renewed.

Nothing stayed the same—that was the message. The wheel kept turning and change happened. Even if we resisted the changes, they would happen all the same.

On September 11, 2001, horror struck and we entered the studio again. The song was harsh at first, but then clickety and complex. Instead of images of burning towers, I saw a jungle with myriad plants at every level—from the mycelia in the soil to orchids growing high up in the canopy. Every leaf, every fern, every bit of bark was earth for another organism: host, ground, soil.

My voice ran up and down staccato scales, tiny stitches sewing together a composite world in many dimensions. A web of strands, visible and invisible, connected the minerals, the plants, the insects, the animals, the human family, the community, the society, the environment, and the galaxy...and held it all in balance. All the relations. There was nothing that did not fit, even evil; everything was part of the whole.

At every point of the web healing could happen. Since everything was connected, every repair helped the whole to heal. Our task was to understand how and then to live it. Easier said than done, perhaps, but there was time. We had all the time in the world, and now was as good a time as any.

I opened my eyes and saw Ted meditating on his cushion. Stubborn and kind, brilliant and tight-minded, he had accompanied me all this way to the change in the world. Even though the question of 'how' was still an unresolved issue between us, after almost half a century we were still willing to have the dialogue.

His beard was gray now and the skin around his eyes crinkled from a lifetime of smiling, but he sat erect with folded knees in my studio, as he would do again tomorrow, and tomorrow. Whatever the differences of our modes of understanding the world, however much we would argue about it, he came to hear me sing.

He came.

Edward, Abram's five-year-old, asked me one evening on the telephone from Michigan, "Grandma, what's in that box on the floor?"

"Oh, it's got some books in it that I'm giving away...wait a minute, can you *see* that?"

"Yah," he replied.

"What else can you see?" I asked tremulously, the hairs on the back of my neck standing straight out.

"Your chair is moving and your eyes are looking down, then up, then down, then up..." I stopped rocking in my rocking chair and paid close attention.

"Go on," I said.

"And there's a lady walking by your house: now she's right in front, now she stopped so her dog can go pee-pee, now she's under the tree, and now I can't see her anymore." Edward was indeed seeing, from two thousand miles away, our neighbor walk her dog past our house.

"What else can you see, Edsy?" I asked softly. He described the pictures on the wall, the bookcase in the hallway, and the flowers on the mantelpiece over the fireplace.

"Grandpa's reading in his chair," he observed, "but his eyes are closed, so he's not really reading." Across the room Ted was indeed dozing over an open book in his lap. Edward and I both giggled.

"You know, sweetheart," I remarked casually, "you've got the gift of seeing." Child of my heart. When we hung up, I just sat there watching Ted sleep. Should I have wakened him to let him hear for himself? Maybe, but it didn't really matter. The new generation was in.

Ted awoke a few minutes later and glanced at his watch.

"Shall we?" he yawned, standing with a slight creak of the knees. We met in the middle of the living room for a kiss—so familiar, still good. Then, linking arms, we went upstairs to bed, murmuring things to each other about the next day, the evening news, the kids. I told him what was new at Abram's house—about their prairie garden and their jobs.

"Want to hear what Edward had to say?" I whispered once we were in bed and he was spooned around me. He wriggled to bring me closer, but it was an instinctive reaction because his breathing had shifted into the gentle snoring of sleep. He hadn't heard me.

I snuggled more tightly against him and gazed into the darkness for a while until my eyes closed, and finally settled with him into the deep, regular rhythms of shared sleep.

THE SACRED MARRIAGE OF
SCIENCE AND SPIRIT

The whole universe is the result of the proliferation
of these vibrations emanating from the primal sound—
the subtle sound that arises at a frequency before noise.

From a creation hymn of the Kashmiri Hindu Shaivites

*D*uring the months I was singing to Ted, the images and insights I received were like teachings from unseen teachers. The personal stories and family histories of the first several weeks began to give way to information about the subtle world: how energy clustered to create matter and form; how universal consciousness was stepped down through the dimensions to be carried into the living body through our DNA; how form was held in place by patterns of intelligent energy. I recognized that I was receiving wisdom of great import, and that I should pay close attention.

After each session, I would excitedly recount the new material to Ted, trying to find mutually understandable language to express the insights I was receiving. He would listen with curiosity, but his response was invariably some version of, "Well, it's interesting, but it's not Science."

Once, he even muttered, "Sounds more like religion to me..." His tone was less than objective.

So what is science, and what is religion? According to the *Oxford English Dictionary*, the word *science* comes from the Latin *scire*, to know, and the word *religion* means to link up, to reconnect, to tie back together again. Both words refer to a knowledge of and connection to the universe. The problem seems to arise when we try to define what we mean by *universe*.

Until Ted and I lost each other in the Kin Kletso ruins in Chaco Canyon, I could never quite grasp why our communications always bogged down when we talked about what was 'real.' I tended to find his scientific views too limited for me, and he thought my insistence upon a wider view was judgmental of him. On that cold winter evening, as we drove down the long canyon road and recounted to each other the experience of our misadventure, I realized, yet again, that Ted and I perceived the world as though through different spectacles.

To him, *the world* was the physical world—a place of form and life and forces and elements and chemicals and astronomical bodies in ultimately measurable space. Humans and their instruments could objectively examine the smallest particles to the farthest galaxies. What was outside the realm of observable reality was not of scientific interest.

To me, *the world* was a boundless universe with multiple interlocking systems of dynamic, intelligent energy on a continuum from invisible to visible, and beyond, which emerged continuously from the Unified Field. What our human senses perceived as material was a part of, but not *all* of a many-dimensioned reality without which our physical world would not exist. To study the material forms without acknowledging the Field from which they emerged, to me did not make sense. I was adamant on this point.

So was he.

For me, the fact that Ted and I had been invisible to each other in the vicinity of the ruin for over two hours was a rare, but entirely possible, phenomenon. Who knew what technologies those ancient peoples possessed? Whoever they were, hadn't they constructed an extensive city of structures in the canyon and beyond? Didn't their artifacts show that they understood complex moon cycles as well as transits of the sun? Hadn't they built a system of roads that still stretched straight as arrows for miles across canyons and *mesas?*

For Ted, convinced as he was that a description of the world could not include hidden dimensions right where he was standing, what had happened to us was impossible. But, as I reminded him more than once, it had happened anyway. For that, he had no answer.

And there is our impasse: one of us entertains the possibilities that fit a material structure of the world; the other entertains possibilities that also include the invisible and unknown.

"Reason can't be the only way of knowing," I have often argued, "and I don't think it's even the best way!" I stomp around the house muttering about closed-minded scientists.

Then he argues back, "Then prove it!"

And I retort in a louder voice, "You disprove it first!"

I wonder, though, why we need to have this argument at all. It seems clear that he and I are simply talking about different ways of looking at the same universe. We look through different lenses, that's all, seeing complementary aspects of the same whole. The world is intrinsically both/and; it is only a limitation of our culture that insists upon things being either/or.

Like the blind men describing the elephant, each of us tends to define the world according to the part of the beast we know the best. But the elephant, of course, is much more than either the tail or the trunk or the legs. By insisting upon only one version of the truth, we are missing the diversity and gorgeousness of the "whole enchilada," as Katsu used to say, and we are making our lives the poorer for it.

Chet Raymo, the wonderful science writer for *The Boston Globe*, has written,

"The battle is not between religion and science, it is between two individually inadequate world views, which might be called 'mystery without science' and 'science without mystery.'"

And something that is not well known about Sir Isaac Newton, whose mechanistic theory of the universe has been the underpinning of Western science for the past three hundred years, is that he was a mystic.

His understanding was that the vital force underlying the universe was the basis for the magnificent clockwork of the mechanistic world, and that a true science investigated both the physical *and* the metaphysical to understand the extraordinary breadth of God's plan. He studied ancient Hermetical texts; he read Plato and Pythagoras; he practiced alchemy. He posited that the physical world was a reflection of the Divine Source, and that everything was held in dynamic, interconnected, mutually responsive balance with everything else. To him, the world was alive and intelligent.

The Church of England suppressed this information, however, nor did the scientific establishment of the time take kindly to it.

It appears that after he had a nervous breakdown, Newton revised his theories to conform to social pressure. His personal mission had been to put together the seen and the unseen in a single, grand theory and present it to the public. But although he wrote volumes—both in Latin and in code—the pressure eventually caused him to back down and present his expurgated research.

One can only wonder about the agonies he endured, and how our culture might be different now had his whole vision been received by his peers.

As it happened, after his work was published he had another nervous breakdown.

I look forward to a time when scientists and mystics can sit at the same table and work together on the current issues facing our society: energy, medicine, education, economics. What won't we be able to dream up together?

I expect that new ways to access unlimited energy from the Unified Field will be discovered, such that, without the political horrors and pollution involved in fossil fuels, all people everywhere will be inexpensively illumined, cooled, warmed, and transported with ease.

I imagine us practicing healing techniques that use sound and touch as well as drugs and radiation. I envision our children being taught reverence in school, as well as spelling and arithmetic, and learning that the intuition is as powerful as the intellect. I see our economies treating the resources of the natural world as gifts to be stewarded with care, recognizing that without nature none of us would be here.

Early in his career, Albert Einstein was said to have stated, "My goal in life is to read the mind of God."

And later, toward the end of his life, he was said to have cried out, "I have run out of mathematics!"

And still, physicists are searching for the Unified Field that encompasses everything. Perhaps it is right here, right now, right where we're standing, waiting to be recognized by our hearts and spirits as well as our minds.

Several years ago I found myself up in the air over the Sonoran Desert with my friend Adriel, who piloted his Ultralight with one knee so both hands would be free to photograph the land below—vivid *palo verde* trees in bloom, erosion patterns in the landscape, the solitary Pichaco Peak from above. We had taken off in the pre-dawn dark of a spring morning on an exploring adventure, and sat exposed in an open cockpit just in front of the wings. With the engine noise drowning out all sound, we communicated through little speakers wired into earphones on our helmets and Adriel pointed out rock formations and the shapes of light as the sun threw its first colors onto the desert.

I loved this man—loved who he was, his grand vision, the gentle quality of his heart. Being up in the air with him and seeing the earth as he perceived it was one of those rare gifts we are sometimes given if we are very lucky. Later, when the sun had erased most of the morning colors, we landed the plane and drove his truck to the base of Pichaco Peak for a hike up to the rim—the same mountain we had just flown over. Carrying sandwiches in our backpacks, we walked up the switchbacks, talking. At one point, following him up and over a boulder in the trail, I heard myself exclaim,

"Thank God you're in the world at the same time I am!"

It's that kind of experience I am talking about here: when you are with a well-loved friend, have seen something of the world together, and are so filled you could burst with the joy of it. Adriel and I knew this mountain's shapes and colors, its spiny plants and resident critters—the crawlers and the winged ones. Walking its flanks now, we had already flown in its airstreams through clouds gathered above its summit and on that day we were intimately part of Pichaco and each other; we were related.

Call it a religious experience, call it a scientific field trip—it doesn't matter. I loved it all, from being up in the air to being down on the ground hiking the hot, dry trail. For that day I was part of it all, along with my friend Adriel.

We were kin—just as Dukie, Danilo, Martine, Katsu, Maud, Ted, and I will always be kin, having shared a time and place in the same world and discovered that love was there with us.

Indigenous peoples everywhere have understood the intimacy of being part of a Divine, coherent field of what is essentially Love, in which we are inextricably related to each other because we are woven from the same fabric. We can listen to their wisdom, remember that we all come from the same ecstatic Wholeness and greet each other as the relatives we really are.

Mayan: *In Lak'ech, I am another yourself.*
Indian: *Namaste, I bow to the God within you.*
Egyptian: *Ua hua, We are one.*

To all our relations, say the Lakota Sioux, *O Matake Oyasin. To all our relations.*

CREATION HYMN OF THE
KASHMIRI HINDU SHAIVITES

The universe originates from one completely subtle sound that gives rise to all the other more gross vibrations. One might say there is a descent of sound from the subtlest and most impalpable to the densest and most palpable. Yet, unlike a hierarchy, there is no separation between levels. The subtlest incorporates the most gross. The untrained person is often aware only of the grossest levels.

Then a throb, a pulse, an urge—a flutter of love—an impulse or desire in the Ocean of Consciousness to create and enjoy. Unlike an ordinary desire or impulse, it emanates from everywhere at once. From that initial movement the whole world comes into being. This Ocean of Consciousness is the Absolute; the throb is its Creative Power.

The Absolute together with the Creative Power equals the Divine Couple. He rests always in His eternal nature and She is eternally active, expanding to reveal and reabsorb the whole of the universe.

She is His first stir, and also the infinite stirring.

This pulsation exists continuously, and exists in all the different states of consciousness. It is the residual, foundational substratum of the manifested world.

This throbbing vibration moves in the atmosphere like a resonance. From this resonance and the interplay of its vibrations, a symphony of energies comes forth. Substance and form are created without ever losing unity in consciousness.

The whole universe is the result of the proliferation of these vibrations emanating from the Primal Sound—the subtle sound that arises at a frequency before noise.

About the Masks

Mask-making is a ritual as old as humankind, and dancing with them on was a sacred practice in early human communities. The masks literally embodied spirits in nature, and the power of deities and demons was brought to life through ritual and story.

Magic happens when the mask I am working on comes into juxtaposition with life events, and life and art oscillate. The energy is so high that at a point in the work life and art merge, and I become dumbstruck, completely in awe at the power of this synchronicity. At critical moments in my life this continues to happen. Then the spirit of the mask is inevitably archetypal.

One such moment of magic happened when Carolyn and I realized that the archetypes of several of my masks matched the archetypes of her characters in *Ecstatic Relations*.

"The Child" was obvious, but then we saw Dani in "The Elf" and "Eve" was clearly Martine. Katsu could be no other than "The Monk" in a cowl of python skin, and the real Maud literally looked like "The Crone" in my Triple Goddess piece.

The masks of the married lovers of the last story are, of course, a portrait of my real friends Carolyn and Herb (or Clara and Ted) as they looked when I first met them.

Carolyn and I celebrate this amazing synchronicity, and the joy of many years of a truly creative friendship.

Sharon Strong
www.beneaththemask.com

Acknowledgments

As many indigenous peoples do, I would like to acknowledge All Our Relations in all the realms, seen and unseen. Without them, this book surely could not have been written.

Many friends and family have read portions of the manuscript at various stages, seen what worked and did not work, and told me about it. To all of you I give deep thanks:

Rebecca Strauss, Kathy Leo, Linda Hess, Sharon Strong, George Durkee, Sara Glaser, Kaila Flexer, Catherine Rose Crowther, Pam Mayer, Christina Bertea, Anne Hudes, Susan Alexjander, Julie Glover, Claudia Walker, Nicole Milner, Kelly Lohman-Basen, Marcelia Yeh, Kathy Yeh, Karin McPhail, Michelle Robbins, Sylvia Blanchet, Jacqueline de Sousa, Deborah Mendelsohn, Patricia Ellsberg, Herb Strauss, Clare Cooper-Marcus, Elizabeth and Robert Cogburn. Carl Pennypacker, Brenda Dunne, Ann Jauregui, Jennifer Biehn.

A few have been particularly involved in the birth and shaping of this book and I am deeply grateful to you all:

Sharon Strong, for our sweet friendship and those extraordinary masks;

Jerry Wennstrom, for the gorgeous cover image from his sculpture "The Sacred Marriage," and for introducing me and Sentient Publications to each other;

Meredith Stout, for the cosmos in a dandelion;

Pamela M. for being, and not being 'Maud';

Efren Solanas, who was there at the beginning;

Sylvia Blanchet, in whose upper room the commentary chapters were born;

Jack Weller, who loved 'Katsu' as much as I did;

Adriel Heisey, who showed me the earth from the air;

Sara Glaser, design collaborator *extraordinaire* for decades;

Eva Sher for offering me time to write at her cozy retreat on Whidbey Island;

Claudia Walker, Julie Glover, Ross Chapin and Deborah Koff-Chapin who sang with me there;

Connie Shaw and everyone at Sentient for including me in on their vision of the consciousness change in the world;

My husband Herb, for his big heart and our years of mutual bafflement as we've tried finding a language that embraces both our philosophies;

Ervin Laszlo, mentor, who sees what I see;

And all the family, neighbors and friends whose skepticism about the unseen world has forced me to find ways of communicating it more and more clearly. You know who you are.

Finally, I bow deeply to the particular beloveds whose stories are told here, and to those whose stories are *not* told here. It is their presence in my life that keeps me connected to the Ecstatic.

About the Author

In her lifelong search for wholeness, Carolyn North has been a medievalist, a midwife in India, a dancer and a writer of novels. She founded the food recovery program Daily Bread, built the first rice strawbale house in the United States and started two Permaculture projects in Northern California.

Currently, she is exploring ways in which improvisational movement and sound, especially in groups, can be used for healing. She believes that whatever generates beauty and deep pleasure has healing power, and that if our intention is clear and loving enough, together we can save our species from self-destruction.

She lives in Berkeley, California with her husband and is the mother of three grown children.

Visit her website at www.healingimprovisations.net.

Photo: Susan Wilson

Sentient Publications, LLC publishes books on cultural creativity, experimental education, transformative spirituality, holistic health, new science, ecology, and other topics, approached from an integral viewpoint. Our authors are intensely interested in exploring the nature of life from fresh perspectives, addressing life's great questions, and fostering the full expression of the human potential. Sentient Publications' books arise from the spirit of inquiry and the richness of the inherent dialogue between writer and reader.

We are very interested in hearing from our readers. To direct suggestions or comments to us, or to be added to our mailing list, please contact:

SENTIENT PUBLICATIONS, LLC
1113 Spruce Street
Boulder, CO 80302
303-443-2188
contact@sentientpublications.com
www.sentientpublications.com